T0331209

"*Fairness in the NHS* should be at the top of the reading list of anyone interested in how we can transform the NHS to meet society's changing needs while still staying true to its founding principles. It makes the case that tackling inequalities makes sense . . . not only ethically, but practically and financially too. It reminds us that 'the values of fairness and kindness are the bedrock of caring.' If we want our communities to be good places to live, work and grow old in then we need an NHS that embodies these values. The contributors to *Fairness in the NHS* have provided a timely guide as to how we can make sure that's the case."

David Fillingham CBE,
Chair of the NHS National Improvement Board

"This book is an important and very timely, incisive review of the future direction of the NHS and discusses the critical debate around the current situation relating to health inequalities, conclusions, and future recommendations. The tone of this book is excellent as it cuts through the jargon and is uncomplicated. Indeed, one of the key areas debated is the thorny issue relating to the fairness of a tax-based NHS provision and the use of public taxation in the UK. It debates the consideration of sustainable approaches with the emphasis on the greatest societal good rather than political principles or personal wealth. Refreshingly, the final chapter offers concise conclusions and makes recommendations regarding the future of the NHS. This is essential reading for policymakers, health workers, and millions of individuals who rely on NHS for their care from our very precious NHS, which is our jewel of the British Institution."

Emeritus Professor Ruth Ashford,
Co-founder and Director, Institute of Professional Development;
Chief Examiner, Chartered Institute of Marketing; former Pro Vice Chancellor,
Manchester Metropolitan University

"This is a timely contribution to the increasing discourse on 'fairness' and 'equity' in the NHS and its future. A wide range of academic and clinical practitioner research outlines influences that fairness and equity do, and should, have planning and delivering healthcare and suggests how greater fairness and equity can be achieved. This book will appeal to individuals working in the public and third sectors, as well as the health and social care sectors. That the book's publication closely follows the election of the new Labour Government may offer a further contribution: a benchmark/framework for assessing the achievement of the Prime Minister's comment that 'government is public service.'"

Eileen Fairhurst MBE,
Chair, Northern Care Alliance NHS Foundation Trust and Co-Chair,
North-West NHS Chairs Forum

"This is an important contribution to the debate about the future direction of the UK National Health Service. In particular, how it might go about addressing the systematic and structural challenges that have created unprecedented internal pressure points. As such, it will be essential reading for those wishing to seek radical and patient-centred solutions to issues that have become so fundamental they are now an embedded part of the national conversation. It will also be essential reading for those charged with implementing the consequent public policy initiatives from the newly elected Labour government."

Dr David Perrin,
Co-founder and Director, the Institute of Professional Development;
Deputy Head of Division, Chester Business School

"How can fairness be promoted in the leadership of our NHS, as well as in other public services? This includes services provided by government agencies, Charities, and other public benefit organisations. The authors present a balanced and thought-provoking discussion of the strengths and weaknesses of modern leadership approaches. They advocate for embedding fairness in public services to align with societal values. This publication serves as a guide for re-evaluating traditional management theories and considering a more compassionate approach that can lead to positive improvements in our well-being. I believe that this publication should be included in all leadership reading lists to explore and advance the theory of fairness and compassion in leadership."

Rachel Peacock,
CEO of Making Space and Trustee of The Association of
Mental Health Providers

"This book offers an evidence-based critique of the NHS and outlines recommendations on how it must adapt to meet changing population needs. Its strength lies in the diversity of the contributions, the role of the editors in distilling key themes and findings, and the practical suggestions for improvement that emerge. It is grounded in real understanding of how the NHS works and what must be done to ensure its renewal."

Professor Sir Chris Ham CBE,
Co-Chair, NHS Assembly, Emeritus Professor of Health Policy and Management,
University of Birmingham

FAIRNESS IN THE NHS

This book is for everyone who is concerned about the successful future of a very special institution – the National Health Service (NHS). It provides the reader with an overview of the complexity of healthcare delivery, and the crucial influence that fairness should have on healthcare planning. The National Health Service Act was approved by Clement Attlee's Labour Government on 5 July 1948. It was created in a great post-war spirit of community with the aim of providing free care at the point of need for everyone, rich or poor. However, right from the start the NHS has faced issues in tackling the challenges that arise in trying to be fair, and of how greater equity in healthcare can be achieved.

The focus is on issues of fairness and equity in healthcare in the NHS, what fairness and equity mean both generally and in the organisational context. It begins with chapters on the inequalities that exist in UK healthcare delivery today. Then a series of chapters focuses on different elements of fairness in healthcare: governance, policy, and leadership; finance and financing; healthcare delivery; the key behaviours required of those working in the NHS and importantly, the patient perspectives.

The conclusions and recommendations will be of great interest to health and social care practice staff, health and social care managers and leaders, politicians and policy makers, health and social care specialists, operational managers within the system, NHS boards and healthcare governors, integrated care providers, primary, continuity and specialist providers, and charities in the healthcare sector. It will also be of interest to academics and others involved in training, research and development, students studying health, social care, and management and to the wider public: to everyone who is concerned about the successful future of a very special institution – the National Health Service.

Mike Thomas is Chair of University Hospitals of Morecambe Bay NHS Foundation Trust, Chair of the Lancashire and South Cumbria Provider Collaborative Board, and Chair of the mental health and learning disability charity, Making Space.

Gay Haskins is former Dean of Executive Education of London Business School and Saïd Business School, University of Oxford, and co-author, with Mike Thomas and Lalit Johri of *Kindness in Leadership*, Routledge, 2018.

FAIRNESS IN THE NHS

Towards a Fairer Future for the
National Health Service

Edited by Mike Thomas and Gay Haskins

Routledge
Taylor & Francis Group

LONDON AND NEW YORK

Designed cover image: Scott Carey, Lancashire Teaching Hospitals NHS
Foundation Trust

First published 2025
by Routledge
4 Park Square, Milton Park, Abingdon, Oxon OX14 4RN

and by Routledge
605 Third Avenue, New York, NY 10158

Routledge is an imprint of the Taylor & Francis Group, an informa business

© 2025 selection and editorial matter, Mike Thomas and Gay Haskins;
individual chapters, the contributors

British Library Cataloguing-in-Publication Data
A catalogue record for this book is available from the British Library

ISBN: 978-1-032-53148-9 (hbk)
ISBN: 978-1-032-52133-6 (pbk)
ISBN: 978-1-003-41056-0 (ebk)

DOI: 10.4324/9781003410560

Typeset in Bembo
by Apex CoVantage, LLC

To the founders of the NHS and all who have worked within it

All royalties received from sales of this book will be donated to NHS Charities Together, the national independent charity caring for NHS staff, patients, and volunteers, helping the NHS go further for everyone

CONTENTS

List of Contributors   *xi*

Preface   *xiv*

The History of the NHS: A Chronology of UK Health, Social
Care and Equity Policies, Statutory Legislation, and Regulatory
Requirements – 1940–2024   *xvi*

PART ONE
Health Care for All?   **1**

1 Our Unequal Health, What Now, and Where Next?   3
   Sakthi Karunanithi

2 Fairness in the NHS: Some Ethical Pointers   20
   Ian Gregory

PART TWO
Governance and Leadership   **35**

3 Fairness in Boards and Governance   37
   Andrew Corbett-Nolan

4 Fairness in Governance in the NHS   50
   Ann Highton

5 Fairness and Finance in the NHS   64
   Mike Thomas

6 Fairness and Organisational Leadership in the NHS   78
   Aaron Cummins and Mike Thomas

PART THREE
Policy and Skills   **97**

7 Questions of Fairness in Health and Social Care Policy
   Decisions – A Socratic Approach   99
   Anthony J Culyer

8 Faith, Spirituality, and the Concept of Fairness   119
   Ian Dewar and Deborah Wilde

PART FOUR
Access, Equity and Fairness of Delivery   **135**

9 Contemporary Specialist Provision: Access, Equity, and
   Fairness of Delivery in the NHS   137
   Mike Thomas

10 Fairness in the NHS: Patient and Employee Perspectives:
   April 2023   154
   Clare Murray

PART FIVE
Conclusion   **167**

11 Fairness in the NHS   169
   Mike Thomas and Gay Haskins

*Appendix A: Fairness in Health and Social Care
Policy Decisions: Socratic Questions – Designed by Anthony J Culyer*   191
Index   195

CONTRIBUTORS

Editors

Mike Thomas is Chair of the Lancashire and South Cumbria Provider Collaborative Board, Chair of the University Hospitals of Morecambe Bay NHS Foundation Trust, and Chair of the Mental Health and Learning Disability Charity, Making Space. Earlier, he was Vice-Chancellor and Professor of Organisational Leadership at the University of Central Lancashire. Professor Thomas trained as a mental health nurse and has a PhD in Psychotherapy. He is the co-editor (with Gay Haskins and Lalit Johri) of *Kindness in Leadership (Routledge 2018)*.

Gay Haskins has over 40 years' experience in management and leadership development and has been Dean of Executive Education at London Business School, Saïd Business School, University of Oxford, and the Indian School of Business in Hyderabad. She has also served as Director General of the European Foundation for Management Development in Brussels. She is the co-editor (with Mike Thomas and Lalit Johri) of *Kindness in Leadership* (Routledge 2018) and (with Lalit Johri and Katherine Corich) of *Mastering the Power of You* (Routledge 2023).

Authors

Andrew Corbett-Nolan is an expert in modern governance and the Chief Executive and Founder of the Good Governance Institute (GGI). He joined the NHS in 1987 and was the first Director for Health Services

Accreditation, Development Director at the King's Fund, and Chief Executive of the Health and Social Care Quality Centre. He sits on the board of the Good Governance Academy, influencing the curricula of universities globally and is a Salzburg Global Fellow for his work promoting good governance as a means of creating social value.

Anthony J Culyer CBE is Emeritus Professor of Economics, the University of York; Adjunct Professor in Health Policy, Evaluation and Management, the University of Toronto; and founder of the *Journal of Health Economics*. In 1994, he chaired a task force into Research and Development in the NHS, resulting in changes in its organisation and funding, and from 1999 to 2004, he was Vice Chair of the National Institute for Clinical Excellence (NICE). A prolific writer, his 39 books include *The Dictionary of Health Economics* (3rd ed. 2014, Edward Elgar).

Aaron Cummins is Chief Executive Officer, University Hospitals of Morecambe Bay NHS Foundation Trust. He began his career in the NHS as a National Graduate Trainee in 2000 and has held several senior positions in the acute and community provider sector since then. He has also held national roles including chair of the Foundation Trust Network Directors' Forum and the Government Procurement Services Customer Board as well as being a member of the National Procurement Council.

Ian Dewar is Lead Chaplain, University Hospitals of Morecambe Bay NHS Foundation Trust (UHMB). He was ordained as an Anglican Deacon in 1992 and priested in 1993. He then worked in East Lancashire and Wigan, becoming a hospice chaplain in 2005 and moving into the University Hospitals of Morecambe Bay eight years later. He sits on the Trust's Clinical Ethics and Organ Donations Committee, is Trustee of a large local Foodbank, and is seeking to establish research around the concept of Compassionomics.

Ian Gregory studied Philosophy at University College London and Balliol College, Oxford, and Law at the University of Hull. His interests are in the Philosophy of Law, the Philosophical Foundations of Criminal Law, Rights Theory, Political and Social Philosophy, Ethical Theory, and the Philosophy of Education. He has considerable expertise in Educational Law, and his most recent writings have been in areas linked to Holocaust Education, Citizenship Education, and Ethics in Research. The majority of his academic career has been at the University of York.

Ann Highton is Strategic Advisor, Radar Healthcare at the Good Governance Institute. Having trained as a physiotherapist, she moved into governance and risk management and now holds several prestigious consultancy positions including governance lead at an integrated care system and has worked on strategic projects including undertaking a board-level governance review for a large acute NHS Foundation. She is also an advisor to the Care Quality Commission (CQC) and has supported several NHS Trusts with CQC inspection preparation.

Sakthi Karunanithi is Director of Public Health, Lancashire County Council, overseeing one of the largest, most populated areas of any UK director of public health (1.2 million people, 12 districts, and five hospitals). His breadth of knowledge covers Population Health Management, Evidence-based policy advice, Epidemiology, Health Promotion, and Healthcare Management. He is an experienced clinician with a demonstrable history of working in the NHS, local government, and industry.

Clare Murray is a consultant organisational psychologist, couple therapist, and leadership coach. Her expertise includes building effective collaboration through the development of trust-based relationships. She has worked for many years at London Business School as a leadership coach, including the NHS Next Generation of Leaders programme. She has co-authored a chapter in the 2018 *Kindness in Leadership* book, interviewing senior leaders in private- and public-sector organisations, including the NHS. Her PhD was in social psychology.

Deborah Wilde is Lead Chaplain at Furness General Hospital, University Hospitals of Morecambe Bay Trust, and has worked in NHS Chaplaincy for 15 years. She was ordained in 2000 to the Methodist Diaconal Order of Great Britain. She has worked in multi-cultural communities throughout her career, researching transition between cultures, bereavement care for children, and compassion within healthcare. Deborah was a founder member of the Paediatric Chaplaincy Network and is Chair of the Cumbria Chaplaincy Collaborative.

PREFACE

Treatment and care in the National Health Service in the United Kingdom are free at the point of access, and this has been the basis for its provision and delivery since its inception in 1948. The budget for the NHS in its infancy was £400 million (1950); by its 30th year, it was over £5,200 million, and by 2021/2022, it was £136.1 billion and continues to rise.

This can be put down to many contributory factors: new technology and advances in treatment, the complexities of modern diagnosis and interventions, the employment of highly trained clinical staff, the research and manufacturing costs of therapies, particularly new drugs, and the rising expectations and growth of the UK population. Health and Social Care is now by far the biggest spending department in the UK government, and consequently one of the most scrutinised.

At the core of the NHS lies a principle that provides the UK population, across its four Nations, with a sense of its values. This underpins the deep and continuing positive emotional relationship between citizens and healthcare. It is the principle that care, free at the point of access but also thereafter, is fair.

Fairness is *the quality of treating people impartially, without favouritism or discrimination* (Cambridge Dictionary) and in a way *that is reasonable right and just* (Collins English Dictionary). Fairness has common attributes such as honesty, justice, and equity, and this last attribute is of particular importance for this book. If fairness is treating people impartially and without discrimination then equity is about ensuring a uniformity of treatment and care, by those responsible for delivery, irrespective of a person's status, wealth, or background.

These values, of fairness and equity, are of more importance today than in the last 80 years, since William Beveridge first published his great work that created the foundation of welfare support in the United Kingdom (Beveridge, 1942). This importance is due to contemporary influences, not least the scrutiny on government spending, the adaptation of a post-Brexit environment, the impact of the COVID-19 pandemic, and the increasing volume of those who cry that the "NHS is broken," and its foundations should be challenged. It is undoubtedly therefore under the most intense pressures since its inception and the burden of delivering a healthcare provision that is fair and equitable is weighty and getting heavier and requires robust responses that provide more hope and compassion to users, carers, and the population.

This book is a call to reinforce the values of fairness and equity in the National Health Service and offers hope and optimism rather than bleak pessimism. Its authors examine different elements of fairness in healthcare: policy, leadership, finance and financing, boards and governance, quality control and enhancement, healthcare delivery, specialist services and the identification of priorities, patient perspectives, faiths and their influence, community and social care, and the impact of technology.

Our aim is the to provide an overview of the complexity of healthcare delivery, the crucial influences that fairness and equity should have when planning and delivering health care provision and how greater fairness and equity can be achieved.

By Gay Haskins and Mike Thomas

THE HISTORY OF THE NHS: A CHRONOLOGY OF UK HEALTH, SOCIAL CARE AND EQUITY POLICIES, STATUTORY LEGISLATION, AND REGULATORY REQUIREMENTS – 1940–2024

1940–1949

1940 – Life Expectancy in UK: 62.3 (www.statista.com)

1942 Sir William Beveridge's Report, Social Insurance and Allied Services: a highly influential publication in the founding of the Welfare State in the United Kingdom

1944 A National Health Service White Paper, detailed the wartime coalition government's vision for a comprehensive, free, and unified health service

1945 General Election, Labour Party Government elected. Clement Attlee, Prime Minister (1945–1950). Aneurin Bevan becomes Minister of Health, responsible for creating the National Health Service

1945 The Family Allowances Bill was enacted, providing a flat rate payment funded from taxation

1946 The National Health Service Act was published

1946 National Insurance Act, extended the scope of the National Insurance Act 1911 by introducing weekly payments to support welfare payments, pensions and grants

1946 National Assistance Act abolished the poor law structures and introduced welfare payment to those who could not pay national insurance contributions

1948 (5 July) Approval of the National Health Service Act, establishing a comprehensive physical and mental health service in England and Wales, free of charge to all and bringing a wide range of medical services under one organisation. Separate legislation was produced for Scotland and Northern Ireland

1948 National Assistance Act: the establishment of welfare benefits through means tested payments and the beginning of community-based care

1948 (10 December) United Nations adopts the Universal Declaration of Human Rights, enshrining the rights and freedoms of all human beings

1948 World Health Organization created, the UN Agency that connects nations, partners, and people to promote health, keep the world safe and serve the vulnerable

1948 21 June HMT Empire Windrush ship docks in London from The Caribbean, the first stop for 492 Caribbean migrants, many veterans of the Second World War

1948 British Nationality Act, defining British Nationality by creating the status of "Citizen of the United Kingdom and the Colonies"

1949 The Nurses Act, reconstitutes the General Nursing Council for England and Wales and makes further provision with respect to the training of nurses

1949. The NHS is given the power to levy a charge for prescriptions

1950–1959

1950 – Life Expectancy in UK: 67.6

1950 General Election, Labour Party Government elected. Clement Attlee, Prime Minister (1950–1951)

1950 JS Colling survey of English general practice is published in *The Lancet*, with criticism of general practice as bad and deteriorating

1950 European Convention on Human Rights signed in Rome, ratified by the UK in 1951

1951 Hugh Gaitskell, Chancellor of the Exchequer proposes new charges for dental treatments (mainly dentures) and spectacles

1951 General Election, Conservative Government elected. Winston Churchill, Prime Minister (1951–1955)

1953 European Convention on Human Rights implemented

1955 General Election, Conservative Government elected. Sir Antony Eden, Prime Minister (1955–1957); Harold MacMillan (1957–1959)

1956 Report of the Guilleband Committee's inquiry into the cost of the NHS is published. It lays to rest fears that the service is extravagant and cannot be afforded

1956 Polio-Immunisation programme commences

1957 Whooping Cough immunisation programme commences

1958 Polio and Diphtheria vaccination programme for all under 15 years of age

1959 The Mental Health Act, abolished the distinction between psychiatric hospitals and other types of hospitals, thereby deinstitutionalising mental health patients and seeing them treated more by community care

1959 General Election, Conservative Government elected. Prime Ministers: Harold McMillan (-63); Alec Douglas Home (-64)

1959 The European Court of Human Rights (the Strasbourg Court) was founded in Rome

1960–1969

1960 – Life Expectancy in UK: 70.6

1960 Royal College of Nursing (RCN) opens membership to male registered nurses

1961 The Human Tissues Act was passed when transplantation was in its early stages. Its terms related to the removal of organs/tissues from cadavers for medical purposes

1962 Commonwealth Immigrants Act restricts access of Commonwealth citizens into the UK

1964 General Election, Labour Party Government elected. Prime Minister: Harold Wilson (1964–1966)

1965 (October) Race Relations Act, the first legislation to address racial discrimination on the "grounds of colour, race, or ethnic or national origins" in public places in the UK. The Race Relations Board was created in the following year

1965 (December) United Nations signs the International Convention on the Elimination of all Forms of Racial Discrimination (CERD)

1966 General Election, Labour Party Government elected. Prime Minister: Harold Wilson (1966–1970)

1966 UK government joins the European Court of Human Rights

1966 The Family Doctor's (GP) Charter, delivered major changes in the way GPs were paid, allowing them to claim 70 per cent of the cost of employing ancillary staff and 100 per cent of premises cost. Financial incentives were introduced for group practices of three or more doctors, pension provision and for undertaking continuing education

1967 The Abortion Act legalised abortion in Great Britain on certain grounds by registered practitioners

1968 Measles Vaccine introduced

1968 The Report of the Committee on Local Authority and Allied Personal Social Services (The Seebohm Report) is published, recommending that separate local authority health departments should be condensed into a single department of Social Services

1968 Ministry of Health and Ministry of Social Security merges to form the Department of Health and Social Security (DHSS)

1968 Race Relations Act, expanded the provisions of the 1965 Act

1969 UK government ratifies the United Nations International Convention on the Elimination of all Forms of Racial Discrimination (CERD)

1970–1979

1970 – Life Expectancy in UK: 71.1

1970 Equal Pay Act, prohibited less favourable treatment between men and women in terms of pay and conditions of employment

1970 General Election, Conservative Government elected. Prime Minister: Edward Heath (1970–1974)

1972 CT scans used in NHS

1973 NHS Reorganisation Act established the posts of Health Services Commissioner for England and Wales, with separate legislation passed for Scotland

1974 Local Authority and geographical boundary reorganisation. Regions and Districts created or renamed

1974 Public Health transferred from Local Authority control to the NHS

1974 14 Regional Health Authorities were formed replacing the regional hospital boards

1974 February, General Election, Labour Party Government elected. Harold Wilson, Prime Minister

1974 October, General Election, Labour Party Government elected. Prime Minister: Harold Wilson (1974–1976); James Callaghan (1976–1979)

1975 Sex Discrimination Act passed, protecting men and women from discrimination on the grounds of sex or marital status

1976 Race Relations Act, providing fresh provision with respect to discrimination

1976 Sharing Resources for Health in England: Report of the Resource Allocation Working Party is published, leads to funding allocation based on population density

1978 Declaration of Alma-Ata, World Health Organization states access to basic health care a fundamental human right, underlining the importance of primary health care

1978 The Warnock Report introduces the concept of "special educational needs"

1979 General Election, Conservative Government elected. Prime Minister: Margaret Thatcher (1979–1990)

1980–1989

1980 – Life Expectancy in UK 73.0

1980 MRI scans used in NHS

1980 The Black Report on health inequalities shows that health inequalities persist, with the main cause being economic inequality

1982 The Körner Steering Group on Health Services Information, established in 1980, reports and builds on existing data systems to improve their usefulness to management

1982 NHS Reorganisation abolishes the 90 Area Health Authorities and creates 192 District Health Authorities (DHAs) in their place

1983 General Election, Conservative Party Government elected. Margaret Thatcher, Prime Minister

1983 The Griffiths Report on management structures in the NHS leads to the introduction of general management in the NHS and heralds a major increase in managers' pay

1983 The Mental Health Act covers the care reception and treatment of mentally disordered people. It provides legislation by which people diagnosed with a mental disorder can be detained in a hospital or police custody and have their disorder assessed or treated against their wishes, informally known as "sectioning"

1984 General management (The Griffiths report) implemented in the NHS

1984 GP contracts include payment for health promotion and prevention activities

1984 The Warnock Report proposes regulatory oversight of IVF (In Vitro Fertilisation) and that a human embryo should not be kept alive for research beyond 14 days

1986 Project 2000 adopted and major reform of nurse training introduced, including nurse education moving into universities

1986 Green Paper on primary care (The Cumberlege Report)

1987 Promoting Better Health, a White Paper proposes improved patient choice and wider roles for nurses and pharmacists

1987 General Election, Conservative Government elected. Prime Minister: Margaret Thatcher

1988 Review of NHS and Public Health Medicine is announced on TV by the Prime Minister

1988 Free breast screening introduced for women over 50 years of age

1989 Working for Patients, a White Paper proposes the introduction of a state-financed internal market in the NHS and a split between purchasers and providers of care and GP fundholders to drive service efficiency

Caring for Patients, places emphasis on NHS to promote community-based care

United Nations Convention on the Rights of the Child

1990–1999

1990 – Life Expectancy in UK: 75.1

1990 The new GP Contract provides incentives for more health promotion and better patient care and results in increases in salaries

1990 The National Health Service and Community Care Act implements internal market in NHS

1990 The Human Fertilisation and Embryology Act, replaces The Abortion Act and states that Abortion is no longer legal after 24 weeks except if the mother's life is in danger, there is extreme foetal abnormality or a grave risk of physical or mental injury to the mother

1991 The Patients Charter stresses the patient as a customer with rights regarding the quality of services they should receive

1992 General Election, Conservative Government elected. John Major, Prime Minister (1998)

1992 The Health of the Nation, a White Paper, identifies several important areas for improving health including cancer, coronary heart disease, mental health, and HIV/AIDS

1994 The NHS Organ Donor Register implemented

1994 Regional Health Authorities reduced to eight

1995 Disability Discrimination Act, makes it unlawful to discriminate against disabled persons in connection with employment, the provisions of goods and services, education and transport

1996 Regional Health Authorities abolished

1996 Primary Care: Delivering the Future White paper published, GP Practices are encouraged to increase flexibility and choice

1996 The NHS: A service with Ambitions White Paper published

1997 Primary Care Act

1997 General Election, Labour Party Government elected. Prime Minister: Tony Blair (1997–2007)

1997 The New NHS; Modern, Dependable published, outlines reforms for the NHS, aiming to replace the internal market and GP fundholding with a more cooperative, integrated system while retaining the purchaser/provider split

1998 A First-Class Service: Quality in the New NHS, sets out a modernisation programme to deliver more consistent and higher quality

1998 The National Institute for Health and Clinical Excellence (NICE) and (in 1999) the Commission for Health Improvement launched, providing guidance on how to strengthen quality and the use of technology

1998 The Independent Acheson inquiry into inequalities in health (The Acheson Report) published with revised targets for reducing infant mortality and increasing life expectancy at birth

1998 NHS Direct established, a national health line providing expert health advice and information

1998 The Human Rights Act allows individuals to defend their rights in UK courts and compels public organisations – including the Government, police and local councils – to treat everyone equally with fairness, dignity and respect

1999 The Royal Commission on Long Term Care, reviews options for ongoing funding of care of older people

1999 Saving Lives: Our Healthier Nation White paper on new NHS strategy with a new focus on health inequality and the economic, social, and environmental causes of ill-health

1999 NHS Reorganization: Primary Care Groups (OCTs) established and GP fundholders abolished

2000–2009

2000 – Life Expectancy in UK: 77.2

2000 (January) Prime Minister Tony Blair makes an apparently impromptu and uncosted promise to raise spending on the NHS to the average European spend

2000 NHS Walk-In centres introduced

2000 The NHS Plan – a ten-year modernisation programme including funding and further reforms and a strategy for more doctors, more nurses, more beds and 100 hospital building schemes by 2010

2001 General Election, Labour Party Government elected. Tony Blair, Prime Minister (–2007)

2001 The Health and Social Care Act begins implementation of the NHS Plan

2001 The Commission for Healthcare Improvement begins assessment of NHS hospitals performance, including rating scores

2001 The Bristol Royal Infirmary Inquiry. The Report of the public inquiry into children's heart surgery at the Bristol Royal Infirmary 1984–1995

2001 Shifting the Balance of Power within the NHS; Securing Delivery is published, setting out changes to develop Primary Care Trusts and creating Strategic Health Authorities and refocusing the Department of Health to do only those things which only it can do

2002 The National Health Service and Health Care Professions Act. NHS Reorganisation: Regional Health Authorities replaced by Strategic Health Authorities (SHAs) and primary Care Trusts (PCTs)

2002 Adoption and Children Act

2002 Homelessness Act

2002 The Wanless Report, Securing our future health; taking a long-term view, leads to increased NHS funding

2003 (June) GP and Hospital consultant contracts renegotiated and agreed. (October) Pay increases for most NHS staff as part of the Agenda for Change and its modernisation of the NHS

2003 The Health and Social Care (Community Health and Standards) Act provides for the establishment of NHS foundation trusts, semi-autonomous acute trusts with greater freedoms, two new inspectorates, the Commission for Healthcare Audit and Inspection and the Commission for Social Care Inspection and the recovery of NHS charges

2003 Employment Equality (Religion or Belief) Regulations, prohibiting employers discriminating on the grounds of religion or belief

2003 Employment Equality (Sexual Orientation) Regulations, prohibiting employers discriminating on grounds of sexual orientation

2004 The White Paper, choosing health; making healthy choices easier, is published promoting the principles of informed choice, individual responsibility, personalisation and working together

2004 First wave of NHS Foundation Trusts established, giving more control over their own services and budgets

2004 Agenda for Change; standardisation of pay and conditions for all NHS staff, except for medical staff, dentists, and very senior managers

2004 Patients Act

2004 The Healthcare Commission replaces the Commission for Healthcare Improvement

2004 Children Act

2004 Gender Recognition Act

2005 General Election, Labour Party Government elected. Prime Minister: Tony Blair (-2007); Gordon Brown (2007–2010)

2005 Mental Capacity Act

2005 The report, Commissioning a Patient-led NHS, introduces practice-based commissioning and calls on the NHS to accommodate and respond to the beliefs, values and agendas of patients as well as of professionals

2006 The Equality Act sets out new provisions to protect individuals against discrimination on the grounds of religion or belief

2006 Childcare Act

2006 Our health, our care, our say; A new direction for community services White Paper published

2006 National Health Service Act

2006 NHS Reorganisation; Strategic Health Authorities reduced from 28 to 10, and 303 Primary Care Trusts reduced to 152

2006 NHS Bowel screening Programme implemented for men and women aged 60–69 years

2006 Employment Equality (Age) Regulations, prohibit employers unreasonably discriminating against employees on grounds of age

2007 Introduction of no-smoking in enclosed places and public places in England

2007 Mental Health Act

2007 Welfare Reform Act

2007 Equality Act (Sexual Orientation) Regulations, outlaw discrimination on the grounds of sexual orientation in the provision of goods, facilities, services, education, the disposal and management of premises, and in the exercise of public functions in Great Britain

2007 Sustainable Communities Act

2008 The Lord Darzi report, High Quality Care for All: the NHS Next Stage Review, makes recommendations on moving on from a centrally driven performance management regime – with a focus on driving activity and meeting targets – to a more sophisticated strategy in preparation for the next ten years

2008 Health and Social Care Act

2008 Human Papillomavirus (HPV) vaccine implemented to all schoolgirls aged 12 years, to protect against genital warts and most cases of cervical cancer

2008 United Nations Convention on the Rights of Persons with Disabilities

2008 Children and Young Persons Act

2008 Human Fertilisation and Embryology Act

2009 NHS Constitution published, establishing seven principles on how the NHS should act, six core values of the NHS in England (working together for patients, respect and dignity, commitment to quality of care, compassion, improving lives, everyone counts) and several pledges to patients and staff

2009 Health Act

2009 Care Quality Commission (CQC) introduced, regulating health and social care in England.

2009 Welfare Reform Act

2009 Autism Act

2009 The Autism Act, focusing on autism awareness, education, employment, health, reducing inpatient care, community support and the criminal justice system

2010–2019

2010 – Life Expectancy in UK: 79.7

2010 Building the National Care Service, Labour Government White paper published on the future of social care funding

2010 General Election, Coalition Government of the Conservatives and the Liberal Democrats parties elected. Prime Minister: David Cameron (2010–2016)

2010 The Public Inquiry into Mid-Staffordshire NHS Foundation Trust was announced

2010 The Equality Act, legally protecting people from discrimination in the workplace and wider society

2010 The Conservative/Lib Dems Coalition Government White Paper, Equity and Excellence: Liberating the NHS, is published

2010 Healthy Lives, Healthy People; Our strategy for public health in England. Coalition government White Paper published, proposing a new organisation, Public Health England

2010/11 The Health and Social Care Bill NHS abolishes Strategic Health Authorities (SHAs), and Primary Care Trusts (PCTs), increases competitive practices and General Practitioner powers in commissioning

2011 The Commission for Funding and Social Care, chaired by Andrew Dilnot, publishes The Dilnot Report, Fairer care funding', calling for major reform of adult social care

2012 The Health and Social Care Bill is passed and formalises recent and upcoming NHS reorganisation. It was opposed by many medical leaders

2012 Roll-out of DNA Mapping for cancer patients and rare diseases

2012 British Medical Association strike action due to changes in NHS Pension schemes: doctors take industrial action for the first time in almost 40 years

2012 The Care and Support White Paper, Caring for Our Future, is published, calling for a reformed care and support system

2012 Welfare Reform Act

2013 The Francis Report of the Mid-Staffordshire NHS Foundation Trust Inquiry is published telling of appalling suffering faced by many patients

2013 Reform of social care funding based on Dilnot report 2011

2013 The "new" NHS comes into being as responsibilities shift to bodies created by the 2012 Health and Social Care Act

2013 Commencement of Coalition government Universal Credit scheme to simplify benefits system and create incentives for work

2013 Jobseekers (back to Work Scheme) Act

2013 Welfare Benefits Up-Rating Act

2013 Marriage (Same Sex Couple) Act

2013 Mental Health (Discrimination) Act

2014 The Care Act introduces more protection for safeguarding adults in care, introduces Health Education England and the Health Research Authority

2014 Children and Families Act

2014 The NHS England Five Year Forward View is published, the first time that a shared view is presented by NHS England, Public Health England, Monitor, Health Education England, the Care Quality Commission and the NHS Trust Development Authority

2014 Immigration Act

2015 General election, Conservative Government elected. Prime Minister, David Cameron.

2015 European Referendum Act

2015 Modern Slavery Act

2016 January – Junior doctors vote overwhelmingly in favour of a strike. New contract agreed in May

2016 The Cities and Local Government Devolution Act lays the foundation for a historic devolution of power to local areas

2016 Monitor (regulator for NHS Foundation trusts) and the Trust Development Authority (regulator for NHS non-foundation trusts) merged into the NHS Improvement body, with regulatory and oversight duties over all NHS providers

2016 June 23rd – UK votes in a referendum to leave the European Union and Brexit begins. David Cameron resigns as Prime Minister and Theresa May takes over

2016 Immigration Act

2016 Welfare Reform and Work Act

2016 Childcare Act

2016 NHS Leaders announce set of measures to regain control of NHS finances

2017 NHS England publishes Next steps on the Five Year Forward View

2017 General Election, Conservative Government elected. Prime Minister, Theresa May (-2019)

2017 Children and Social Work Act

2017 European Union (Notice of Withdrawal) Act

2018 Funding settlement announced for the NHS ahead of 70th Anniversary.

2018 Governments revised mandate to NHS England for 2018/19 sets pout strategic objectives

2018 Health and Social Care (National Data Guardian) Act

2018 Assaults on Emergency Workers (Offences) Act

2018 Homes (Fitness for Human Habitation) Act

2018 European Union (Withdrawal) Act

2019 A new contract for general practice is agreed between the British Medical Association (BMA) and NHS England. This opens the way for

GPs to deliver a much wider range of services, to build larger primary care networks and to develop wider multi-disciplinary teams involving pharmacists and physiotherapists as first contact providers

2019 NHS England publishes the Long-Term Plan, aiming to set the direction of the NHS to 2028. It includes ambitious goals to reduce deaths from cancer, heart disease and stroke and to put in place rapid response crisis care teams. It calls for GPs to join networks and to offer online consultations. Local health and social care services are to come together as "Integrated Care Systems

2019 Mental Capacity (Amendment) Act

2019 Children Act 1989 (Amendment) (Female Genital Mutilation) Act

2019 General Election, Conservative Government elected. Prime Minister: Boris Johnson (2019–2022); Elizabeth Truss (September–October 2022); Richi Sunak (October 2022–July 2024)

2020–2022

2020 – Life Expectancy in UK: 81.1

2020 January – the UK officially leaves the EU

2020 European Union (Withdrawal) Act

2020 European Union (Future Relationship) Act

2020 UK Internal Market Act

2020 NHS Funding Act

2020 Windrush Compensation Scheme (Expenditure) Act

2020 March Coronavirus Act. Covid-19 is declared a global pandemic by the World Health Organization. Lockdown begins in the UK and NHS England's Chief Executive declares Covid-19 the greatest challenge the health service had ever faced

2020 December Covid-19 mass vaccination programme implemented in UK

2021 November NHS waiting times hit new levels

2021 Medicines and Medical Devices Act

2022 The Health and Care Act reorganisation of the NHS abolishes Clinical Care Commissioning Groups and introduces Integrated Care Systems, Integrated Care Boards and Provider Collaborative Boards. It also places emphasis on partnership and collaborative ventures in the local delivery of healthcare services

2022 Nationality and Borders Act

2022 Downs Syndrome Act

2022 Charities Act

2023 NHS England introduces National General Practice Improvement Programme

2023 Health Education England, NHS Digital and NHS England merge to form a single organisation called NHS England

2023 NHS Long Term Workforce Plan

2023 Levelling up and Regeneration Act

2023 Worker Protection Act. Amendment of 2010 Equality Act to provide better protection from sexual harassment by prioritising prevention

2023 Social Housing Act

2023 British Nationality Act. Regularisation of past practices into single act

2023 90% of Trusts and Foundation Trusts to have electronic records by December 2023 and 95% by March 2025. 80% of Care Quality Commission registered adult social care providers should have digital social care records in place by March 2024

2023 The NHS Constitution for England provides guidance on NHS principles and rights of patients

2024 March The government's 2023 mandate to NHS England updated. Sets out formal targets and spending ambitions to 2025

2024 April Martha's Rule implemented in the NHS. Provides for patients, families, carers and staff to access a rapid review of a patient's condition from a separate clinical team

2024 Consultants pay reform deal 24/25 agreed and ends consultants' industrial action

2024 May Conservative Government calls General Election

2024 June 27th to July 2nd Five Day Strike by Junior Doctors, the 11th Action in their long-run pay dispute (44 days of strikes since March 2023)

2024 July 4th UK General Election held. Labour Government elected. Prime Minister: Sir Keir Starmer (2024-)

Sources of Data

Acts of Parliament https://www.parliament.uk

House of Commons Library https://commonslibrary.parliament.uk

Legislation https://www.legislation.gov.uk

UK Parliament Acts https://www.lexisnexis.co.uk

UK Parliament Bills https://bills.parliament.uk

PART ONE
Health Care for All?

1

OUR UNEQUAL HEALTH, WHAT NOW, AND WHERE NEXT?

Sakthi Karunanithi

Introduction

On Friday, 26 July 1946, the National Health Service (NHS) Bill was debated and read for the third time in the United Kingdom (UK) Parliament. It was passed with the belief that it is the men and women outside the House of Commons who can make the NHS a living reality and eventually, it will be there to serve sick people of the country, the weak, and the distressed[1] who would not have to fear the costs at the point of care. The NHS is still regarded as a crown jewel of the British Institution across the world.

The enjoyment of good health is considered basic to our happiness, harmony, and security. Our understanding of health as a state of complete physical, mental, and social wellbeing and not merely the absence of disease or infirmity; as one of the fundamental rights of every human being without distinction of race, religion, political belief, economic, or social condition has largely been the principle behind the creation of the Welfare State, especially after the Second World War.

Having good and effective healthcare is important for both an individual and a community, but it is only a part of the picture. We need to consider to what extent healthcare contributes to our health compared with genetic factors, our behaviours, our income, education, employment, environment, and our national and local policies that shape and influence them. Various estimates show that the contribution that healthcare makes to our overall health is far less than 50 %.[2-4] It is the social, economic, and environmental determinants

DOI: 10.4324/9781003410560-2

of health that are the building blocks of our health and health inequalities. Figure 1.1 shows the system map of the causes of health inequalities.

Our Unequal Health

Whilst there is a rich history of public policies aimed at improving health and reducing health inequalities in the UK, the general public understanding of health is mainly associated with access to the National Health Service and how people experience care when they are ill.[5] As a society, we seem to have largely conceptualised being healthy as equivalent to taking personal responsibility for healthy behaviours and having access to safe, timely, and effective health care.

Despite being one of the world's wealthiest countries with a publicly funded welfare and healthcare system, the UK continues to grapple with significant variations in the health status between individuals from various socio-economic and cultural backgrounds.

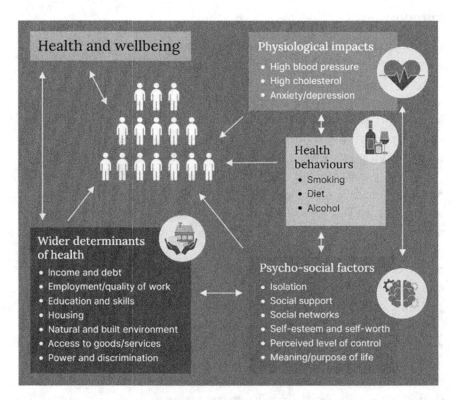

FIGURE 1.1 System Map of the Causes of Health Inequalities – Adapted Labonte Model.
Source: https://www.nice.org.uk/about/what-we-do/nice-and-health-inequalities

Health inequalities in the UK have long been part of the national debate, reflecting unwarranted variation in health outcomes, its determinants including access to healthcare services among different population groups. At its core, health inequality is unfair and an avoidable variation in the distribution of health and wellbeing across different segments of the population. Unfair to the extent that the variation in our health outcomes is determined by the unjust distribution of underlying social, economic, and environmental factors affecting our health, avoidable to the extent that they are determined by the policy options chosen by those that govern and steward public and private goods, services, and resources. Figure 1.2 presents the four broad dimensions of health inequalities.

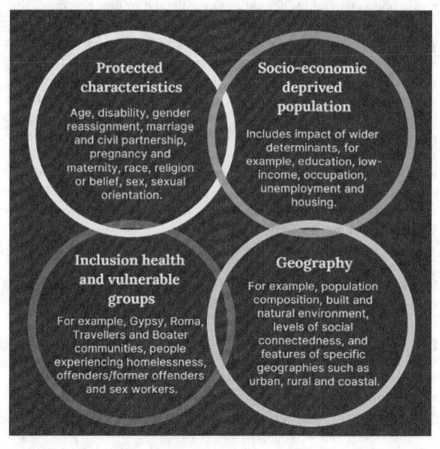

FIGURE 1.2 Dimensions of Health Inequalities.
Source: https://www.nice.org.uk/about/what-we-do/nice-and-health-inequalities

The analysis of the Office of National Statistics (ONS) shows that health inequalities are worsening. We have seen statistically significant increases in the inequality in life expectancy at birth since 2015. From 2018 to 2020, males living in the most deprived areas were living 9.7 years fewer than males living in the least deprived areas, with the gap at 7.9 years for females.[6]

These inequalities manifest in not just how long we live but also how well we are during our lifetime. Females living in the most deprived areas were expected to live less than two-thirds (66.3%) of their lives in good general health, compared with more than four-fifths (82.0%) in the least deprived areas. Male disability-free life expectancy at birth in the most deprived areas was 17.6 years fewer than that in the least deprived areas from 2018 to 2020; for females it was 16.8 years fewer. Ibid.

The COVID-19 pandemic has had a significant impact on health inequalities in England, exacerbating existing disparities and creating new ones. The pandemic has affected the population's physical and mental health, hampered access to care, and led to a syndemic in which two or more illness states interact poorly with each other and negatively influence the mutual course of each disease trajectory. The higher mortality and morbidity rates amongst the most vulnerable[7] have not only replicated existing health inequalities but, in some cases, increased them, through their disproportionate impact on certain population groups.[8] Analyses have shown that older age, ethnicity, male sex, and geographical area are associated with the risk of getting the infection, experiencing more severe symptoms and higher rates of death.[9]

Geographical location also plays a pivotal role in health disparities. Different regions in England exhibit significant variations in health outcomes and healthcare provision. These disparities have far-reaching implications for individuals, communities, and the overall societal wellbeing. Overall, the analysis by Health Equity North shows a worrying pattern of lower life expectancy, higher infant mortality rates, and worse health and wellbeing in the North of England. There were 144 extra infant deaths in the North in 2021 above expected numbers if the North of England had the same rates as in the best performing regions. Of the 72 local authorities in the North of England, 59 (82%) had a disability prevalence higher than the national average. Our three Northern regions (North West, North East, and Yorkshire and Humber) also report above-average levels of care provision of at least 50 hours per week. The top five local authorities across the country with the highest levels of economic inactivity due to long-term sickness or disability are in the North.[10]

Factors such as air quality, availability of green spaces, and access to healthy food options can differ substantially between urban and rural areas. This can lead to divergent health outcomes, with some regions experiencing higher rates of chronic diseases, mental health issues, and overall lower life expectancies.

Ethnicity and race further contribute to health inequalities. Black, Asian, and minority ethnic groups in England face disproportionate health challenges. Black women are four times more likely than white women to die in pregnancy or childbirth in the UK.[11] Black African and Black Caribbean people are over 11 times more likely to be subjected to Community Treatment Orders than White people.[12] In Britain, South Asians have a 40% higher death rate from coronary heart disease (CHD) than the general population.[13] Whilst these disparities are multifactorial, they also often stem from systemic discrimination, cultural barriers, and differential access to healthcare services. Language barriers and cultural insensitivity within the healthcare system can limit effective communication and lead to suboptimal care for individuals from minority ethnic backgrounds.

Gender-based health inequalities are also noteworthy. While women generally have a longer life expectancy than men, they may experience specific health challenges related to reproductive health and gender-specific diseases. Men, on the other hand, tend to have higher mortality rates from preventable causes like heart disease and certain types of cancer. These disparities reflect complex interactions between biological, social, and cultural factors.

Efforts to address health inequalities in England have spanned multiple decades. Government policies, public health campaigns, and targeted interventions have aimed to reduce disparities and promote equitable health outcomes. Initiatives have focused on improving access to healthcare services, enhancing health education in underserved communities, and addressing the social determinants of health, such as housing and employment opportunities.

However, progress has been slow and uneven. Persistent health inequalities underscore the need for a comprehensive and sustained approach that considers the intricate web of factors contributing to these disparities. This includes not only healthcare interventions but also broader societal changes that address socio-economic inequities, discrimination, and access to educational and employment opportunities.

The challenge of health inequalities in England is multifaceted and demands urgent attention. Do they? If so, what is the imperative? Why now?

Do we really understand the wide-ranging implications of addressing the unequal distribution of health outcomes rooted in socio-economic status, geography, protected characteristics, and vulnerable groups? If so, what needs to happen? Who is responsible? Who do we hold accountable? What is the role of the NHS?

These questions have prevailed over decades spanning before and after the creation of the NHS. Successive governments have taken actions with varying degrees of success. This remains a grand strategic challenge of the 21st century for nations across the world. And here in the UK too. Especially as we emerge from the COVID-19 pandemic and move towards a general election in 2024. We have an opportunity to make lives better for all. Will we grasp that?

WHY SHOULD HEALTH INEQUALITIES MATTER?

Whilst there are moral, policy, and economic imperatives to address health inequalities, not addressing the underlying socio-economic inequalities risks undermining the fundamental values of modern democracies.

Moral Imperative

Woodward and Kawachi put forward four key arguments for reducing health inequalities on the basis that they are unjust, they affect everyone indirectly, they can be avoided without levelling down the healthiest, and finally, they are cost-effective for the use of public resources.[14] They conclude that the moral justice argument is the most compelling although they raise further questions on the extent to which inequalities can be reduced solely on the basis of justice theories.

In 2010, an estimate undertaken for the Marmot Review suggested that each child born in 2010 could expect to live for around two extra years if they were born in households that have the same distribution of health outcomes as the top decile of neighbourhoods by income.[15]

Policy Imperative

Under the Levelling Up and Regeneration Act 2023, the government committed to laying a Statement of the 12 Levelling Up Missions before Parliament. These serve as an anchor for policy across government, as well as a catalyst for innovation and action by the private and civil society sectors. This includes a specific ambition that by 2030, the gap in healthy life expectancy (HLE) between local areas where it is highest and lowest will have narrowed, and by 2035, HLE will rise by five years.[16] The current health policy imperative stipulates integrated care systems tackle inequalities in outcomes, experience, and access. The Core20PLUS5 approach, developed by NHS England, is a national approach to inform action to reduce healthcare inequalities at both national and local system levels.[17]

Economic Imperative

The estimate for the Marmot Review in 2010 described the economic costs in England arising from lost productivity as £33 billion per year, and the costs to the government through reduced taxes and welfare payments as £20 billion per year. In addition, the paper suggested that total treatment costs would be 15% lower in the absence of health inequalities. Given a total treatment budget of £37 billion at the time, this implied a direct cost to the NHS of £5.5 billion as a result of health inequalities.[18]

Analysis by researchers at the University of York in 2016 estimated that socio-economic inequalities cost the NHS acute sector £4.8 billion each year. They found that people living in the most deprived fifth of neighbourhoods had 72% more emergency admissions and 20% more planned admissions than those living in the most affluent fifth of neighbourhoods.[19]

Similarly, the British Red Cross estimated in 2021 that high-intensity usage of A&E, closely associated with health inequalities, cost the NHS £2.5 billion per year.[20] Although the cost and evidence base for interventions within the NHS will vary depending on the place, without additional resources like the Hewitt review recommended (1% increase in NHS spending over the next five years), this will inevitably involve redistribution of the existing NHS resources that may not be feasible.

As of June 2023, approximately 29.6 % of people who were economically inactive in the United Kingdom were on long-term sick leave, reaching a peak of 2.58 million people in the same month.[21]

The Health Foundation analysis forecasts the number of people living with major illnesses to increase by 37% – over a third – by 2040. This is nine times the rate at which the working-age population (20–69-year-olds) is expected to grow (4%). This burden is inevitably going to fall on the vulnerable creating additional pressures on us all to care for and fund a growing population with high health and care needs.[22]

Imperative to Uphold Fundamental Values of Society

In their contribution to the Institute of Fiscal Studies review of inequalities,[23] Satz and White argue that there are very good fundamental reasons to be concerned about the consequences of economic inequalities namely, politics, tax, and opportunity. They point out that democracies guarantee that each citizen has the formal right to vote and are founded on the idea that all citizens are equals in the making of law and policy. This gets undermined in a system where the wealthy can donate large sums of money to their preferred candidates and influence political outcomes. These further cement the tax inequality, which in turn undermines a society's collective efforts to promote equality of opportunity, by sequestering the public resources required to give every child a best start in life and support everyone to achieve a better-quality life.

> The case pertaining to health inequalities and indeed our NHS is one of the canaries in the coal mines of the State, its institutions, and the civic society.

In examining the underlying socio-economic, cultural, and wider determinants of health and the various imperatives for reducing health inequalities, one cannot escape the fact that this goes way beyond the realm of the National Health Service and how firmly it rests on the fundamental world views and values of our society and how we choose to govern it, especially of those in the leadership roles that can steward the common good.

At this point, it is fitting to pause and look back on our track record as a nation and ask: "What can we learn from our own history about current health inequalities?"

Lessons From Looking Back on Our History of Tackling Health Inequalities Across England

Our immediate memory might take us to the idea of the creation of the NHS and the social security system as part of the post-war welfare state in 1948. The Second World War had changed public attitudes. Post-war recovery was a national priority. Another major priority was the welfare of the people, directly involving the National Health Service (NHS). The need to treat large numbers of citizens gave people access to health care they had never experienced before. The state and its institutions had also controlled almost every aspect of people's lives during the war, so the idea of government looking after the population's health did not seem strange. Nonetheless, personal social services, long-term care for most elderly people, and responsibility for wider determinants of health like the environment, housing, roads, education, and employment remain the preserve of local and central government to date.

Medical Officers of Health, the historical avatars of current Directors of Public Health, were first appointed in 1848, 100 years before the establishment of the NHS. The Public Health Acts of 1872 and 1875 made it a statutory duty for districts to appoint medical officers of health with responsibilities to tackle communicable and infectious diseases and improve the environment, water supply, sewerage, removing public nuisance, and maintaining infectious disease hospitals. Public Health responsibilities were transferred into the NHS in 1974 and subsequently transferred back into Local Authorities in 2012.

The first major attempt to investigate the scale of health inequalities was commissioned in 1977 by the then government to investigate the variation in health outcomes across social classes and consider the causes and policy implications. The working group on inequalities in health, chaired by Sir Douglas Black, showed in detail the extent to which ill health and death are unequally distributed among the population of Britain and suggested that these inequalities have been widening rather than diminishing since the establishment of the National Health Service in 1948.[24] It found differences in mortality rates across the social groups, with those in lower social groups suffering higher rates of mortality. The report also found inequalities in access to health services, particularly preventive services, with low rates of uptake by the working classes. The report concluded that these inequalities were not mainly attributable to failings in the NHS.

The 1980 Black Report identified four possible explanations for the social class inequalities. These were as follows: artefact explanations, theories of natural or social selection, cultural/behavioural explanations, and materialist explanations. Members of the working group concluded that "Intellectual honesty demands that we make clear our belief that it is in some form or forms of the 'materialist' approach that the best answer lies," highlighting that the health inequalities arose from inequalities in income, education, housing, diet, employment, and conditions of work. By the time of publication, there had been a change in government and the government did not accept or endorse the recommendations to implement a wide range of social policy measures to combat inequalities in health due to the proposed scale of expenditure.[25]

There have been further significant investigations into health inequalities. They include The Whitehead Report in 1987, The Acheson Report: "Inequalities in health: report of an independent inquiry" in 1998 and more recently The Marmot Review – Fair Society, Healthy Lives in 2010 with a further update in 2020.

Positive Change Is Possible

Whilst we need to be really concerned about the recent widening of health inequalities, Britain has a successful track record of protecting the poor, old, sick, and vulnerable. The attempts of successive governments in addressing societal inequalities can be traced back at least 400 years to the 16th century. Professor Szreter, in the 2015 annual lecture at the Behaviour and Health Research Unit, Cambridge[26] highlighted that "The welfare state of England is not something invented after World War II by Beveridge; it has a full 400-year history." He discussed the Elizabethan Poor Law (1601–1834), also known as the Forgotten Poor Law, a foundational institution in Britain's early economic success which was extremely good at protecting the poor with 2 % of the national income allocated towards social security. He highlights the crucial role of taxation-based funding of the welfare state, the importance of working with local authorities, and incentivising civil society to continue to undertake charitable activities in providing indoor and outdoor relief for orphans, widows, sick, and the poor. This idea and the apparatus still exist after 400 years. In addition, his lecture also highlighted the scale of tax evasions and frauds that still exists is comparable to the public funding that might be needed to support public services.

The Elizabethan Poor Law had been successful in reducing fundamental health inequalities. Demographic analysis of parish records after 1623 showed a lack of evidence regarding national or regional famine crisis mortality and no correlation between grain price rise and mortality in England after 1623. This contradicted what was happening in Western Europe at the same time where the periodic rise in grain price coincided frequently with high mortality rates. Unfortunately, in 1834 new Poor Law saw a 50% reduction in national spending towards the poor which was seen as the enemy of the working class.

The government's national health inequalities strategy 2000–2010 set key targets: to reduce the life expectancy and infant mortality gaps between the 20 % most deprived local authorities (so-called Spearhead areas) and the English average by 10 %. Reductions in health inequalities were broadly achieved by 2010.[27] The gap in male life expectancy was 1.2 years smaller, and the gap in female life expectancy was 0.6 years smaller than it would have been if the trends in inequalities before the strategy had continued.[30]

Similarly, the gap in infant mortality rates between the most deprived local authorities and the rest of England narrowed by 12 infant deaths per 100,000 births per year from 2000 to 2010.[27] Between 2001 and 2011, the gap in mortality amendable to health care between the most deprived and least deprived local authorities fell by 35 deaths per 100,000 for men and 16 deaths per 100,000 for women.[26] Each additional £10 million of resources allocated to deprived areas was associated with a reduction in four male deaths per 100,000 and two female deaths per 100,000.[28,29]

Inequalities in the UK have also been particularly prone to global financial crisis in the late 2000s, and indeed, the underlying structural inequalities made us even more vulnerable during the pandemic.

Perhaps, a specific national intent, concerted cross-governmental action combined with increasing the proportion of national welfare spending have all been the essential hallmarks in reducing health inequalities.

What Can We Learn From Our History of Reducing Health Inequalities?

Universal social security apparatus funded through progressive taxation policies along with engaging local government and civic institutions has protected vulnerable citizens from dying due to poverty and famine for nearly 250 years since the 1600s.

In fact, such welfare spending policies have been shown to have facilitated UK's economic progress during the early modern era and industrial revolution.

Whilst major gains have been achieved in improving life expectancy through economic progress and investing in the NHS in the early 20th century, this has not resulted in narrowing the gap of health inequalities.

Concerted cross-governmental action, as we saw during the first decade of the 21st century between 2000 and 2010, with a stated national goal to reduce health inequalities, can indeed lead to achieving the goal.

And not having such a cross-governmental national goal to reduce inequalities combined with reduced welfare spending, as we have seen during the 2010s and 2020s, can certainly make our nation more prone to widening these inequalities, especially when recovering from the global financial crisis and the pandemic.

In the years immediately after the Second World War, there was a "post-war "consensus" when the major political parties agreed on the country's main priorities like recovering from the war and generally co-operated in improving the welfare of the people, including the creation of the National Health Service (NHS).

The government of the day had a huge majority. Organised labour still had a sway on national policies. Globalisation was not a major phenomenon. Baby boomers were infants. Infectious diseases such as tuberculosis, infant, and maternal mortality were key indicators of how healthy we were. Greater emphasis was placed on emerging health care technologies like vaccinations and lifestyles.

Economic depression and the financial market crisis led to a reduction in welfare spending, with very limited success in the subsequent decades to narrow inequalities. In-depth studies showed the effect unequal distribution of socio-economic determinants was having on health inequalities.

Acting on Health Inequalities in the 21st Century

We have had a better understanding of inequalities as a society during the last 75 years. We have had seminal reviews like "Fair Society, Healthy "Lives" published in February 2010 concluding that reducing health inequalities would require action on giving every child the best start in life, enabling all children, young people and adults to maximise their capabilities and have control over their lives, creating fair employment and good work for all, ensuring healthy standard of living for all, creating and developing healthy and sustainable places and communities, and strengthening the role and impact of ill-health prevention.[30] A further review of 10 years included tackling racism, discrimination, and their outcomes along with pursuing environmental sustainability and health equity together.

In 2023, the report, "Covenant for Health: Policies and partnerships to improve our national health in 5 to 10 years"[31] was published. It highlights the need for urgency and suggests that we should be able to help three million people quit smoking, halving our smoking rate; help four million people avoid becoming obese; help at least four million be more active; help more children be physically and mentally healthy, fewer at risk of obesity; reduce the 30,000 deaths a year from poor air quality; help five million people to reduce their risk of cardiovascular disease (CVD), still 24% of all deaths; help the people and places where health is worst. It also points out that the traditional public health playbook is broken and proposes that

"we must be realistic, not romantic, and recognise that there are vested interests to be tackled, unfair economics to be challenged, damaging social policies to be overturned and nasty politics to be navigated, and this can only be done with a solid political strategy"

and calls for a more resilient political architecture that is based on social justice, economic case, mobilised NHS, and personal responsibility.

Furthermore, reviews like The 2019 *Institute for Fiscal Studies (IFS) Deaton Review* seek to understand inequalities of all kinds including an examination of the role of policies, from taxes and benefits to trade policy, education policies, the labour market, regional development, competition policy and regulation, and big forces ranging from technological change, globalisation, labour markets, and corporate behaviour to family structures and education systems will no doubt shine further light on what people perceive to be fair and unfair, and how those concerns relate to the actual levels of inequality and what can be done about them.

This leaves us with some fundamental questions that are likely to determine how equal or unequal we become in the coming decades.

Is the post-pandemic world of the 21st century equivalent to the post-Second World War world of the 20st century? With general elections due in 2024, where do we look to next beyond 2024, and what should we do as citizens, the NHS, and civic society?

Levelling up is indeed a national government priority. It is, however, questionable whether we really have a collective convergence akin to the "post war "consensus" as a nation to prioritise welfare spending to reduce inequalities. Even if we assume there is a unified will for a fairer nation, the statistics and the indicators are not yet showing the impact of our collective action. At the same time, the consequences of social unrest, war, and climate change-related migration are likely to become more prominent determinants of inequalities across the world.

With indicators of health inequalities being the tip of the iceberg of underlying socio-economic, cultural, and environmental inequalities, markers of how equitable our NHS and social care systems have again become canaries in the coal mines of the 21st-century statecraft that will shape our lives, especially those of the vulnerable and voiceless. These are not hard-to-reach people, they are hardly reached communities! The NHS and care systems need to specifically demonstrate how they have made care even more accessible to communities based on their cultures, strengths, and needs. In addition, they also have a role in redistributing resources proportionate to the needs of various communities and becoming stronger anchor institutions in providing better life chances.

Every Local Authority should publish a Health Inequalities Covenant, similar to their Local Plan, to describe how they will narrow the gap in education, income, health, housing, and environmental inequalities within the area over the next 30 years. This should be used as a building by the national government as a key input to review progress against the Levelling Up Plan.

Reducing health inequalities cannot be left to the NHS, Department of Health, and Social Care or through a separate Department of Levelling Up, Housing and Communities. The moment we departmentalise inequalities, we have compartmentalised them and therefore missed the whole point that this is fundamentally about economic, social, cultural, and environmental inequalities and that it requires cross-government action as an expressed top priority for the Government. A No. 10 Fairer Society Unit should be established to report on the national progress on an annual basis to the Parliament. Anything less is a lack of understanding of what is required to make lives fairer and even worse, will convey a flawed assumption that a utilitarian approach in improving the averages will narrow the gaps too, and make our nation fairer. This is neither what history has taught us nor what the situation warrants.

Public expectations of the NHS remain high, yet public understanding of what causes unequal health and the actions needed to reduce them is low. We have experienced better engagement with communities during the pandemic through greater access to data and information. Most of this is presented on administrative boundaries, and very little is expressed as stories of people's lives. We need to democratise data on health inequalities, so it is more clearly linked with places people live and work. Office for National Statistics (ONS) data should be presented on the basis of political constituencies. Local community leaders, Voluntary, Community, Faith, and Social Enterprise organisations, and higher education institutions (HEIs) should be encouraged to convene more conversations in our communities about our health inequalities as not just a private matter for individuals but also a common good that matters to all of us and our environment. We need to mobilise people to express their agency and not remain as bystanders, onlookers, and mere customers in a market-based economy and a market-mimicking State.

We also have a greater understanding of how commercial determinants influence our social, physical, and cultural environments through their business actions and societal engagements. They affect our health, directly or

A No. 10 Fairer Society Unit should be established to report on the national progress on an annual basis to the Parliament. Anything less is a lack of understanding of what is required to make lives fairer and even worse, will convey a flawed assumption that a fragmented and utilitarian approach in improving the averages will narrow the gaps too, and make our nation fairer. This is neither what history has taught us nor what the situation warrants.

indirectly, positively, or negatively. They affect everyone, but especially young people from unhealthy commodities that worsen pre-existing economic, social, and racial inequalities. This raises the question of whether the "market "mimicking" governance of the state, promoting the idea of gross domestic product (GDP), inflation, reducing spend on welfare as the way out of reducing national debt prevails as the primary mode of governance and measuring success. Whilst the commercial sector has a greater responsibility in protecting and promoting our health, where should fairness and justice fit within a market mentality? To what extent can money buy fairness and justice? Or should we be asking if there are any moral limits of markets? Exploring the moral narrative and collective consensus for acting on inequalities should take the mainstage during the 21st century and will go a long way to understand how our society is organised and how we make it a fair and just one.

References

1. https://hansard.parliament.uk/Commons/1946-07-26/debates/90cc1d97-d6cb-4afd-ae4f-c6907813ef01/NationalHealthServiceBill?highlight=bevan#contribution-f3db5dd5-ea3c-4b1e-af85-b023237b24fc
2. McGinnis, J.M., Williams-Russo, P. and Knickman, J.R. (2002) The case for more active policy attention to health promotion. *Health Affairs* 21 (2), pp. 78–93.
3. Canadian Institute of Advanced Research, Health Canada, Population and Public Health Branch. AB/NWT 2002, quoted in Kuznetsova, D. (2012) *Healthy places: Councils leading on public health*. London: New Local Government Network. Available from New Local Government Network Website.
4. Bunker, J.P., Frazier, H.S. and Mosteller, F. (1995) The role of medical care in determining health: Creating an inventory of benefits. In *Society and health*, ed. B. Amick III et al. New York: Oxford University Press, pp. 305–341.
5. https://www.health.org.uk/publications/long-reads/building-public-understanding-of-health-and-health-inequalities
6. https://www.ons.gov.uk/peoplepopulationandcommunity/healthandsocialcare/healthinequalities/bulletins/healthstatelifeexpectanciesbyindexofmultipledeprivationimd/2018to2020#main-points

7. Bambra, C., Riordan, R., Ford, J. and Matthews, F. (2020) The COVID-19 pandemic and health inequalities. *Journal of Epidemiology and Community Health* 74 (11), pp. 964–968, https://doi.org/10.1136/jech-2020-214401

8. Public Health England, *Disparities in the risk and outcomes of COVID-19*. London: Public Health England, 2020, p. 4.

9. Public Health England, *Beyond the data: Understanding the impact of COVID-19 on BAME groups*. London: Public Health England, 2020, p. 4.

10. https://www.healthequitynorth.co.uk/app/uploads/2023/04/HEN-REPORT.pdf

11. MBRACE-UK, *Saving lives, improving mothers' care: Lessons learned to inform maternity care from the UK and Ireland confidential enquiries into maternal deaths and morbidity 2016–18*, https://www.npeu.ox.ac.uk/mbrrace-uk/presentations/saving-lives-improving-mothers-care

12. https://digital.nhs.uk/data-and-information/publications/statistical/mental-health-act-statistics-annual-figures/2021-22-annual-figures/community-treatment-orders#community-treatment-orders-by-higher-ethnic-group

13. https://www.nhsrho.org/what-we-do/improving-health-outcomes/

14. Woodward, A. and Kawachi, I. (2000) Why reduce health inequalities? *Journal of Epidemiology & Community Health* 54, pp. 923–929.

15. https://www.instituteofhealthequity.org/file-manager/FSHLrelateddocs/overall-costs-fshl.pdf

16. https://www.gov.uk/government/publications/statement-of-levelling-up-missions/statement-of-levelling-up-missions#mission-7-health

17. https://www.england.nhs.uk/about/equality/equality-hub/national-healthcare-inequalities-improvement-programme/core20plus5/

18. https://www.instituteofhealthequity.org/file-manager/FSHLrelateddocs/overall-costs-fshl.pdf

19. Asaria, M., Doran, T. and Cookson, R. (2016) The costs of inequality: Whole-population modelling study of lifetime inpatient hospital costs in the English National Health Service by level of neighbourhood deprivation. *Journal of Epidemiology and Community Health* 70, pp. 990–996.

20. Nowhere else to turn: Exploring high intensity use of Accident and Emergency services. https://www.redcross.org.uk/about-us/what-we-do/we-speak-up-for-change/exploring-the-high-intensity-use-of-accident-and-emergency-services

21. https://www.statista.com/statistics/280292/uk-economic-inactivity-by-reason/

22. Watt, T., Raymond, A., Rachet-Jacquet, L., Head, A., Kypridemos, C., Kelly, E. and Charlesworth, A. (2023) *Health in 2040: Projected patterns of illness in England*. London: The Health Foundation, https://doi.org/10.37829/HF-2023-RC03

23. https://ifs.org.uk/inequality/debra-satz-and-stuart-white-give-their-views-in-prospect/

24. https://pubmed.ncbi.nlm.nih.gov/7118327/

25. https://navigator.health.org.uk/theme/black-report-health-inequalities

26. BHRU annual lecture 2015: What can history tell us about current health inequalities? https://www.bhru.iph.cam.ac.uk/video-of-bhrus-annual-lecture-2015/

27. Barr, B., Bambra, C., Whitehead, M. and Duncan, W.H. (2014) The Impact of NHS resource allocation policy on health inequalities in England 2001–2011: longitudinal ecological study. *British medical Journal* 348, https//doi.org/10.1136/bmj.g3231

28. Robinson, T., Brown, H., Barr, B., Fraser, L., Norman, P. and Bambra, C. (2019) Investigating the impact of New Labour's English health inequalities strategy on geographical inequalities in infant mortality: a time trend analysis. *Journal of Epidemiology Community Health*, https//doi.org/10.1136/jtech-2018-211679

29. https://www.appg-leftbehindneighbourhoods.org.uk/wp-content/uploads/2022/01/Overcoming-Health-Inequalities.pdf
30. https://www.instituteofhealthequity.org/resources-reports/fair-society-healthy-lives-the-marmot-review
31. https://medium.com/@Covenantforhealth/report-990529772639

2

FAIRNESS IN THE NHS

Some Ethical Pointers

Ian Gregory

Introduction

This chapter will concern itself with those ethically salient features finding expression in the NHS and its Constitution and buttressed by Equality Law. How those features inform, or certainly should inform, the day-to-day concerns of the NHS will be highlighted. All issues broached could themselves be the subject matter of a chapter in their own right. My own work has been in the fields of philosophy and law: the text mirrors this background.

The Origins and Development of the NHS

In its inception and its various incarnations since, the UK National Health Service (the NHS) has set itself the most demanding of tasks, the provision of a Universal Access Health System delivering health care to all who need it within the UK, free at the point of delivery, "from cradle to "grave" when and as needed.

The NHS was launched on 5 July 1948. Its origins lay in recognition that for far too many for far too long, whether they received health care at all, what the quality of that care might be was determined by considerations largely a consequence of socio-economic status. The better off financially could buy a level of care for illness and disease and enjoy the benefits of care that further enhanced their already existing social advantages. Poverty made relief from ill health that much harder and confirmed the divisions within society, born of money and social privilege.

DOI: 10.4324/9781003410560-3

The post-war Labour government of the time, led by Clement Attlee, deemed that a situation in which money and social status determined access to decent medical care was so unjust, so systematically discriminatory that the State should take upon itself the task of providing, very largely through general taxation, health care for its citizens (and indeed at the time anyone within its boundaries).

It is worth remarking that in the 75 years since its beginnings, the status of the NHS as the responsibility of the Central Government has been reaffirmed time and time again. No matter where the UK Political Parties have stood on the issues surrounding the role of the State within the lives and affairs of its citizens, privatisation of health care provision has not been canvassed as a serious alternative to the delivery of a universal care system for the UK. The setting up of the NHS as funded out of general taxation allowed for a small private health care sector, a price Aneurin Bevan, the then Secretary of State for Health and Social Care for the UK, felt compelled to pay to get consultants on board, "stuffing their mouths with gold" as he put it. (Bevan, 1948)

Universal-access health care systems are a feature of countries with well-developed economies. The form and ambition they take reflect the different histories and cultures of such countries. No matter the scope of ambition, the hope is that if someone falls within the relevant categories of ill health or health promotion of the given system they can be catered for.

The Underlying Ethics

What is striking about the NHS as revealed in its setting up, its principles and Constitution, buttressed by the law governing its operations, is the underlying ethic. The Constitution in outlining its pursuit of improving health and wellbeing highlights "Principles that guide the NHS." (NHS Constitution for England, updated August 2023).

A striking commitment to Fairness and Equality is to be found in Principle 1, which states that the NHS exists to provide a comprehensive service to all irrespective of gender, race, disability, age, sexual orientation, religion, belief, gender reassignment, pregnancy, and maternity or marital or civil partnership status. In this context respect for the human rights of all is at the forefront. The pursuit of equality through the services offered is seen as part of a wider social policy. And in keeping with Principle 1 particular attention is to be paid to ensuring that all sections of society benefit from NHS provision, as and when needed (Ibid.)

Principle 1 sets the scene for an ethically charged enterprise. Principle 2 emphasises that clinical need is the determinant of treatment, not the ability to pay. Principle 3 focuses on high-quality care that is safe, effective, and focused on patient experience with Respect, Dignity, Compassion, and Care being at the very heart of how patients and staff should be treated. Principle 4 affirms the importance of the patient being at the very heart of everything the NHS does. Principle 5 highlights that the NHS works across organisational boundaries and with a commitment to working jointly with other local authority services, other public-sector organisations and a wide range of private and voluntary sector organisations to deliver improvements in health and wellbeing. Principle 6 alludes to the NHS providing the most effective, fair and sustainable use of finite resources. And finally, Principle 7 emphasises the accountability of the NHS to the public, communities, and patients it serves (Ibid.)

The NHS Constitution is replete with good intent as it spells out its responsibilities to those in need, its dealing with staff and how staff themselves should conduct themselves in their dealings with patients. It emphasises what the public has a right to expect from the NHS as it seeks to discharge its responsibilities in the matter of providing appropriate health care provision. Further reaffirmation in all of this lies in the role of Equality Law in giving possible redress if the NHS falls short of its ambitions. Importantly, pledges are given expressing the determination to meet and even go beyond commitments on issues such as waiting times in Accident & Emergency (A&E), ambulance response times, and the like. And the legal protection afforded to the individuals and groups listed in Principle 1 earlier reinforces the ethic of fairness and equality finding expression in the Constitution.

What must be true is that if the NHS is true to its fundamental principle that need is the determinant of treatment and that all have an equal right to treatment as and when needed, if the treatment on offer raises the suspicion that considerations of gender, race, and sexual orientation, etc., might be influencing the provision of treatment and if there is any suggestion of policy denying such groups ready access to appropriate treatment when needed, the accusation of systematic discrimination will be justified. As will the complaint that such discrimination is unfair and illegal.

The ambition behind the NHS is demanding. All governments, whatever their hue, have been very conscious of the requirement to check on how well the NHS is meeting the demands placed upon it, whether ambition and reality are of a piece. As it pursues the end of delivering health care meeting individual and social needs, the NHS is committed to providing the best value for taxpayers' money.

Increasing Inequalities

Recent research, however, suggests that health inequalities are getting worse, especially in poor and deprived areas and regions. The 10-year follow-up report on the original 2010 Marmot Report, set up to look at health inequalities within the nation and how they might be addressed, stated unequivocally that in England "health is getting worse for people living in more deprived districts and regions, health inequalities are increasing, and for the population health as a whole is declining". (Marmot Review 10 Years On, 2020). The data that this report brought together also showed that for almost all the recommendations made in the original Marmot Report (Marmot Report, 2010), the country has been moving in the wrong direction and that, for those towards the bottom of the social hierarchy, lives had been made more difficult.

At the time of writing almost never a day goes by which does not carry in the media further examples of a health system falling way short of its best hopes and ambitions. The problems confronting the NHS, its shortcomings in delivering on its promises to provide healthcare to whoever needs it, clearly demand the most urgent and radical attention. Others, economists, politicians, medical practitioners of all kinds across the board, and the general public, all have a role to play in putting the NHS back on more secure foundations.

The philosophical task in part is to remind us of those values and ideals finding expression in the NHS and its constitution, what they commit us to, and why they matter so much. The task of rebuilding the NHS should not lead us to forget its original inspiration grounded in the belief that all individuals are of equal value, all need health to enjoy the possibilities life has to offer, and that being denied such possibilities is a moral affront to fairness equality and justice. While all the time recognising that resources are limited, hard choices will have to be made, hopefully in the light of best evidence. And that in the very nature of things fresh problems and challenges will emerge, decisions will have to be revisited, new outcomes be delivered. But always while striving to sustain the ethical concerns finding expression within the NHS Constitution.

The Importance of Need

Arguably the most fundamental notion informing the ambitions of the NHS is "Need". Need is the determinant of care. Putting it at its crudest and simplest, if a person is ill, care will be forthcoming at no cost to the patient.

It is need that generates the moral concern to put in place health care provision that allows those in need to live better lives than would otherwise be the case.

Not all needs have importance morally. Statements of need are mostly statements of fact, what must be done or be the case if some end is to be satisfied. "I need to be in by three pm to receive Mary's telephone call." "I need to practice hard if I am to have any chance of beating him." Needs come in many guises and according to context can be satisfied in so many ways. The need for exercise can be met in a hugely diverse range of ways, at the gym, playing football, going for a run at night, and so on. The need to relax can be satisfied by going to the cinema, listening to one's favourite music, and having a chat with friends. To a very large degree, how the diversity of needs is met is a matter of personal choice, of cultural and social possibilities. But some needs seem more basic, more fundamental in the lives of all humans. They seem to carry moral weight and have a greater moral significance than those needs reflecting our wishes and desires of the moment.

A key element in the debate surrounding needs has been around accounts of why some needs seem so basic that they seem to demand being satisfied because necessary to any form of human life. And perhaps so basic that any State seeking reasons for its population to be loyal to it takes on board responsibilities associated with the meeting of those needs. What is generally common to all these accounts, no matter how they might vary in detail, is the recognition of health care as such a need because of the harm caused if considerations of health are not catered for.

Opinions differ about the precise nature of the harm to individuals if illness and health are not met by a system of universal health care. For example, some think health is a necessary precondition for participating in any kind of human life. Others see health as a necessary precondition for participation in the form of social life within which individuals pass their lives. No matter where one stands on these debates, it seems patent that one basic need demanding satisfaction is health – fundamental to individuals living a minimally decent existence. Illness is to the detriment of human lives and health to their benefit.

The emphasis upon the meeting of individual needs, the respecting of human rights, the respect to be paid to all seeking and receiving care, and the meeting of needs irrespective of the ability to pay, all speak to an ethic which is non-consequentialist and rights driven. This stands in contrast to an ethic that talks of value for money and sees the pursuit of efficiency within the NHS as of paramount importance. The pursuit of efficiency and laying proper emphasis upon the importance of individuals, their needs and rights, while not antithetical to each other, nevertheless can sit uneasily one with other. The more consequentialist, the more utilitarian cast of mind is inclined to lose sight of persons affected by the need for care born of illness. The separateness of persons rather drops out of the equation. Very crudely, £100 spent on 20 patients is deemed to represent better value for money than the same sum spent on two individuals no matter who they are and the nature of their plight. This always possible tension haunts health care provision at all levels, the individual and the collective.

The Allocation of Resources

The provision of health care is hugely expensive and becoming more so. The allocation of resources to the NHS raises key issues. While UK governments all reaffirm their commitment to the NHS as funded out of general taxation, the claims of the NHS must be set against other claims that governments must meet. Defence, Social Care, and Education, for instance, are funded from the same source, and some way of meeting those competing claims has to be found. Determining priorities is a task making great demands upon a government struggling with accommodating these different but compelling claims.

Allocating resources within the budget set by the government for health care provision is just as problematic. The issue is how to allocate resources between categories of patients whose needs go from the most urgent to the less urgent. In a world with limitless resources, the acute nature of the choices to be made in a context where resources are limited would be largely absent. The choices had to be made arise at all levels of concern within the NHS. Individual practitioners dealing with patients within their care must sometimes choose between meeting the needs of one patient or set of patients against those of others. At the macro level, choices that must be made as to which conditions and category of patients are to be the recipients of care and resources can have implications for the health welfare of others who are also in need of care appropriate to their conditions.

To particularise the foregoing general comments, a nurse may only have a limited amount of a drug to hand to help patients. How does he or she choose (say) between giving the drug to a young child with the condition and someone in their 70s similarly afflicted who, without the treatment, will die? What about choosing between policies meeting the needs of a relatively few children who will have entire lives to lead if treated with a new drug as against devoting the money involved in treating hundreds of (say) women with a drug that enhances the quality of life of women suffering acutely from menopausal symptoms? The examples are far too sketchy to do justice to the complex issues confronting how to meet the demands of fairness, equity and justice within the NHS. They do, however, point to the tensions involved in making such decisions. The question now is as follows: how are they to be made, who is to be involved in the making of such decisions, and is there any reason to suppose outcomes will go some way, at least, to satisfying the demands of fairness and equity?

Other chapters address issues of fairness relating to the conduct of the NHS in areas such as specialist provision, governance, and leadership. What-ever the dimension of concern addressed, the ultimate end is the delivery of health care resources that across the board deliver better outcomes, individu-ally and collectively, for those deemed in need of health care. There needs to be some agreement on priorities, which conditions cry out for urgent attention and demand recognition as having the first claim upon resources. Talk of illness, health, and wellbeing embrace a range of conditions that can be to the detriment of "quality of life" to some recognisable degree. What degree of impact upon quality of life is necessary to attract health care provi-sion is part of the ongoing debate. Given the NHS commitment to ensuring the delivery of value for taxpayers' money and the most effective, fair, and sustainable use of finite resources, there is clearly a need to keep accurate records of where and how and to whom what medical conditions, mental and physical, are being treated along with record of success or otherwise of treatments. It seems entirely reasonable when thinking about value for money, that issues relating to health conditions, quality of life consequential upon treatment, and how successful treatment has been in terms of keeping alive, should be part of the currency informing how money (finite resources) should be spent. Competing intuitions are to be expected on the issues aris-ing from such reflection.

At the level of policy, the way forward in keeping with the NHS constitu-tion is to engage as many stakeholders as possible in the making of decisions. And always to be as transparent as possible as to what policy is and how arrived at. Disagreement is always to be expected over the fairness or not of given situations. In the context of the NHS, need is the elemental ground driving judgement about what is fair. Within the context of the allocation of health care provision, distinctions will be drawn as to the urgency of need. The rights-driven ethic of the NHS, the insistence that the patient will be at the heart of everything the NHS does, seems to preclude a wholesale embracing of the more utilitarian ethic informing best value for money aggregating as it does without reference to the individuals who are ill and in need of care.

It is important to emphasise how non-consequentialist the ethic of the NHS is. Talk of compassion, respect for persons, dignity, human rights, and patience at the heart of everything speak to the importance of the individual as an object of moral concern. This is not to say that outcomes and best value for money are of no moment, but it is to insist that a proper concern for the individual should always be part of moral deliberation when they are affected by the outcome of any issues under consideration.

Policy sensitive to the requirement and desire to avoid discrimination, conscious of the claims of equity upon the providers of health care can nevertheless in the delivery of policy find itself falling short of its best ambitions. Experience and research can highlight the incidence of health inequities within a population. Still too often there is evidence that racism, ageism, sexual orientation, and other legally protected considerations blight access to and the enjoyment of appropriate health care. And more generally still the case that the benefits of health care are enjoyed by the better off. Socio-economic status is still too often key to the guarantee of adequate health care. What as a matter of reason should determine health care is the conditions able to benefit from the appropriate health resource. Whether the claims of reason can easily be met in the matter of best practice, given the limited resources available, is a matter of considerable doubt.

Determining Priorities

If the best value for money is the goal, if resources are not unlimited, if there is recognition one must make do with what is at one's disposal, then talk of the determination of priorities, talk of the need to ration health care resources is inevitable and necessary. The implications of such realism have to be confronted.

In keeping with the ethical temper of the NHS Constitution, all decisions regarding the setting of priorities and the rationing of care should recommend themselves to both morality and reason. Expensive treatment might keep someone in a desperate plight alive but the costs involved might be used to transform the lives of many persons less ill and with much more to offer, not only on their own behalf but also the community at large. Determining priorities involves making such decisions. No matter what model of health-care provision is involved, whether state-funded or not, decisions on who gets what health care and why and whether its cost can and should be met by the state or other providers can never be avoided. What we know is that the costs of healthcare are on the rise. Given the expense often involved in new treatments and drugs, it is incumbent that a case for their employment be made. And if the case is successfully made, it will likely have implications elsewhere in the system for the prospects of care for others. Rationing is the inevitable outcome of an increasingly expensive healthcare system that cannot rely upon an endless expansion of resources (money) being allocated to it.

The very idea of the rationing of resources brings in its wake the consideration of policy. Talk of the determination of priorities is part and parcel of deliberation about where resources should be directed, to whom and at what cost. The serious pursuit of the best use of resources demands scrutiny of how those resources are being used. What this suggests is that the crucial issues about the allocation of resources should not be left to individuals. Rather they should lie with the body or bodies charged with the final determination of where resources are directed, to whom and at what cost. A multitude of individual decisions taken by doctors as to how any individual will be treated according to the moral intuitions of the given doctor or what they deem the best use of resources is a recipe for chaos, both medically and economically. Fairness is best served if there are appropriate guidelines which can be referred to by both the medical practitioners and patients outlining what in the given circumstances are the justified expectations of the patient in the matter of treatment.

Guidelines themselves may occasion significant debate. Decisions that can carry momentous implications for the health and wellbeing of patients in desperate need and which it is within the medical capacity to alleviate will always excite great concern, moral and otherwise. This brings to the fore two key issues bearing upon the shaping of health care provision. What are the key considerations to be borne in mind? How are decisions to be arrived at? There needs to be a currency in which debate and deliberation around such fraught matters is conducted. Always bear in mind that the currency of debate itself could well become a matter of contention.

Any reflection upon the fruitful use of resources, any concern for value for money in respect of such allocation of resources must look to the impact of health provision in terms of easing or enhancing the lot of those in need, physical and mental. Absolutely crucial to the judgements to be made about the allocation of resources within a healthcare system is the careful and accurate recording of the impact the different illnesses have on individuals, to which groups individuals belong, how long the evidence suggests such a recipient of care might live while enjoying a quality of life, and what impact directives based on such evidence might have upon the community. The numbers touched or potentially so touched could be an element in the making of final judgements about the allocation of healthcare resources within a given community.

Cost-effective analysis of some kind must be made available to decision-makers within the NHS. How could detail on how effective given treatments are in meeting patient need and at what cost not be germane to the issue? Take as an instance policy touching our increasingly ageing community. In the very nature of things, the amount of life still to be enjoyed after treatment, even if successful, will typically be many fewer years. Illness, expensive treatment, and diminished life expectancy, all combine to raise questions about value for money and the best use of resources. We know alternative uses of resources devoted to the oldest and illest of patients could easily be found. Resources that would make a great difference in the lives of many more with a great deal still to contribute to the lives of others around them over many more years. Denying how anguished such decision-making can be is silly. For some, priority should be given to the desperately ill. For some, numbers matter and are the crucial determinant of the allocation of resources. Given conflicting intuitions, how can we resolve matters having such a potential influence on the policy of rationing limited resources? Any resolution should be based on evidence germane to the allocation of resources of health care provision.

However arrived at, there is little reason to suppose there will not be disagreement on the part of some on what is decided. What must be hoped for is that there is recognition that decisions having such an impact on individual lives should be occasions of the most serious deliberation. In keeping with the NHS Constitution, all key NHS stakeholders should be consulted. An ethical seriousness should be key to the final discussion outcomes. Along with an acceptance that issues should be revisited if experience suggests that any decision has had untoward consequences for the lives of those affected. Competing intuitions, different standpoints on the very nature of moral principles and their rationale brought to bear upon evidence relating to the urgency of need, the condition to be alleviated or promoted, the significance attached to life expectancy, and the numbers involved in treatment almost guarantees no unanimity on how resources are to be allocated. But if all parties engage seriously in the pursuit of the most rational and moral outcome while recognising that in the light of experience issues may need to be revisited, a way forward can be found. Underlying this optimism is the belief that ethical discussion is a species of rational discourse and not simply a matter of emotion. Why someone recommends a particular moral stance is always open to reasons advanced and challenged. The give and take of such debates frequently offer a way forward that can be lived with.

So much of the current debate around the NHS suggests its inadequacies are a function of inadequate resources. In recent years the decline in the fortunes of the NHS has seen a corresponding increase in the numbers having recourse to private medicine. Central government might well be tempted by the prospect of a greater role for private medical care going hand in hand with a more modest scale of ambition on the part of the NHS as a way forward for a system struggling for resources. All would be guaranteed free-of-charge treatment appropriate to their category of need as allowed for under the new dispensation. What to some degree is already a "tiered" system of provision would be accepted as a way forward easing the pressures upon the NHS budget. How to give flesh to such a recasting of the balance between NHS provision and the private sector is deeply problematic. Talk of minimum standard of adequate care is easy but difficult to give substance to. There needs to be a mechanism for deciding just what constitutes minimum adequate care.

What might ease its way into favour for Governments of a certain hue is that, under the proposed recasting, both Equality and Liberty get a hearing. The present system arose out of an overwhelming commitment to some Principle of Equality to the detriment of the Principle of Liberty. Libertarian sentiment sees the exercise of choice as fundamental to the moral status of persons. If there is in place minimum free healthcare provision that adequately meets most citizen's medical needs, why shouldn't citizens who so choose spend their money on health care as they see fit? Why not embrace a larger role for the private sector? There would need to be clarity as to the respective roles of each party in meeting medical needs within the wider community. The claim might be that economic realism compels such an outcome.

Fairness in the Workplace

It is important to remember that the NHS is the largest employer of people across the UK. It employs 1.3 million people or one in every 25 working-age adults, three-quarters of whom are women. (www.longtermplan.nhs.uk). It is those people who collectively deliver the resources and health care which is the business of the NHS. It is important to further recognise that fairness is as desirable a goal in the treatment of staff as it is in the allocation of resources. The Constitution reminds us that Respect, Dignity, Compassion, and Care should be at the core of how patients and staff are treated not only because that is the right thing to do, but because patient safety, experience, and outcomes are all improved when staff are valued, empowered, and supported. In the event of a conflict between employer and employees, accommodations must be found that in process and outcome are aimed at a fair and equitable set of outcomes to all parties with a stake in the NHS – the NHS as an employer and NHS staff at all levels. Talk of Respect and Dignity demand nothing less.

Workers, be they be nurses, junior doctors, or ambulance drivers, for instance, have within their ranks individuals of ethnic minorities, different religions, different classes, and differing sexual orientations. They have the right to expect treatment and working conditions allowing them to fulfil their designated roles to the best of their ability and with due recognition of their efforts. The Constitution backed by Equality Law means that racism, sexism, ageism, and the other forms of discrimination highlighted in the Constitution and Equality Law are not to be tolerated. It does not matter whether the discrimination is direct or indirect. Direct because the difference in treatment is because (say) someone is of a "protected group", indirect in that if while not deliberate is occurring and causing harm which is avoidable once due note is taken. Both morally and in law due regard should always be given to the danger of discriminating against our "protected groups" in the workplace.

There certainly seems to be no shortage of evidence that members of the protected groups feel that they have been the victims of discrimination, direct and indirect. The evidence suggests that in the workplace the incidence of such discrimination is significantly higher among members of people of colour than among their white indigenous counterparts. Reported discrimination takes the form of unfair denial of promotion, doubting the quality of work, undue harassment, verbal abuse, bullying, and so on. Perhaps it should be no surprise that the discrimination against certain groups within the wider society with which we are so familiar should also manifest itself within the NHS. There is a need to confront discrimination wherever it is to be found and thought must be given to programmes of action and education that seek to mitigate the impact of discrimination with the NHS.

If the ambition is to get the best value for money, turmoil, and discontent within the ranks of NHS staff almost guarantee that the best value for money will be unattainable. The quality of care the NHS exists to deliver is ultimately dependent on its staff at all levels of the organisation playing their part to the full. The NHS as the employer has a moral duty to treat its staff with dignity, fairness, and respect. A consequence of staff feeling disrespected, feeling unfairly treated, and not accorded proper regard is bad labour relations. Failures in retention of staff and recruitment suggest something amiss. Strikes across the NHS by junior doctors, consultants, nurses, and radiographers among others speak to a degree of alienation among staff that must be to the detriment of quality delivery of care.

The underlying issues are, of course, very complex. An important element in all these disputes involves issues of perceptions of fairness on the part of the respective parties. The invoking of fairness as somehow key to the resolution of the disputes highlights the importance of parties' sense of what are their justifiable expectations – that wages should not have fallen so far behind the rate of inflation, that a group of workers should not have been disadvantaged as against other groups within the system, that a given group of employees should have been properly rewarded for their special excellence and commitment. Government, in turn, will talk of fairness to everyone, given the state of the economy. The invoking of fairness sets the scene for the ongoing debates. Out of this conflict over time and through the give and take (one hopes) of discussion between the parties, will come outcomes all parties can persuade themselves are fair to an acceptable degree to all concerned. Such challenges will always be part of the life of the NHS.

Final Thoughts

Talk of crisis and chaos within the NHS is part of the currency of the times. Targets are not being met. Waiting lists and levels of dissatisfaction are at a historic high. It is claimed the NHS is reaping the effects of long-term inadequacy of resources. A British Medical Association (BMA) analysis of the period 2009/2010 to 2021/22 claims that the cumulative underspend on the NHS over the period reached £322 billion in real terms (BMA, 2023). If made available, this money would surely have eased the problems of the NHS over recent years.

The problems blighting the NHS are going to make great demands on those charged with the running of the service. But solutions there must be if the NHS is going to fulfil its historic role of providing the nation with free, high-quality healthcare for those in need. Government, local authorities, unions, NHS Trusts, medical practitioners, managers and administrators, patients, and the public, all have a crucial role to play in the turning around of NHS provision. The solutions demand an expertise, experience, knowledge, and commitment appropriate to the resolution of such issues.

The final vindication of the NHS lies in its meeting the health care needs of those who look to it for help. The alleviation of ill health, the promotion of better health, born of recognition of how fundamental to human flourishing at both the individual and collective levels meeting health needs are, informs the moral imperatives at the heart of NHS provision.

The bottom line is that with all else in place – the size of the budget for medical care, the personnel to deliver – everything turns on the allocation of resources to meet medical needs. Difficult decisions cannot be avoided, decisions arrived at as between different categories of medical need and groups within society and their claims on the budget demand on occasion anguished debate as to the most rational and reasoned moral allocation of resources.

The likelihood that disagreement will always haunt decision-making around the allocation of resources to meet medical needs is built into the fabric of such debate. But if the ethic finding expression in the Constitution of the NHS permeates all that is done in the name of the NHS, wealth as the determinant of the quality of individual health care provision will be much diminished. The NHS is premised on the fundamental proposition that need should be the determinant of care. Taken seriously, the unreason of wealth, colour of skin, gender, sexual orientation, or religion bearing upon access to appropriate health care is plain.

The question for the government is, while recognising the normative salience of health care needs, just how far does it go in pursuing its ambition to provide free health care for its citizenry alongside the other claims on the public purse, like Education and Defence? The NHS has transformed so many lives over its existence. The irrationality of wealth being the determinant of health care has been significantly diminished. What would be intolerable and morally to be deplored is for the State to cease recognising health is as a morally salient consideration for which it should accept responsibility to as great an extent as it is able. A too-ready acceptance of private wealth as a key element in the meeting of medical needs would run the risk of bringing about a return of those unfairnesses the NHS was set up to some 75 years ago to end. Not a state of affairs to be desired.

Bibliography

Easily accessible and authoritative expositions of the issues thrown up by the ethics of health care provision are to be found in the online Stanford Encyclopedia of Philosophy. I would particularly recommend Brock, Gillian and David Miller *"Needs in Moral and Political*

Philosophy" Summer 2019 Edition, Edward Zalta (ed.). and Daniels, Norman *"Justice and Access to Health Care"* Winter 2017 Edition, Edward N Zalta (ed.). Both articles can only be read with advantage and in addition have extensive bibliographies listing key works relevant to issues thrown up by the allocation of health care resources.

References

Bevan, A. (1948), Source and Quote, *The Guardian*, http://www.guardian.co.uk/soci ety/2004/jul/03/NHS.politics, updated 2 July 2004

BMA, Health Funding Data Analysis, www.bma.org.uk, updated 10 August 2023

Marmot Review Report, Fair Society Healthier Lives (2010), Available from Institute of Health Equity Health Equity in England: The Marmot Review 10 Years on, Institute of Health Equity, https://www.instituteofhealthequity.org/resources-reports/fair-society-healthy-lives-the-marmot-review, updated February 2020

NHS Constitution for England, Chapter 4: NHS Staff Will Get the Backing They Need, 4.1, www.longtermplan.nhs.uk, updated August 2023

PART TWO

Governance and Leadership

3

FAIRNESS IN BOARDS AND GOVERNANCE

Andrew Corbett-Nolan

The Aims of This Chapter

Governance is often considered a dry activity that, at best, stops bad things from happening. In this chapter we look at how effective and impactful governance actually has a strong ethical underpinning with a broad sense of fairness at its heart. The chapter explains how this concept of acting fairly to all stakeholders has a history as old as corporate governance itself, and through tussles with crude capitalist profit aims this sense of caring for the wellbeing of all prevails in modern governance thinking, if not universal practice.

Explaining the way in which governance has developed over the last 175 years to support an understanding of this narrative, the chapter focuses on modern legislative changes in Wales and England for public services, particularly healthcare, and how governing for now and the future places a responsibility on the NHS and other public-sector boards to act fairly.

The chapter describes how fairness is not just a virtuous end in itself for boards but a crucial element of success, and how fairness promotes more effective strategies and solutions that are agreed and delivered by both public- and private-sector boards. Consideration of what this means for the characteristics and behaviours of board leaders is tied to the Nolan Principles.[1]

DOI: 10.4324/9781003410560-5

Good Governance: What Does It Mean?

The Chartered Governance Institute defines governance as

> a system that provides a framework for managing organisations. It identifies who can make decisions, who has the authority to act on behalf of the organisation and who is accountable for how an organisation and its people behave and perform.[2]

In the UK public bodies and organisations providing a public purpose (such as charities or community interest companies) are governed in a number of different ways ranging from leaderships appointed through suffrage, such as in local government, through to approaches more usual in the corporate sector of accountable directors as part of a unitary board appointed against skills and experience, such as in our NHS.

Directors are accountable for governance. Boards have responsibilities around:

- **Mission/vision** – what is the "point" of the organisation? If the organisation did not exist, what would the world be missing?
- **Strategy** – the plan to make the mission/vision happen
- **Leadership** – selecting the executive leadership and setting the tone and culture of the organisation through such means as agreeing on the risk appetite, stipulating the ethical framework, and setting the reward structure
- **Assurance** – on behalf of the various stakeholders being sure that the organisation behaves and delivers as planned and operates within any relevant regulations
- **Transparency** – being ready and able to explain why the organisation took the decisions it did and what evidence it used to support these
- **Stewardship** – the summarising feature of governance which is looking after something that does not belong to you and handing it on to the next custodian in better fettle than you received it in

Good governance means doing all the above, but in doing so achieving beneficial change and impact. It is the understanding principles of governance and applying them in a way that delivers meaningful outcomes – in short, governance that creates positive benefits for the organisation and its stakeholders. The concept of meaningful outcomes in governance was first described by Mervyn King in his King IV report[3]:

- **Ethical culture** – in the course of making decisions in the best interests of the organisation, the governing body should ensure that a stakeholder-inclusive approach is adopted which takes into account and balances their legitimate and reasonable needs, interests, and expectations

- **Value creation** – the governing body should lead an audacious value creation process by appreciating that strategy, risk and opportunity, performance and sustainable growth are inseparable elements
- **Effective control** – governing risk and opportunity in a way that supports the organisation in defining its core purpose and how it sets and achieves its strategic objectives. It should ensure that assurance results in an adequate and effective control environment and the integrity of reports for better decision-making
- **Legitimacy** – setting the tone and leading the organisation ethically and effectively to ensure it is a responsible corporate citizen and delivers improvements to the wellbeing of staff, society, and the environment as well as governing

This system of organisational control initially developed within the commercial world and is routed back to the industrial world. These crude beginnings were an essential element of prospering capitalism and economic growth.

Fairness and Governance: Historical Context

Governance comes from the Greek word kubernaein [kubernáo] meaning "to steer" which emphasises the sense of strategy and purpose However, the origins of modern corporate governance are better routed in thoughts around protection, control, and indeed fair play, coming as they do from the various companies and limited liability Parliamentary Acts and associated regulations between 1844 and 1855. It is worth exploring the antecedents of fair play in the boardroom to explain why the concept of fairness is hard-wired into governance from its history.

Prior to the Joint Stock Companies Act of 1844 corporate incorporation was complex, and prior to the Limited Liability Act of 1855 liability for a business' failure was shouldered personally by the shareholders and investors. This meant that commerce was a high-risk business which could, and did, mean that investors found themselves held to account for business losses often resulting in personal bankruptcy and, worse still, imprisonment as a debtor. During the 18th and 19th centuries in England, upwards of 10,000 people were imprisoned for debt each year. A prison term did not alleviate a person's debt with inmates usually required to repay the creditor in full before release. Often families would need to also support debtors by paying for the cost of imprisonment. Special debtors' prisons in London included the Fleet and Marshalsea prisons and it was in the latter of these that Dickens' father found himself. The Debtors' Act of 1869 curtailed the ability of the Courts to commit debtors to prison but the practice continued. The idea of commercial risk was hard-wired into our language. For example, another debtors' prison, The Clink in Stoney Street near today's Borough Market in London, gives us the phrases "in the clink" and to be "stony broke".[4]

With commerce being structurally unattractive to investors because of the significant personal risks, capital was more usually invested in a limited range of other types of property and in particular land. This held back economic progress and became significantly problematic after the emancipation of slaves by the British government in 1833 and the subsequent Slave Compensation Act of 1837. This Act provided the obscenity of former slave owners receiving financial compensation for their "loss" and unleashed some £20 million into the investment market in one go. The compensation, administered by the Bank of England, was in the form of 3.5% government stock that only finally expired in 2015, but much was immediately sold with the consequent risk of creating inflation in land prices at a difficult time of rural poverty. These factors fuelled the desire for safer investment in commerce through some means of limiting risk via protected incorporation. This was facilitated through legal reforms that allowed straightforward corporate importation. Indeed prior to the Joint Stock Companies Incorporation Act 1844, the only way of achieving incorporation was through the complicated and expensive means of obtaining a Royal Charter. This was followed by the Limited Liability Act of 1855, which, as the name suggested, limited a shareholder's liability to the unpaid portion of their shares.

But what would now protect those lending money to commercial enterprises if the owners enjoyed the privilege of limited liability? The quid pro quo by way of fair play to all was a system of governance, with the stewards of limited liability incorporated entities identifiable as the directors who had certain duties to act with due consideration for those who were stakeholders in the company's success – principally those lending money or providing credit. This initially meant the banks and trade creditors, but over the last 175 years, this has been extended to include stakeholders of all kinds including shareholders, staff, customers, the wider public, suppliers, and regulators. Directors demonstrate their stewardship duties through compulsory transparency measures, such as the publication of accounts, shareholder details, and details of privileged debt. Thus, early governance systems tended to start with a focus on the financial aspects of a company's affairs, but over time this has been dramatically extended. In the last 50 years in particular, the primacy of the shareholder as the stakeholder of highest concern has been systematically eroded to a much broader and more equitable interpretation of stewardship duties for directors – in short, fairness. This is particularly so in modern public sector and public purpose organisations.

Governance and Fairness: Linguistic Insights

Words do indeed matter. As socio-linguist Norman Fairclough asserts "existing language practices and orders of discourse reflect the victories and defeats of past struggle."[5] By way of example, the development of governance arrangements for our NHS provides an important opportunity to foster revised understandings of governance and to ensure that the language of governance is engaging for all, including crucial in an NHS context, clinicians, and the public as well as the existing cadre of NHS board members. Word association for governance is thus crucial to get NHS organisations on the right track. Often the word "governance" finds itself, in a public-sector setting, associated with "assurance," "compliance", or phrases such as "holding to account," but this is an unsatisfactory description for an organisational system as rich and fruitful as governance needs to be.

In 2014 the Good Governance Institute (GGI) published a White Paper for NHS England on the language of governance.[6] At this time, Clinical Commissioning Groups (CCGs) were starting to operate with their in-built clinical majorities on their governing bodies. One significant challenge, therefore, was to get a broad group of general practitioners to engage with their governance. Language was seen as a key means of unlocking this or in the obverse acting as a block to getting clinicians involved. Through a series of interactions on social media, a survey (n214) and focus groups the White Paper's authors at GGI developed three linguistic narratives for governance and tested with different audiences which resonated best.

The three linguistic narratives were:

1.   Governance is about *control and assurance*. It sets firm rules that lay out how an organisation is run. There is a focus on policies and procedures that help all understand what they must and must not do.
2.   Governance is about *leadership and strategy*. In CCGs this means making sure that the clinical voice leads the debate. In a well-governed organisation, a clear strategy has been set and governance helps ensure the organisation works towards this. Governance is about creating real change.

3.   Governance is about *fairness to all* and ensuring that no one stakehold-
     er's interests dominate. Those running organisations are responsible for
     making sure that all stakeholders are thought about when decisions are
     taken. Governance has an ethical basis and ensures that the right things
     are done.

In this chapter we are interested in governance and the concept of fairness,
but it is worth noting before focusing on this in more depth, that this report
found that overall there was no strong preference for one narrative over others, although general practitioners preferred narrative 1 (control and assurance) and 3 (fairness), and the most marked overall antithesis was to narrative
1 (control and assurance). The factors that turned participants "on" or "off"
for each narrative were as follows:

1.   *Control and assurance*

     Turn on: Assurance, help all understand
     Turn off: Firm rules, control, mustn't do

2.   *Strategy and leadership*

     Turn on: Leadership, strategy, real change
     Turn off: Clinical voice

3.   *Fairness*

     Turn on: Ethical basis, fairness to all, right thing is done
     Turn off: Fairness to all, right thing

Drilling down into fairness, why should fairness be a valid narrative for
governance?

Fairness and Stakeholders

With directors the accountable stewards of an organisation, who should they
be fair to? The privilege of limited liability allows directors to take measured
risks with assets that belong to others on the expectation of fair profit and
thus gain. In the crude financial sense this means the capital provided by
shareholders and lenders can be put at risk against expected gain, the lenders
being rewarded through interest and the shareholders through profits, divi-
dends, and an increase in the value of their stake. However, the view of who
comprises a valid stakeholder that directors need to consider has been mas-
sively extended beyond shareholders and creditors over time, and in today's

world, and in particular in the public sector, directors need to consider being fair to staff, customers, beneficiaries (such as patients or students), local residents, and even the general public, who all have their stakeholder rights enshrined in one way or another by the law. The stakeholder agenda speaks to the modern concept of value creation over simple profit creation. It is the understanding that shareholder profit cannot be effectively subsidised by damage to stakeholders. Value creation is where directors elevate the benefits to the broader stakeholder group thereby generating broader enrichments than simply shareholder return. Strategically, the business model is a central cog in the value creation process which turns valuable resources and relationships (inputs) into results (outputs) that create value for stakeholders and society (outcomes and impacts).

This was a hard-won conflict that dominated corporate governance throughout most of the 20th century. Some of the totems of this change along the way are interesting. In 1919 the Ford Motor Company defended and lost a case brought against them by two major shareholders John and Horace Dodge. The Dodge brothers, who were later to set up their own motor manufacturing company, owned 10% of Ford and through this court case successfully stopped Henry Ford from using the accumulated company profits, which by 1916 amounted to $60m, to fund an ambitious growth strategy, which involved lowering the prices to consumers and at the same time increasing the salaries of his workers. Those accumulated profits were deemed to belong to the shareholders and should, the judge in the case found, be paid out to shareholders.[7]

If Dodge vs. Ford Motor Company was one of the first volleys in the route march of shareholder supremacy the zenith was the Friedman Doctrine of 1970. Friedman stated in his famous article in the New York Times that

there is one and only one social responsibility of business – to use its resources and engage in activities designed to increase its profits so long as it stays within the rules of the game, which is to say, engages in open and free competition without deception or fraud.[8]

The thinking was that it was not fair of company directors to apply a business' resources to social purposes as this was spending someone else's money. In the same article Milton Friedman wrote,

Insofar as [a business executive's] actions in accord with his "social responsibility" reduce returns to stockholders, he is spending their money. Insofar as his actions raise the price to customers, he is spending the customers' money. Insofar as his actions lower the wages of some employees, he is spending their money.

The doctrine is flawed, however, and as the 20th century progressed there was a realisation that natural assets were finite and that ecological overshoot had been reached, namely companies and individuals were using natural assets faster than nature was regenerating them: unsustainable development. Shareholder profits were being subsidised, for example, by damage done to the environment or the social wellbeing of other stakeholders. As Mervyn King wrote in 2018 "corporate leaders are rethinking the role of business in society. Investors are increasingly focusing on companies' social and environmental practices as evidence mounts that performance in those areas affects returns over the long term."[9] Describing the genesis of the Environmental, Social, and Governance (ESG) movement, in the same article King wrote,

> The outcomes-based approach of integrated reporting is to look at the value creation chain from inputs into the company's business model, its output, being its product or service and the effects that that product or service has when it goes out into society on the three critical dimensions of sustainable development, the economy, society and the environment.

Recognising that by the year 2000, only around 30% of the stock market value of quoted companies could be accounted for as a result of financial and physical assets, and 70% of the value was concerned with intangibles such as patents, knowledge, reputation, and other forms of value, the 2004 United Nation report "Who cares wins" states

> Companies that perform better with regard to these issues can increase shareholder value by, for example, properly managing risks, anticipating regulatory action or accessing new markets, while at the same time contributing to the sustainable development of the societies in which they operate. Moreover, these issues can have a strong impact on reputation and brands, an increasingly important part of company value.[10]

Public-Sector Bodies, Stakeholders, and Their Boards

So, fairness to all makes sound business sense and maximises long-term value creation over short-term profit. How does this translate to those organisations, particularly public bodies, where the aim has never been to make profit but to provide services? The tension is not around immediate profit vs. longer-term value creation, but one of immediate performance against goals and creating more sustainable communities. Intellectually the battle is already won, but politically the conflict is a very real tension for boards.

The Health and Care Act 2022 which created Integrated Care Boards was a unique piece of legislation where the inspiration came from the knowledge of those running care services rather than policy makers translating political dogma. It was based on the NHS Long Term Plan of 2019 which the NHS England website describes as "developed in partnership with those who know the NHS best – frontline health and care staff, patients and their families and other experts." As medical science has found ever-more inventive ways of extending life expectancy and the population has become older, sicker, and fatter, a tsunami of need has reared up at NHS care services. This tsunami was detectable years out and consistent national policy documents stated that unless the determinants of ill health and population morbidity were addressed then, as the 2020s progressed, addressing the impact of these solely through treating the consequences of ill health was unsustainable. Sharpening service efficiency through the internal market had reached its limit, and a policy change to promote collaboration over competition would support channelling funds into building resilience in communities and health into populations: population health management (or PHM). PHM aims to optimise the health of populations over individual life spans and across generations. Population health management is the nexus that brings together an understanding of population needs (public health) through big data, patient engagement, and healthcare delivery to embrace the triple aim of experience of care, the health of populations, and cost-savings. Success for NHS boards in achieving this will largely depend on a change in culture, reflecting the shift away from simple transactional performance management in the NHS. In introducing population health management, system leaders will need to be prepared to go beyond this in enabling its success. As a marker of success, a well-defined governance model and strategy will align partner organisations and their stakeholders in a shared vision of population health management and patient engagement. A strategy capable of aligning multiple players will be crucial.

For the NHS and its partners, a successful system working means being able to provide services to patients in the future as well as now. It therefore depends on advancing the governance model away from directors simply thinking of the wellbeing of their own organisation and today's performance figures. It demands a concern for the sustainability of all partners and the broader benefits to the local population in the longer term, as well as immediate needs for those using services today. This is true value creation through a credible fairness approach by boards. In terms of the board working day to day, month to month this means being fair to all partners and beneficiaries but not just for the needs of the here and now but for tomorrow's market too: fair to the future.

This means that board directors of NHS organisations need to govern for both now and the future. In Wales, there is a specific duty placed on all public bodies under the Wellbeing of Future Generations (Wales) Act 2015. It requires public bodies in Wales to think about the long-term impact of their decisions, to work better with people, communities, and each other, and to prevent persistent problems such as poverty, health inequalities, and climate change. The Act gives a legally binding common purpose in the form of seven wellbeing goals to national and local governments, the health service, and other specified public bodies in Wales and specifies how these public bodies must work, and work together, to improve national wellbeing.

In England, the Health and Care Act 2022 focuses more on the NHS than the Welsh legislation but it does have similar ambitions in the sense that it lays out the purpose of Integrated Care Boards being to:

- improve outcomes in population health and healthcare
- tackle inequalities in outcomes, experience, and access
- enhance productivity and value for money
- help the NHS support broader social and economic development.

The aims all have fairness at their heart. For example, enhancing productivity and value for money enables resources to be focused on addressing needs, not subsiding inefficiency and waste.

Being a Director in an Organisation That Values Fairness

Fair organisations thus work better, have more impact, and create longer-term, sustainable value. But what are the characteristics of directors of high-performing boards that push for excellence and rise above transactional aims? In his 2023 article on ethical decision-making Dr Andrew George writes,

> Virtue ethics promotes striving for high performance. Deontological or utilitarian approaches encourage behaviour that is "good enough". If you follow the rules, or if you ensure that you do more good than harm, then you have satisfied these ethical frameworks. There is no call to do better. However, virtue ethics promotes one to do and be the best that one can.[11]

Dr George, who has sat on several NHS boards, is interested in Aristotle's concept of the "virtuous organisation" that is characterised, at the most simple level, as being led by leaders who work within an ethical framework. Dr George's key premise is that "The key premise is that a 'good' person will behave appropriately and an individual should develop the virtues that enable them to do that." This echoes the Nolan Principles that guide the behaviours of leaders who hold public office. These are as follows:

- **Selflessness:** Holders of public office should act solely in terms of the public interest
- **Integrity:** Holders of public office must avoid placing themselves under any obligation to people or organisations that might try inappropriately to influence them in their work. They should not act or take decisions in order to gain financial or other material benefits for themselves, their family, or their friends. They must declare and resolve any interests and relationships
- **Objectivity:** Holders of public office must act and take decisions impartially, fairly and on merit, using the best evidence and without discrimination or bias
- **Accountability:** Holders of public office are accountable to the public for their decisions and actions and must submit themselves to the scrutiny necessary to ensure this
- **Openness:** Holders of public office should act and take decisions in an open and transparent manner. Information should not be withheld from the public unless there are clear and lawful reasons for so doing
- **Honesty:** Holders of public office should be truthful
- **Leadership:** Holders of public office should exhibit these principles in their own behaviour. They should actively promote and robustly support the principles and be willing to challenge poor behaviour wherever it occurs

Introduced in 1995 these values are now enshrined in codes of conduct across the public sector. In Scotland the principals have been extended further to include:

- **Public service:** Holders of public office have a duty to act in the interests of the public body of which they are a board member and act in accordance with the core tasks of the body
- **Respect:** Holders of public office must respect fellow members of their public body and employees of the body and the role they play, treating them with courtesy at all times

Conclusion and the Challenge for the Future

The post-pandemic global economy is a real mess, and post-truth politics set a concerning context for those responsible for public bodies. Governance matters in a way as it has never mattered before and the governance approach mindset need is one that is holistic and has legitimacy from being seen to be fair. The leadership of the Post Office, for example, have become the focus of outrage through the illegitimate prosecution of around 1,000 sub-postmasters. Subsequently, their non-executive directors have found themselves hauled up before Parliament to apologise for and explain paying – whilst this scandal was unfolding – massive, flawed bonuses to the executive directors. Fair play matters to the public and toxic totems of unfairness such as the Partygate antics of political leaders during the pandemic have understandably enraged the public. Remembering that legitimacy and an ethical culture are two of the four meaningful outcomes of good governance those occupying seats at the board tables of public bodies need to look at how they interpret their role as well as their own behaviours.

In his 2020 "Three Kings" series of broadcasts, Mervyn King, who served as Governor of the Bank of England from 2003 to 2013, describes the context for directors today as one requiring collaboration and compromise, and of directors very aware of their moral compass. To conclude this chapter, there are no better words than Professor King's own:

> *Directors have to apply their minds because they are the conscience of the company. The company, as we all know, is an artificial person which is incapacitated. It has no mind, no soul, no conscience. I've spoken for years about the innocent company because when its corporate leaders make a business judgement call which turns out to be adverse to the environment for example, society turns its wrath against the company and the company, like an incapacitated child, is absolutely innocent. It's the conduct of its corporate leaders.*[12]

Notes

1. Lord Nolan, *First Report of the Committee on Standards in Public Life*, HMSO, May 1995
2. CGI Website, *Understanding Governance*, Charter Governance Institute, 2024
3. ME King, *King IV Report on Corporate Governance*, Institute of Directors for Southern Africa Johannesburg, 2016
4. JE Burford, *In the Clink: The Story of Britain's Oldest Prison*, New English Library, January 1978
5. N Fairclough, *Language and Power*, Longman, 2001

6. A Corbett-Nolan, C Smith and D Sutton, *Language and Governance*, Good Governance Institute, 2014

7. Dodge v. Ford Motor Co., 204 Mich. 459, Michigan Supreme Court Docket No 47, February 7, 1919

8. Milton Friedman, "A Friedman Doctrine: The Social Responsibility of Business Is to Increase Its Profits", *The New York Times Magazine*, September 13, 1970

9. Mervyn E King, "Mervyn King in His Own Words", *Festival Review 2015–2018*, Good Governance Institute, 2018

10. The Global Compact, *Who Cares Wins Executive Summary*, pp I–II, United Nations Environment Finance Initiative, 2004

11. Andrew George and Susan Rose, *Ethical Decision-Making: Virtues for Senior Leadership in Higher Education*, Management in Education, 1 May 2023.

12. GGI, *Three Kings Series*, GGI YouTube Channel, 2020, https://www.youtube.com/watch?v=Z3jP49AMelU

4

FAIRNESS IN GOVERNANCE IN THE NHS

Ann Highton

Introduction

The focus of this chapter is placed on governance in the NHS and how fairness and governance interact with each other to continually improve patient safety.

The reach of governance and fairness in the NHS covers every organisational system and process, and therefore, the potential remit of the chapter was vast; a methodology was developed to gather the thoughts of like-minded governance professionals to identify whether there were any consistencies in thought.

A group of five governance professionals participated in a Teams call to discuss how fairness and governance are linked. The call was limited to one hour and five questions were posed for discussion. A further four individuals were asked the same questions individually. The outcome of these sessions has formed the content of this chapter where themes common to all contributors emerged. The contributors were as follows:

Julie-Ann Bowden, Head of Professional Standards, National Health Service England.
Len Richards, Chief Executive Officer, Mid Yorkshire Hospitals NHS Trust
Talib Yaseen OBE, Chief Nursing Officer, Mid Yorkshire Hospitals NHS Trust
Caroline Keating, Director of Corporate Affairs, NHS Trust

DOI: 10.4324/9781003410560-6

Julie Garrity, Independent Consultant

Siobhan Obodai-Payne, Head of Clinical Governance, Remedy Healthcare Solutions

Steve Connor, Non-Executive Director, Mersey and West Lancashire Teaching Hospitals NHS Trust

Tracey Martin, Independent Consultant

Caroline Finnegan, NHS Specialist Trust

My thanks are due to all contributors for their valuable input.

The five areas for discussion were as follows.

- What is governance?
- What is fairness?
- Thinking about the definitions, what is your view of the relationship between governance and fairness within the NHS?
- What could be achieved if governance and fairness were linked?
- How could we work differently to achieve this?

Definition of Governance

The word "governance" is one which is now used widely in the NHS. Most Trusts have one or more Directors, Associate Directors, and Heads of Governance who generally hold the relevant level of responsibility for events, complaints, and litigation management, and some roles also include corporate governance, health and safety, risk management, and others.

It is the opinion of the author that governance is very rarely defined and if a Trust Board were to be asked to define it all answers would be different. It is a specialised role that has a title which is not well known, such as "nursing" for example. For the sake of this chapter, it was agreed that to ensure a standardisation of thought, a definition of governance needed to be agreed. The same approach was agreed for the definition of "Fairness."

Participants were asked to consider the three commonly used definitions of governance and agree on the one to be used throughout the discussion.

1. A system that provides a framework for managing organisations. It identifies who can make decisions, who has the authority to act on behalf of the organisation and who is accountable for how an organisation and its people behave and perform.

2. Governance encompasses the system by which an organisation is controlled and operates, and the mechanisms by which it, and its people, are held to account. Ethics, risk management, compliance, and administration are all elements of governance.

3. Structures and processes that are designed to ensure accountability, transparency, responsiveness, rule of law, stability, equity and inclusiveness, empowerment, and broad-based participation.

The discussion highlighted that no one definition was correct and a blend of them all would be more appropriate. Six of the participants thought that number three was the most appropriate and the remaining two preferred number one. Some thought that number one felt more "technical."

Comments reflected the need for the wording of the definition to be understandable so that everyone in an NHS organisation understands what it means to them as individuals and the organisation as a whole; any employee should be able to explain what governance is to their colleagues. A discussion about the gap between governance, the strategic direction of the Board, and what employees are expected to deliver resulted in a need for the definition to consider the link between the two.

Therefore, the group agreed on their own definition of governance within the NHS: *How an organisation ensures that its aims and objectives are consistently being met by all employees whilst maintaining a high quality of service.*

Definition of Fairness

Perception of fairness may differ, depending on an individual's culture, the situation, or personal values and preferences. The NHS is a mixture of differing cultures and professional and personal backgrounds, all of which are expected to work to common definitions. This difference provides the environment for the consideration of alternative approaches, but it also poses an organisational strategic challenge if everyone has different definitions of the same function; expectations may differ. To address this for the purposes of this chapter, participants were asked to consider the three definitions of fairness listed later and agree on the one to be used throughout the discussion.

1. The quality of treating people equally or in a way that is reasonable.
2. The quality of being reasonable, right, and just.
3. The quality of treating people equally or in a way that is right or reasonable.

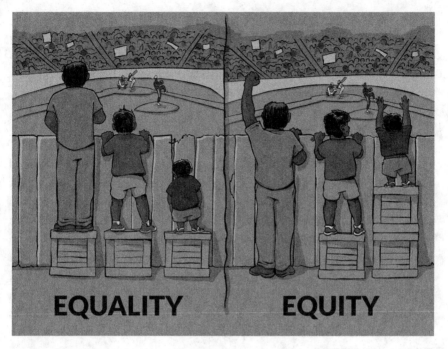

FIGURE 4.1 Evolution of an Accidental Meme: Equality vs. Equity.
Source: http://interactioninstitute.org/illustrating-equality-vs-equity

Six participants thought that definition number three was the most applicable; however, the word "equally" generated a lot of interesting discussion. Figure 4.1 "Evolution of an Accidental Meme: Equality versus Equity" demonstrates that treating people equally will not have the same outcome for everyone as people's experiences are different. Treating people equitably is very important.

The group also discussed how "opportunity" was key to fairness and equity, that is, if patients have the same experience, they will have the same opportunity to respond.

The outcome of the discussion relating to the definition of fairness resulted in a new definition being written. The definition includes the "comfort" words such as equity and opportunity and is as follows:

> *"Ensuring equitable opportunities for all."*

The Relationship Between Governance and Fairness

The next topic of discussion focused on identifying the relationship between governance and fairness within the NHS.

Governance is the structure that underpins and reinforces fairness.

An organisation with good governance will have a library of robust procedural documents for example strategies, policies, procedures, and guidance. These documents define the organisational values and behaviours, setting the procedural boundaries which should advocate for fairness.

Achieving Fairness: Procedural Document Processes

The group felt that if the procedural document processes were embedded consistently, fairness would be achieved. This consistency is dependent on the culture of the organisation. If an organisation is not committed to an "open" culture where staff feel confident to report deviations from the normal processes, then fairness may be compromised. James Reason argues that human error is universal and inevitable and that it is not intrinsically bad as without error we cannot learn from our mistakes. (Reason, 1991) Therefore, to maintain fairness in the NHS, an open reporting culture is crucial to enabling the identification of occurrences of unfairness and subsequent implementation of improvement actions to restore a fair culture.

Achieving Fairness: Speaking Up

The 2022 staff survey reported that only 61.5% of staff said that they felt safe to speak up when things concerned them, suggesting that 38.5% of NHS staff do not. (NHS Staff Survey, 2022)

The group also discussed the function of the "Freedom to Speak Up Guardian" (F2SU). This role operates independently within Trusts; it is completely confidential and exists to provide support to staff who have experienced unfairness. During the discussion one group member shared the following example.

Staff member A. complained about unfair behaviour from their senior manager. The F2SU process was initiated and resulted in the F2SU guardian undertaking a full internal and subsequent external independent investigation into the allegation.

The depth, time to complete the process and the time spent responding to the enquiries placed the senior manager in a position of extreme anxiety, which impacted on their confidence, emotional wellbeing, and perception of their position within the senior leadership team. Due to the culture of the organisation the HR function provided no emotional support to the senior manager who had to source wellbeing support externally. The investigation resulted in "no case to answer."

This is an example where the F2SU process is conceptually fair, that is, in response to the issue raised by staff member A. However, in this example the process failed the senior manager.

The Care Quality Commission (CQC) is the independent regulator of health and adult social care in England. It aims to ensure that health and social care services provide people with safe, effective, compassionate high-quality care. It monitors, inspects, and regulates services and where poor care is found through the CQC activities then the organisation uses its regulatory powers to intervene and expects a compliant response (https://www.cqc.org.uk/).

This approach may be fair and equitable if the inspection model is applied consistently across all organisations by all inspectors. However, the system fails when there is an inconsistency in approach.

The inspection process uses standardised "Key Lines of Enquiry" and more recently "Quality Statements" along with homogenous questioning to provide the framework to gather the required evidence. However, this standardised approach is compromised by the human interaction of inspectors who do not understand the NHS as a whole and more specifically the explicit differences found in the NHS.

An example of this is the inspection of "Specialist Trusts" such as Maternity where inspectors are required to use a generic methodology which may, due to its generality, not be able to collect the specific information relevant to the organisation. Even though all inspectors receive standardised training in the data collection methodology, they do not all have the knowledge and experience to use the general inspection framework and then ask deeper questions more relevant to individual Trusts.

A competent interviewer draws out more relevant information from the interviewee as opposed to taking the first answer given by an inexperienced interviewer.

Linking Governance and Fairness

The next question asked of the group was: What can be achieved if governance and fairness are linked?

In response to this question much of the group discussion focused on the need to develop and embed an open culture which encourages the identification of events that challenge fairness and systems of good governance and supports staff who are involved in the event. There was an agreement within the group that strong solidarity between governance and fairness would directly increase psychological safety.

If we consider the definition of psychological safety as: "a *shared belief held by members of a team that it's OK to admit mistakes – all without fear of negative consequences*."

In this context the team could be the organisation, a directorate, or individual teams within each directorate. Governance should be the spot check to identify situations where fairness is not being considered, this subsequently has a direct impact on the morale of employees and the degree of psychological safety. There is a huge opportunity for the improvement of psychological safety (and fairness) through the empowerment of staff who feel confident to report adverse events and speak up knowing that they will be treated fairly, without punitive retort and that the outcome will be an improvement in patient safety. In a culture of psychological safety staff will have the confidence to challenge those senior to them when they believe something is not right and expect remedial action to be identified and implemented and, where appropriate health and wellbeing support to be provided.

An example is in NHS Trusts during theatre procedures where surgeons are required to complete a safety checklist. The aim of the checklist is to reinforce required safety practices and foster better communication and teamwork between clinical disciplines thus improving the safety of their operations and reducing unnecessary complications and surgical deaths. If staff who are working in the theatre suspect noncompliance with the required process, they are required to call a "halt" to the process so that a review can be undertaken to establish if there are any compromises to patient safety.

In a culture of psychological safety this will receive a fair response from the clinician and be a positive experience for the person calling the "halt." They will feel that they have positively contributed to patient safety, the patient will have a positive outcome and the organisation will maintain a reputation of being safe. The calling "halt" process fails when the response to the halt call by the clinician is punitive, disciplinary or fails to acknowledge the importance of the call. This type of behaviour has a significant impact of the morale of staff. In the situation where psychological safety is compromised staff will be reluctant to identify when things go wrong, the consequence being the potential to reduce patient safety and organisational learning.

A Just Culture

The comments at the beginning of this chapter have identified that fairness in the NHS is underpinned by good governance and psychological safety. Neither of these will be able to flourish without another factor which requires discussion, that of a "Just Culture."

In 2019 NHS England and NHS Improvement published the "NHS Patient Safety Strategy" (NHS England, 2019). The strategy refers to the following quote from John F Kennedy, *"We are not here to curse the darkness, but to light the candle that can guide us through that darkness to a safe and sane future"* (Kennedy, 1960).

It refers to the need for safer systems and learning to hear more, learn more, and improve care.

Good governance requires sound systems of internal and external control, these are reflected in the procedural document management portfolio which are representative of the organisational culture.

A "just" culture which incorporates fairness relies on two elements, firstly the procedural documents which define the structure of organisational systems and processes and secondly the willingness of staff to follow the desired procedures. The culture of an organisation is defined by the organisation's strategy. The strategy states the values and beliefs of the organisation which must be upheld and embraced by everyone. In some organisations staff choose not to engage with the organisational culture and in this situation, fairness is compromised. For fairness to flourish, staff must engage with the culture and believe in the values of the organisation. This can be measured by initiatives such as patient safety surveys, staff surveys, adverse events, and complaints.

There have been many publications referring to fairness in the NHS, for example in 2021 NHS England published a report entitled "A Just Culture Guide" the purpose of which was to encourage managers to treat staff involved in a patient safety incident in a "consistent, constructive and fair way" (NHS, 2018). In 2019 NHS Resolution suggested that a just and learning culture is a balance of "fairness, justice, learning – and taking responsibility for actions" and their publication entitled "Being fair 2" aimed to promote the value of a person-centred workplace that is "compassionate and fair" (NHS, 2023).

It is one thing to talk about employees engaging with the culture and therefore encouraging fairness but for the statement to be meaningful it needs to be measured. The question of how NHS organisations know that the actual culture is consistent with the espoused culture is answered through the annual NHS Staff Survey. (NHS Staff Survey, published annually)

In the annual NHS staff survey question 18a asks:

18. *To what extent do you agree or disagree with the following*

   a. *My organisation treats staff who are involved in an error, near miss or incident fairly.*

However, this process poses a further challenge when the response rate is low and requires remedial action.

Staff Opinion of Fairness

It can be said that the identification of staff opinion on whether or not fairness is evident in an NHS organisation is a priority for the NHS.

Taking positive action to address the issues raised through the survey process will result in staff seeing that the organisation is committed to quality improvement and therefore patient safety which will in turn promote a just, fair, and open culture. Improvement plans are developed and overseen by the relevant committee, group, or Trust Board. Outcomes from Staff Surveys are reviewed as part of the CQC inspection process where organisations are held to account for improvement initiatives. However, do organisations implement change to satisfy external scrutiny or because the organisational values and culture really believe in the benefit of the process?

Barriers to Fairness and Good Governance

The next discussion point with the group focused on what they felt were the barriers to achieving fairness and good governance in the NHS.

The group Trust CEO representative felt that organisational focus is disproportionately placed on policies, procedures, and targets instead of prioritising fairness. Two examples he shared related to different ethnic groups working together in a theatre and ward environment.

Theatre nurses complained that there was an infection, prevention and control risk posed by others wearing a hijab. To establish the facts underpinning the issue the Chief Nurse visited the unit to discuss it with staff and was met by a clinician who was wearing a "Guns and Roses" bandana. The ensuing discussion resulted in the conclusion that as long as both headdresses were washed according to protocol there was no difference between the wearing of the two. What emerged as the actual issue was the perspective of those working in the unit and the fairness of their acceptance of cultural differences.

Another example described an allegation that a nurse from Nigeria was making a phone call home from the ward phone. An investigation was initiated, and several staff were asked to provide a statement of accounts relating to the event. At a subsequent meeting between the accused nurse and management representation the outcome produced no evidence to support the accusation. The Nigerian nurse queried why nobody had checked the phone records prior to the start of the investigation and whether the Trust would have initiated an investigation if it had been a nurse from the local area who had been accused of calling home. The nurse felt that she had been treated unfairly and undervalued.

Overseas employees are a desired resource in the NHS of today. These examples challenge organisational tolerance to a multi-cultural workforce which if it is allowed to prevail will have a detrimental effect on the NHS overseas recruitment ability and consequent waiting lists.

Fairness and Leadership

Leadership plays an important part in fairness and the lack of good leadership will compromise the openness required to develop a just culture. Individuals in organisations whose values contradict those of the organisation and who abuse their position of power can breed a culture of defensiveness, apathy, and lack of empowerment, the consequence being staff fear retribution if they challenge superiors. This has been highlighted in the recent Lucy Letby case where leaders did not listen and act on information shared by colleagues. This case was widely covered in the press at the time (https://www.theguardian.com/uk-news/2023/aug/18/lucy-letby-how-did-a-nurse-commit-such-unthinkable-murders).

Effective communication of the organisational values was placed as a high importance by the discussion group. It was thought that if employees understood what was required, and why it was important and saw themselves as being an important part of the process, there would be greater clarity and appetite for engagement, ownership, and accountability.

Good communication ensures that information is shared in a way that everyone throughout the organisation can understand. For example, a key barrier to effective communication was thought to be the use of medical jargon or fancy words instead of using plain English. All too often in the NHS information is not conveyed at a level that is understandable to all the people who will be reading it.

Some examples are clinicians using clinical terminology which is too specific and technical for non-clinical employees. Or lengthy NHS policies which contain more information than is required resulting in staff not reading the document due to the time required to read or understand it. Consequently, staff disengage. It is unfair for organisations to expect employees to comply with processes that they cannot understand.

The group discussed the impact that "status" has on fairness; the conclusion being that in some organisations people in executive, senior and clinical positions have strong opinions of how things should be done. They appear to have a closed mindset to positive enquiry which manifests as arrogance and a lack of professionalism and professional courtesy, the effect on staff being reluctance to challenge and a loss of psychological safety.

Apathy

Another discussion point was that of "apathy." There are certain departments, people, or groups within the NHS who have the belief that they have been doing something for such a long time there is no point in changing as it will not change anything which is important to them.

An example of this is staff who do not comply with the manual handling regulation requirements which set out specific guidelines for manual handling. The phrase "I've been lifting like this for years and I'm not going to change now" can be heard from individuals who do not believe in the benefits of safe handling. This may be accepted favourably as individual choice, but it has an unfair impact on other staff when handling tasks are undertaken with more than one and the other handler is placed at risk of injury and on patients when the incorrect technique is compromised.

Fair Compensation

Another discussion focused on the "people" aspect of fairness in the NHS. More specifically on the effectiveness of the "Agenda for Change" process and how fair its impact is on NHS staff. Agenda for Change (AFC) is the NHS pay grading structure which was introduced in 2004 to provide a harmonised approach ensuring that employees are compensated within a common framework. (NHS Employers). It places a requirement on managers to evaluate job roles against standardised knowledge and skills frameworks which are linked to a structured salary scale.

The desired result of the approach is that all staff are paid fairly and consistently across the NHS. The group felt that the process was fair if applied accurately and truthfully by the senior leader completing the evaluation. However, the evaluation process is open to individual interpretation; it reveals inconsistencies when the AFC criteria are misinterpreted or manipulated, and the criteria of the job role are aligned to a higher pay band. The result being individuals are placed on higher pay bands than others due to the discrepancies. Consequently, staff may be working in similar roles receiving different salaries.

The resolution to this is a sound quality assurance process which unfortunately does not always function effectively enough to identify the failures. An example was shared (which was not felt to be uncommon) of a staff member requesting a salary increase stating that they had another job confirmed and would leave if the increase was not approved, the individual was subsequently offered an increase in salary. This was in direct conflict with the AFC process.

Another staffing-related factor which influences fairness is that of "role creep." In this situation employees (usually the more junior staff) complete the AFC process mentioned earlier and are aligned to an appropriate pay band linked to their role; however, over time additional responsibilities are attached to their portfolio without the appropriate increase in salary. This situation creates an environment where employees are exceeding the requirements of their job description and not receiving the relevant salary and requests to align the role are met with the explanation that the funding to increase the pay is not available. More responsibility without reward causes frustration, conflict, and low morale.

Fairness and Nursing Care

The fairness of nursing care is challenged in some NHS organisations that have moved away from the traditional form of a "ward" to where each patient is cared for in their own individual room. In the ward situation there is a centralised "nursing station" where nursing staff oversee all patients who are cared for in bays holding several patients. Patients can interact with and support each other, and nurses have oversight of multiple patients at one time. In this model there is the potential for the control of infection to be compromised but robust infection prevention procedures will control the situation. Caring for patients in individual rooms is considered to reduce the risk of infection. However, it has the potential to cause loneliness, isolation, and subsequent fear. It is difficult for nurses to respond to calls from patients due to the high number of rooms within the overall environment. This scenario has particular significance when patients are being cared for on a one-to-one basis and there is a requirement for one person to be always with the patient; this is difficult to achieve in these days of significant staff shortages. In this example fairness is challenged by the potential for infection.

Working Differently

The group was asked how they could we work differently to achieve fairness in Governance and the NHS?

A Clearer Definition of Governance

Define governance. The role of "governance" is often misunderstood in the NHS environment. It is an entity that usually lacks a definition, for example if one talks about "pharmacy" most people understand what it is and what it does in the NHS, but that is not so for governance. Definitions of governance within the NHS generally differ, indeed if eight people sitting around a table were asked to define governance, it is a high probability that each definition would be different. Governance should be the spot check that is used to bring fairness back into a process. If poor governance processes are in place the normalisation of unfair outcomes in given situations will become embedded.

Streamlining Processes

Organisational policies can be far too long and therefore staff are understandably reluctant to read them; this is a problem when the document is a statutorily required one. Procedural documents are crucial to the NHS as they govern the behaviour of the organisation ensuring that it is operating fairly and in line with the values and goals. Organisations must eliminate overly complicated documents.

Encouraging Conversations

Having an environment which encourages challenging conversations is key. Leaders must empower staff to raise concerns so that they feel confident in the knowledge that if they challenge a situation they will be treated fairly. The term "professional curiosity" needs to replace words such as "challenge" so that it becomes seen as a positive response.

Listening

Leaders need to demonstrate deep listening when individuals share their concerns about unfairness. They need to be committed to what the speaker is saying and demonstrate empathy, "putting themselves in their shoes." This will make staff feel that their opinion is valued and encourage "buy-in." Treat others as they would like to be treated themselves.

Conclusion

This chapter has highlighted examples of where fairness is compromised and has also suggested ways in which to improve fairness. The three key messages to take away from reading this chapter are.

The NHS has robust systems and processes in place which if adhered to, will enable a culture where everyone is treated fairly. Human behaviour compromises these safe systems and if left unchecked has the potential to normalise deviated behaviour.

A culture of psychological safety is crucial to ensuring that staff feel supported when they report adverse events. This culture must be defined in the strategy and communicated in a way that ensures organisational commitment.

Continued strategic focus needs to be placed on the importance of openness and learning. NHS Resolution has published three documents "Being Fair," Being Fair 2," and the "Just and Learning Charter," which all highlight the importance of a reflective and just approach.

Like the chicken and the egg question, the group discussed the question of what comes first governance or fairness. The answer was neither: one can't exist without the other.

References

Kennedy, John F. (1960). *The New Frontier.* Convention Acceptance Speech.

NHS Employers. (2023). *NHS Terms and Conditions Annual, Hourly and HCAS Pay Values Scales for 2023/24.* NHS Employers.

NHS England. (2018). *A Just Culture Guide.* NHS England.

NHS England. (2019). *Patient Safety Strategy.* NHS England.

NHS Resolution. (2023a). *Improving Organisational Culture in the NHS.* NHS Resolution.

NHS Resolution. (2023b). *Being Fair 2 – Improving an Organisational Culture.* NHS Resolution.

NHS Resolution. (2023c). *Just and Learning Culture Charter.* NHS Resolution.

NHS Staff Survey. (2021). *Working Together to Improve NHS Staff Experiences.* NHS Staff Survey.

NHS Staff Survey. (2022). *Mike.* https://www.nhsstaffsurvey.com.uk.

Reason, James. (1991). *Human Error.* Cambridge University Press.

5

FAIRNESS AND FINANCE IN THE NHS

Mike Thomas

Introduction

This chapter was written following conversations with experienced NHS finance experts who have contributed their thoughts, insights, and views to the issue of fairness and finance in the NHS. Their knowledge of healthcare finances and their hands-on experiences have been central to how I considered my approach to this chapter. I decided to place emphasis on governmental approaches to NHS funding allocations and the impact of their decisions on the frontline for those wrestling with managing large budgets as demand for healthcare rises and the cost of pharmaceutical and technological advances increases. I am grateful to the experts who have contributed to Chris Adcock, the Chief Finance Officer (CFO) at the University Hospitals of Morecambe Bay NHS Foundation Trust, and Bill Boa, experienced NHS finance director and independent finance leader, whose contributions provided context from the front line of NHS finance and leadership roles over many years, across a number of different systems and NHS organisations.

The Early Days of the NHS

Following its inception in 1948, the National Health Service has always faced financial challenges. In fact, even during its passage through parliament before it was formed there were arguments around funding. Aneurin Bevan, the Health Secretary in Clement Attlee's 1945 post-war labour

DOI: 10.4324/9781003410560-7

government overcame several Treasury hurdles to enable universal health care in the United Kingdom. His eventual resignation from the Cabinet over disagreements with charging for certain health care products and activities (spectacles and dental work) provides some insight into the high levels of principles some parliamentarians attached to a tax-funded NHS.

Bevan agreed, after a prolonged argument with the British Medical Association, to pay consultants a higher salary than first envisaged (but still less than the figures found in private practice) and to permit self-employed contracts and the freedom to have fee-paying beds in NHS hospitals.

Bevan was also the chief proponent of a tax-funded health service, rejecting an insurance-based model as unfair to those from poorer communities who would proportionally pay more (Portillo, 1998). The Attlee government brought local authority and voluntary-run hospitals under central control, which meant that the different health provider agencies were collectively put into a public-sector framework. Added to the various hospitals were Ambulance Trusts, Community provision, and mental health services, and what we all know as the National Health Service.

This makes the UK National Health Service unique in funding terms, with nearly 93% funded via Treasury control. Elsewhere in Europe there are no examples of such high tax-funded models. The Netherlands, widely accepted as one of the world's best healthcare providers, funds healthcare through a mix of approximately 85% of social and private insurance and less than 10% is funded through taxation. A similar picture applies in France, and in Germany where health and social care are jointly funded.

The Treasury being the only real source of funding created pressure right from the beginning. In Bevan's time as health secretary, costs began to rise as demand for eye care, dental services, and drugs reached unprecedented heights. The UK population was not healthy, the demand for healthcare was, and has, always been very high. The drug costs alone in 1948 were £13 million, by 1950, just 24 months later, it had risen to £41 million (Kynaston, 2007), and today those figures are dwarfed by the £17.2 billion spent in 2021/2022 (LSE, 2023). In 1948 health spending was £138 million; by 2022/23, this had increased to £181.7 billion.

NHS spending is always a political source of differences and spending does fluctuate depending on political philosophies and priorities. By 1955 a conservative administration spent 4.5% in real terms (by real terms I mean the actual amount spent after adjusting for the rate of inflation), on the NHS and over 5% during the early 1970s. This was more than the Labour administration which spent less than 3.5% during its time in office during the mid-1960s and the 1970s.

Approaches to Funding Policies 1980–1997

The real political break from a general political consensus that the NHS should be supported came through the political and fiscal policies of the Thatcher-led conservatives of the 1980s and early 1990s. The impact on funding was severe. Her government cut health spending to the lowest since its inception, spending only 2.5% in real terms. Rogers and Pilgrim (2001) noted that the Thatcher administration introduced an American-influenced approach to centrally funded welfare services, departing from the post-war consensus of a funded Welfare State to one which was based on a mixed-market economy involving the public, private, and voluntary sectors working either alongside or preferably in competition to deliver healthcare.

The original premise that the NHS was tax-funded, centrally directed, and created as "a monopoly provider of health" (Hutton, 1996, p. 211) was widely accepted politically for over 30 years as a more egalitarian approach to health through the provision of "free" services at the point of entry, typically via a first assessment by GPs. For the 1979 Conservative government with their market-focused political philosophies, the NHS monopoly was seen as inherently inefficient. Thatcher and her ministers worked hard to reinvent the NHS as a market.

This ideological approach broke with the past, and by the late 1980s, in full stride, Thatcher brought in an internal market to further encourage competition between health providers. The objective, later proven to be unfounded, was that market forces would deliver improved productivity, increased efficiency, and in turn lower the central government funding contribution to the NHS. The introduction of complex funding models led to inequality, the so-called "postcode lottery", as often funding packages were based on population size, the number of GP practices, or where care was commissioned by fundholders within regions, rather than a whole-of-nation approach.

The quality and spread of provision were uneven, and care was differentiated across regions. It was widely perceived as unfair because the quality-of-care provision depended on where one lived, not on population health needs. As the impact spread, Will Hutton predicted in 1996 that the competitive market model would lead to more inequalities, more specialisation of services (often far from where the patient lived), and pressure to reduce costs rather than spend to meet the healthcare needs of the population. His prediction came true.

Approaches to Funding Policies 1997–2010

Labour had to quickly reform the internal market from 1998 onwards, but in doing so the Blair and Brown governments had to dig deep into the Treasury to support the NHS recovery and have spent the most since the NHS was launched, 5.5% from the late 1990s and throughout the early years of this century. Labour's reforms, which provided General Practitioners with new NHS contracts in June 2003, allowing them to run like small businesses, paid for more multi-disciplinary practice-based delivery. The new contract arrangement freed General Practitioners from the responsibility for 24-hour services, and they received extra income for taking on additional contract work.

The days of a recognisably named GP was ending, however, as nearly two years later, in April 2005, the practice of GPs becoming contract providers was introduced through the creation of Primary Care Trusts (PCTs), who "commissioned" provider contracts. In this model, general practitioners were further allowed to keep any proportion of saved contract funding within their practices. By December 2006 the PCT model was rolled out across all of England. It is unclear whether large swathes of the population realise how changes over the years impact on their health provision. Most people still hanker, years after the Blair reforms, for a named GP, and most do not seem to realise that General Practices are small businesses, most of which are reliant on NHS-commissioned contracts to survive.

Yet although the Blair government spent the most on NHS funding, in real terms, it was not easy and not sustained. Between the years 2007 and 2011 NHS spending was reduced to 4% of the treasury allocation (down from the previous 5.5%), and although the funding appeared to increase (from £90 billion in 2007 to £110 billion by 2010), in real terms the funding could not match rising NHS costs and impacted on NHS provision. For example, in Mental Health Services it led to a 20% shortfall in spending requirements (Lester and Glasby, 2010).

The Austerity Years 2010–2017

The austerity years of the Cameron-led Conservative and Lib-Dem coalition has spent the least since 1948, around 1% in real terms, a huge decline from the Labour years. The last decade of Conservative rule has not exceeded

2.8% in real terms. Its current plans for the years 24/25 indicate an increase of only 0.1% (The Kings Fund, 2023).

Experienced NHS finance director, Bill Boa suggests that notwithstanding some of the NHS productivity challenges the NHS has been running at, or close to, 100% capacity for years, and this means it had limited if any flexibility in a pandemic. Bill has a view that "Presumably this will be commented on by the current enquiry, [the COVID-19 inquiry]; however, at least since the start of Austerity, the NHS infrastructure and capacity has been significantly negatively impacted." (Boa, 2023)

These are important issues, often lost in the blame game prevalent in politics; the evidence overwhelmingly indicates that sufficient funding of the NHS is fairer and more equitable in terms of the nation's health. The Blair reforms of the NHS, alongside its increased funding in real terms, led to increased productivity, performance, and outcomes. But from 2010 all these have declined, initially due to the governmental austerity measures and therefore sharp reductions in annual funding increases, and poor workforce planning.

Added to this situation has been the complete lack of much-needed social care reforms. By 2014, Trusts, for the first time in such numbers, were experiencing widespread deficits and encountering their first year of failing to hit waiting list targets. This has continued for the past ten years with services across the NHS with data demonstrating decline, including Mental Health Services, Learning Disability provision, General Practice, and across Primary and Acute Care (Ham, 2023).

The conservative administration of Rishi Sunak aimed to spend £168.8 billion on commissioning in 2023/2024, less than the £181.7 billion spent in 2022/2023 whilst demand continues to rise. The Institute for Fiscal Studies recognises that additional top-up funding has been given to the NHS during and after the pandemic, but they also acknowledge that it is not enough to compensate for the increase in NHS staffing costs, higher inflation, lower productivity, and pharmaceutical costs compared to pre-COVID data (Warner and Zaranko, 2022).

Contemporary Impact of Funding Policies

Increased staffing costs have occurred paradoxically alongside a reduction in real-term bed numbers and a rise in staff sickness as they feel the burden of doing more with less. Social Care has also experienced severe reductions in funding which has inadvertently led to a major challenge for NHS Trusts which are struggling to discharge patients out of hospital. In 2022, 40% of all patients in hospital for more than 21 days experienced delayed discharges (Warner and Zaranko, 2022), mainly because of a lack of resources to support patients to be cared for outside the hospital. This situation also leads to a reduction in the number of patients who can be admitted.

This is attributed to the lack of funding and resources in the social care sector and increases costs across both the NHS and social care providers. The spending plans for 2024/25 would require an additional £4 billion to manage the real-term additional costs to the NHS. And this funding is predicated on real-term growth in the economy, including a reduction in global energy, food costs, and reduced inflation and interest rates, alongside increased GDP growth and export income.

Bill Boa suggests that when considering equity,

> We need to start with clarity about what we are planning to be equitable about. Health and well-being is made up of a multitude of things . . . and health is undermined if social care, housing, education and employment isn't in place. For example, the 20% cut across social care will significantly impact on the other wellbeing factors. The health allocation process is a management tool within a constrained resource and whilst the allocation process does this, it can't pretend to be equitable. Whatever you do with the allocation of healthcare resources it will not be equitable or work as intended if the other elements have been drastically cut or inadequately resourced.
>
> *(Boa, 2023)*

Following the 2022 NHS Health and Care Act, the dissemination of funding continues to rely on commissioned contracts, but the market-focused competitive reforms introduced in 2012 have gone, replaced with more emphasis on collaborative delivery and local systems working. The previous commissioning groups have been abolished and replaced with integrated care systems overseen by 42 statutory Integrated Care Boards (ICBs), with responsibility for local delivery, mainly along local authority, or city boundaries.

Financial oversight of each system lies with the ICBs. In the year ending 2022/23 34 of the 42 ICBs in England were thought to be in deficit; in fact at year end this was almost halved to 16 ICBs which failed to achieve their targets of breakeven. It was thought that for 23/24 a total of 15, will collectively bring in a £750 million deficit (Lister, 2023) It is early days, the ICBs have yet to be established and fully integrated into place, but the early signs are more funding restrictions, reduced commissioning contract envelopes, and a drive to reduce deficits. It is perhaps predictable that unplanned Treasury uplifts will be required to ensure sustainability in some regions.

Fairness and Equity

How equitable will be the funding balance remains unclear. Bill Boa notes,

> Parity of care/distance from target is often used so that changes do not drastically destabilise systems, but this leaves questions about the speed at which any system can therefore move towards a more equitable solution . . . there is another challenge in this. We don't manage the underlying data well and such data is used to draw the conclusions from these allocative processes, (especially in respect of aligning primary care, acute care, and wider demographic information), and going forward we somehow need to draw this together. This requires a national discussion about the use of data in the NHS. The public are being turned off by data overload yet health data, ONS data, and social care data need to combine. In London the e-child system [an electronic patient record system], has it all, but they cannot get at the primary care data . . . inevitable we must look beyond health to ensure equity, but within health we must look at, and use the right data.
>
> *(Boa, 2023)*

More Reform?

The temptation for the existing administration or a new incoming government to do something to wrestle the costs downwards is compelling. It may not be the right response. Wickens and Brown (2023) examined different approaches and models and concluded that it may be more prudent to *not* seek alternate models of funding. Their Kings Fund article looked at several proposed reforms in policy discourses such as social insurance, private provision, health and social care merger, NHS charges, and hypothecation of tax (the practice of ring-fencing a percentage of tax revenue for specific purposes). They all appear to have too many challenges, being either too costly or too disruptive to continuity of care. Others add an additional layer of administration to the existing system, or there is a lack of current NHS capacity. Wickens and Brown suggest that better improvement of the current model would be more efficient and effective, and therefore fair.

Bill Boa considered how the UK Public Health has become fragmented and attempts to deal with an ageing population. In the context of population ageing it is likely that where Japan is now will be the future challenge for the NHS, how to manage the challenges of demand rather than any particular funding model. Bill argues that there must be a discussion on what the health system does for the population overall as the current model looks to be unsustainable. He further argues that the way that capital is allocated is outdated and questionable regarding its fitness for purpose.

Revenue constrains the allocation so can only cover so much cost of capital. However as with all change, it needs to be understood that the current structures cannot replace broken and outdated infrastructure without the revenue to support it. Any replacement systems with a poor capital base are likely further disadvantaged. Businesses never look at capital and revenue separately and the current capital processes for the NHS are badly joined up. Bill feels that there should be more focus on inequality as a basis for capital allocations and not redistribution in asset wealth.

Financial leadership has been significantly challenging in the NHS over the last 14 years with declining real-term funding and increasing demand for services. Longer term planning is necessary to address the health inequalities and future and well-articulated public health challenges and the needs of an ageing population – specifically, the step changes which will result from the "baby boomer" population reaching their mid-80s and beyond – is too often deferred or de-prioritised due to the financial crisis response required today.

The Public Sector financing regime, whereby there are Departmental Expenditure Limits ("DEL"), means that a pound of capital spend ("CDEL") to be equivalent to a pound of revenue spend ("RDEL"). This is very different to any other industry and therefore leads to short-term decision-making based on affordability and whatever reflects the political priority at the time. The NHS regime operates within the context of how overall public finances operate and therefore it is questionable whether NHS arrangements could be effectively overhauled without change to this.

Chris Ham (2023) proposed a more effective funding model where the NHS annual funding is in line with long-term average revenue targets. Ham also calls for an urgent focus on funding to bridge the gap in provision for patient discharges as well as a general focus on social care funding. In recognition of the fragility of public and population health efforts he suggests that the government should ensure that public health, primary, and community care be prioritised alongside a credible workforce plan. Ham recognises the shortfalls in both funding and policymaking during the last decade and encourages cross-departmental and Treasury support to tackle the wider determinants of health; this should include more focus on personal responsibility and individuals being more active agents to support and maintain their own healthcare and wellbeing.

Different Approaches to Planning

Leadership time to implement financial plans through to completion is required. Too often Finance leaders find themselves overwhelmed with further priorities, which frequently divert attention and resources way from planning schedules and activities. Mike's own observations suggest that lengthening the period of uncertainty in planning cycles is an added stress for leaders, particularly when the time allocated to bring certainty to a situation is supplanted by sudden and unplanned priorities by the very leaders who originally pushed for pace in agreed planning cycles and subsequently added further financial pressures on budgets.

Extended planning timelines have become more commonplace during this period, and this appears to be linked to the scale of the financial challenges faced by the NHS alongside expectations of what can be achieved within available resources.

The recent pattern of an annual "crisis" approach will not promote meaningful and longer-term sustainable approaches to dealing with the NHS financial challenges. More inclusion of collaborative partnerships between community, primary care and acute providers needs to be harnessed to meaningful reform in social care and local authority responsibilities.

Local systems must give real focus and attention to the effective development of local financial frameworks which best fit the local circumstances and challenges in pursuit of the best patient outcomes and the effective deployment of resources. Individual provider organisations need to come together more effectively to plan and contract together, share the delivery, and measure the impact of their actions on patient experience and on population health. It should be noted that recently issued planning guidance further reinforces the requirement for and importance of system collaboration in this way.

Organisational and budgetary boundaries can get in the way of the achievement of these objectives if the parties to agreements are differentially exposed to risk. For example, overstretched primary care resources are not adversely impacted when patients go to A&E because they can't get an appointment, and secondary care budgets are not directly impacted by the increasingly expensive care packages required in the community. The development of more flexible and joined-up system financial frameworks could promote a more holistic approach to patient-centred care.

Local system financial frameworks and contractual agreements should promote and reward shared financial and budget approaches to service delivery and patient outcomes.

Reflection Points

Context

The NHS has been in existence for over 75 years. Its tax-based model through central funding and a generally shared belief in a universal healthcare provision was dominant in its first 30 years. The principle of free at the point of access was seen as being a fair and equitable model of delivery. The political philosophy of Thatcherism brought in a new model, more market-driven and competitive with attempts to bring in different funding approaches. Her government caused a dramatic shift in the post-war political consensus, and evidence suggests that healthcare delivery and provision became more unfair and inequitable. The Blair years demonstrated more productivity and access to healthcare, with increased spending correlated with improvements in population health.

The years of austerity leading to, and through, the pandemic, have currently caused a constant race to catch up because of previous deteriorating funding, and the race has been constantly lost during the last 13 years. Contemporary data indicate that the health of the nation has deteriorated and is struggling to improve, waiting lists have continued to rise, and long bed occupancy in hospitals prevents efficient throughput for care (Warner and Zaranko, 2022). This has often led to top-down, instrumental, and directive instructions, which has been shown to repeatedly fail to shift efficiency in the right direction. Instructional top-down orders have a negative impact on staff engagement and productivity, whilst emotionally intelligent leaders have the opposite impact. Michael West (2021) stresses that effective and positive staff engagement with compassionate leaders positively impacts on care quality and financial improvement.

Fairness and Politics

The year-on-year real-term funding reduction (the funding allocated after the effects of inflation) is a contentious point. The question has to be asked, does decreasing real term spending on the NHS make it unfair? In a political context this can be debated. The recent conservative government would have challenged this and have argued that the NHS budget has been protected, even if they had conceded that it has not grown. The Treasury does not keep funding at a level that copes with sudden and often sharp rises in pharmaceutical costs, new technology or energy prices. Governments choose the priorities to meet their manifestos and often believe they are mandated by the population to do so. Much depends on your viewpoint and attitude towards the NHS being tax-funded and controlled by the government. Ultimately, the question of real-term increase in NHS funding is an issue of choice. Mike believes that it is unfair to patients and users if real-term increases are not provided.

Traditional conservative ideology stresses a small State, less regulation, and the encouragement of a free market. Such ideology believes that the market regulates and conducts itself through profit and loss, growth, acquisitions, and so on and is best placed to demonstrate increased productivity and efficiency. Within such an approach the public sector is either stereotyped or demonised, often seen as a drain on resources, unproductive, slow to be entrepreneurial, and steeped in fixed cultures and practices. It also prevents the State from being smaller.

The opposite ideology, such as held by labour administrations, sees the public sector as the safety net for those who are in lower socio-economic positions, with opportunities for improved education, employment, and life prospects, and often essential for the good working of society, whether in social care, health, education, or local authorities. Business principles can be seen as profit-orientated rather than existing for the common good, that unregulated markets create conditions, which dispossess the poor, sick, and frail, causing the state to intervene on their behalf. Within this philosophy, the State is seen as the utilitarian guardian of the population and intervenes to enrich the lives of as many as possible.

The issue of fairness in this context may therefore depend on your political leaning. Perhaps the real question around fairness is whether it is fair for governments to claim a mandate to act on behalf of citizens when they receive the most votes in an election, but not the votes of most of the population. Thirteen years of attempting to create a smaller state-orientated government has been hampered by the pandemic, where they were required to do the reverse, which may lead to the view that the NHS is under a form of "managed decline" to engineer an increase in market intervention and lessen the funding burden for the Treasury.

However, if there is little, if any, profit to be made in the field of social care for example, and these services have experienced huge government funding reductions without the instigation of any type of reforms, that such a strategy would lead to a market intervention of this type would be much less likely. It is more likely that NHS funding has decreased in real terms because of short-term priorities, reactive responses to immediate issues, and perhaps the impact of a government administration at the end of 14 at times tumultuous years lacking the policy and vigour to intervene. Declining real-term funding has not kept up with the demands of ageing infrastructure, technological advancements, and the costs of increased patient demand.

Public Confidence

An important point to consider is whether the public has confidence in robust government interventions to ensure fairness in NHS funding. The witnesses for the national COVID-19 Inquiry provide a picture of politicians who generally did not, and could not, understand or interpret basic science-based data, who decried expert advice (who can recall Michael Gove, a government minister throughout Covid, and his earlier claim that the population had had enough of "experts"?), and who at times seemed dispassionate with regard who would die or not during the pandemic.

Allocation of Funding

A further reflection question: where do you think the balance lies between central oversight, an ever-increasing demand for services, individual organisation performance and productivity, and budget planning? Bill Boa notes that,

> Our processes are always behind the curve on the changes that occur in respect of our allocative arrangements. It is patently obvious that there is an issue regarding coastal communities and still no change at all in the allocations. It may be that the Office of Budget Responsibility or equivalent needs to take an independent view across health and social care.

And this should be considered in the context that the NHS took up approximately 27% of government spending under Gordon Brown and is now above 40% and heading for 50%. One colleague did articulate their view that a model that provides care for free is unlikely to be sustainable in the context of an ageing population. There have been several calls from commentators nationally for cross-party working groups to look at the challenge and viability of the NHS funding model in the context of the provision of free at the point of need for all, in the context of an ageing population, technological advances and rising demand. We would support this approach as a priority.

The future of the NHS cannot be deliberated without accepting that funding must be tackled. It is a huge challenge for policymakers and governments, and one which should include a public voice. The future wellbeing of the population will be influenced by the decisions that are made.

Final Reflections for the Reader

Some questions for you to consider:

Do you feel that the NHS productivity would increase with additional funding? (And what is the basis for your answer?)

Do you think that political ideology should influence the finances and planning of the NHS?

Should the health of the nation be a cross-party issue that would benefit from agreed five-year planning periods?

Do you think there is enough public awareness and scrutiny of NHS funding?

And does this reflect on whether the population accepts year-on-year real term decreases in NHS spending because they feel this is a government objective, or a tired administration?

Has cynicism in political policymaking gained traction amongst voters to the extent that disinterest is becoming an accepted norm?

Is it an equal relationship where both the government and the NHS plan funding together? Or should the current model stress that any decrease in year-on-year real funding requires providers to adjust through increased efficiencies?

Do you think the NHS should, or can, continue in its present form with existing funding?

Should a new model be explored, and if so, which one would you propose? (Ie. The models from Europe with a mix of social insurance and tax funding? The reintroduction of a mixed market model? Private and personal insurance funded provision?)

Or do you think we should keep the NHS with realistic tax-based funding?

References

Boa, B. (2023) *Notes of conversation with Chris Adcock*. University Hospitals of Morecambe Bay NHS Foundation Trust, 29 June.

Ham, C. (2023) *The rise and decline of the NHS in England 2000–20: How political failure led to the crisis in the NHS and social care*. The Kings Fund, 12 April. www.kingsfund.org.uk

Hutton, W. (1996) *The state we're in*. Vintage.

The Kings Fund. (2023) *The NHS budget and how it has changed.* www.kingsfund.org.uk

Kynaston, D. (2007) *Austerity Britain; 1945–51.* Bloomsbury Publishing PLC.

Lester, H. & Glasby, J. (2010) *Mental health policy and practice.* 2nd Ed. Palgrave Macmillan.

Lister, J. (2023) *NHS England bosses crack the whip over ICB debts.* The Lowdown, 4th August. www.lowdownnhs.info.

LSE. (2023) *LSE news: Costs of expensive new drugs threaten financial sustainability of NHS while pharma industry lobbies for increase on medicines spending,* 5 June. www.lse.ac.uk.

Portillo, M. (1998) The Bevan legacy. *BMJ,* 317(7150):37–40, 4 July. doi:10.1136/bmj.317.7150.37.

Rogers, A. & Pilgrim, D. (2001) *Mental health policy in Britain.* 2nd Ed. Palgrave Macmillan.

Warner, M. & Zaranko, B. (2022) *NHS funding, resources, and treatment volumes.* Institute for Fiscal Studies, 14 December. www.Ifs.org.uk.

West, M. A. (2021) *Compassionate leadership – sustaining wisdom, humanity and presence in health and social care.* The Swirling Leaf Press. www.swirlingleafpress.com.

Wickens, C. and Brown, T. (2023) *The NHS in crisis – evaluating the radical alternatives.* The Kings Fund, 31 July. www.kingsfund.org.uk.

6

FAIRNESS AND ORGANISATIONAL LEADERSHIP IN THE NHS

Aaron Cummins and Mike Thomas

Introduction

This chapter was written using several sources which vary from published research, think tank reports, parliamentary papers and interviews with leaders who practice leadership on a day-to-day basis. Personal perspectives of fairness and leadership in the NHS were written from the experience and research of the two authors, Aaron Cummins (Chief Executive Officer (CEO), University Hospitals of Morecambe Bay NHS Foundation Trust), and Mike Thomas (Chair of the Lancashire and South Cumbria NHS Provider Collaborative Board) and through discussion group interviews conducted by Aaron Cummins with experienced healthcare leaders. Contributors included system and place leaders Kevin Lavery, the CEO of the Lancashire, and South Cumbria Integrated Care Board (LSC ICB), Jane Scattergood, who is the Director of Health and Care Integration, LSC ICB, Cumbria, Louise Taylor, a fellow Director of Health and Care Integration LSC ICB, Lancashire, and Dr David Levy, the Medical Director of the LSC ICB.

Amongst CEOs of hospital trusts were Trish Armstrong Childs, the CEO of Blackpool Teaching Hospitals NHS Foundation Trust, Chris Oliver, the CEO of Lancashire & South Cumbria NHS Foundation (mental health) Trust and Foluke Ajayi, the CEO of Airedale NHS Foundation Trust. And from a regional and national perspective were Jackie Hanson, Chief Nurse, North-West, National Health Service Executive, and Sue Holden, CEO of

DOI: 10.4324/9781003410560-8

Advancing Quality Alliance (Aqua), NHS. We are grateful for their time, insights, and valuable contributions.

The Development of Modern Leadership Within the NHS

As with much of the public sector, leadership within the NHS has always been a focus of interest for policymakers, politicians, and aspiring managers. This can be rationalised by the fact that the NHS is funded through tax and is directly responsible and accountable to the government of the day who act on behalf of the public. Among the public, there is an expectation of value for money, efficiency, effectiveness, and high standards of public service amongst the leaders of the NHS.

1979–1997

Prior to Margaret Thatcher's conservative government from 1979 onwards, the leaders of the NHS received little attention. Clinical services were managed and operated by lead clinicians, and the leaders who currently hold the nomenclature of Chief Executive Officers were more often titled Hospital Administrators. Margaret Thatcher and her ministers took the view that the whole structure of management in the NHS needed to be modernised and the practices of commercial companies introduced throughout the publicly funded health system.

In 1983 her government asked Sir Roy Griffiths, a Director of J Sainsbury's plc to lead a formal inquiry into NHS effectiveness, focusing on manpower and efficiency. His report concluded that the NHS lacked any clear definition of management functions and led to the introduction of a new general management structure (Gorsky, 2013). Under the following Prime Minister, John Major's conservative administration between 1990 and 1997 further reforms included the introduction of the Citizen's Charter and separately the Patient's Charter which both underlined the principle that users of public services and the NHS were to be perceived as consumers and was the beginning of the continuing trend to have measurable targets of productivity and efficiency such as fixed waiting times for assessments (House of Commons, 2008).

1997–2010

Following these reforms, there were a number of leadership development policies which continued into the next Labour government of Tony Blair in 1997. These included Making a Difference (1999), which strengthened nursing leadership, the NHS Plan in 2000 which established the NHS Leadership Centre, Liberating the Talents (2002) which supported primary care leadership, Choosing Health in 2004 which promoted Public Health leadership, and Our NHS, Our Future (2007) which called for leadership to be strengthened within the curricula of education and training programmes. This was carried out alongside several other "reforms", controversial at the time, such as the introduction of fees for certain dentist procedures, spectacles, prescriptions, and rehabilitation equipment which had previously been provided free of charge.

Although Margaret Thatcher's and John Major's conservative governments always stressed that the essential founding values of the NHS were maintained, such as free healthcare at the point of access, it was clear that the conservatives had introduced a more market-influenced National Health Service with certain aspects of health intervention now requiring personal financial costs beyond the previous tax-funded provision. This new, private-sector-focused NHS required a different approach to leadership and more focus was put on developing managers who would concentrate their energies on increasing productivity, doing more with less funding, and adopting commercial practices in their approach to running a "business" rather than a hospital. The previous consensus approach to management was swept away as not fit for purpose, at all levels, with managerialism the chosen model to replace it.

Leaders have been scrutinised since for their effectiveness within a pseudo-market economy which stressed skills which supported developments within a more private industry-driven approach to health delivery (targets, productivity output, etc.). Different government administrations, Conservative and Labour continued with this approach for 20 years believing in effective leadership as one which had at its heart a "business" perception of how to lead organisations. The Blair government, for example, introduced league tables of best and worst performing hospitals (based on their fixed metrics), believing that publicly shaming organisations and leaders would improve delivery.

This model is widely believed to be ineffective and lacking the confidence of practitioners though it is still in use today through regulatory bodies such as OFSTED (The Office for Standards in Education, Children's Services, and Skills) in the educational field and other government-funded regulatory bodies (a finding which the Care Quality Commission seems to have considered as they have altered their previous "inspections" to a more collaborative and supportive process) (CQC, 2024).

2010–2024

The pseudo-market model reached its height with the Conservative/Liberal Democrat Coalition government (2010–2015). It introduced an austerity programme that introduced the reforms which has consistently led to year-on-year real-term financial reductions in the NHS. For example, the Health and Social Care Act, 2012, abolished local Primary Care Trusts and the regional Strategic Health Authorities and introduced many hundreds of local Clinical Commissioning Groups (CCGs). These were in turn abolished under the 2022 Health and Social Care Act, which were predominantly organised and managed by local General Practitioners. Nearly £80 billion of funding was transferred into the new CCGs so they could commission, or contract, local delivery of healthcare.

Following a growing realisation by the subsequent conservative administration that market competition, with hundreds of local commissioning contract systems which encouraged inter-provider rivalry, and private-sector approaches to health-based contracts was damaging healthcare delivery and increasing population health inequity the focus altered with the NHS Health and Care Act, 2022, with its different emphasis on collaboration and partnership. However, this legislation must be taken within the context of the conservatives' principles of reducing spending on public sectors and creating a smaller state.

The drive for increased productivity remains hugely important, as does improved effectiveness and efficiencies, but the emphasis, supported by legislation, is for these to be demonstrated through leadership in partnership, collaboration, and multi-agency working across the healthcare sector. Contemporary healthcare leaders, who have spent three decades in a market-driven environment with competition, acquisitions and a more directive leadership style are now finding the new skills requirements are facilitation, persuasion, relationship-building and sustaining networks. This moves away from a hierarchical centralised leadership model with its top-down command and control style towards a more relational model with skills in compassionate, kind leadership, and building collaborative consensus coming to the fore and bringing opportunities for NHS leaders to redefine issues of fairness in their leadership approaches to locality and place provision and delivery.

Contemporary NHS Operating and the Political Environment

Contemporary NHS operations are strongly influenced by the political environment. Former Prime Minister Rishi Sunak put the fortunes of the Conservative administration to the test by emphasising five pledges which his government would improve upon. One of those five pledges was to bring down NHS waiting times, but this was not to be achieved before the 2024 General Election. The knock-on effects of industrial action by NHS workers, particularly medical staff, meant appointments were cancelled whilst the numbers waiting for first appointments had to wait longer.

The poor investment and the lack of political will to reform Social Care also means that the NHS has, in July 2024, the highest number of in-patients in its history who are unable to meet the criteria for discharge because of a lack of social and local authority resources to ensure they are discharged to a safe environment. This takes up beds and reduces the number of people that could normally be seen, adding more pressure on waiting lists. And there is a focus by political leaders on funding within healthcare due to a growing frustration that, in their perception, the NHS is getting additional funding, a larger workforce (compared to pre-pandemic time), and new technology, yet productivity has worsened (Warner and Zaranko, 2023).

Centrally directed operational plans have meant the NHS Executive is therefore under pressure to deliver political objectives, and this flows down the hierarchy with regional, and local leaders expected to adapt their own plans to ensure a more nation-wide approach to healthcare. This political oversight, which has been utilised by every government since 1948, requires NHS leaders at the national level who can manage both politics and politicians. Most of the time senior NHS executives somehow cope with the hugely pressurised environment within which they work but not always. For example, it has come clear through the interviews in the COVID-19 Inquiry that senior civil servants, scientists, and health advisors struggled to get their voices heard within the political elite, and on occasion were not given full attention because of the tension between priority political objectives and opposing population needs.

NHS Leadership and Fairness

There is a strong link between compassionate/empathetic leadership and fairness, even if it isn't always self-evident. Compassion and empathy are *emotional* perceptions and responses and so influence our approaches and actions towards others and situations. Fairness can be seen as more *behavioural,* and action orientated. Approaching leadership through the more skilful utilisation of compassion would suggest that kind actions are perceived as fair. In contrast imagine leadership judged as unkind or lacking compassion. Can such an approach be seen as fair in practice? It is appropriate to see compassionate leadership approaches as the application of high emotional intelligence, and fairness as the application of just actions and behaviours.

Fairness is a critical underpinning of kindness. Alison Gill reflected in 2018 that without the foundations of firmness and fairness, kindness somehow cannot flourish (Gill, 2018). Aaron agrees strongly with this view, believing that kindness and fairness require a strong belief foundation so that the individual can remain firm when experiencing the day-to-day buffeting of leadership experiences.

This issue of firmness is often overlooked, it is more appropriately termed as being resolute. Too often compassionate and therefore fair leadership is perceived as rather woolly or "softer" than leadership through giving instructions and hierarchical command. But demonstrating compassionate leadership is much harder than barking orders to people. The level of emotional intelligence required is much higher, the complexity of co-ordinating different individuals, viewpoints and approaches much more challenging, and remaining resolute and therefore consistent requires a firmer understanding of the impact of one's own leadership, in other words a higher degree of insight. It's tougher to be a compassionate and fair leader.

Fairness is essential to organisational processes, and not just in healthcare. John Mackey, the joint CEO of Whole Foods Market in the USA, and Raj Sisodia, Professor of Global Business at Boston, are firm in their view that fairness should be integral to policies and processes of recruitment, promotion, work allocations, shift patterns, discipline, and exiting an organisation. To quote them, "people are prone to envy, and any perceived unfairness exacerbates this tendency, giving it the energy of justification." (See Thomas and Rowland, 2018, page 148).

The work of Professor Michael West has shown that compassionate leadership has a positive and deeply profound practical impact on health outcomes for both healthcare users and employees, on increased productivity, costs, and better use of resources. (West, 2021). West argued that compassionate, and in this context of behavioural practice we can include the principle of fair leadership, should be practised across the whole health and social care system, from national leaders to locality leaders. Leadership that is kind and considerate recognises the values of listening to, and hearing the other (think of the lack of acknowledgement of the other in the Post Office scandal), arriving at a shared, rather than imposed understanding of the challenges facing health and social care, actively caring for colleagues, and being consistent in our behaviours and actions towards others.

The main themes running through the practice of compassionate leadership for West are empathetic listening, understanding the pressures and challenges that colleagues face, sustaining learning rather than a blame culture, and encouraging and sustaining collaborative and engaged decision-making. This approach still retains the discipline required to ensure high quality of care, sound financial and auditing management, and high levels of operational and strategic planning. These are attributes which all our interviewees consider relevant to their working lives, and which all take seriously in their approach to decision-making.

This is an important point as these behaviours are not only cited in the annual NHS staff surveys as the underpinnings of fairness demonstrated through the actions of NHS managers but also perceived by staff as a more appropriate and professional approach to direct patient care and personalised healthcare delivery.

Contrasting Command With Compassionate Leadership

Compassionate and fair leadership is often held in direct contrast to the arguably required command and control approach taken during the COVID pandemic, with its hierarchical control structures, management directives, and instructions that required compliance. A health crisis, whether for the individual or the population, often requires such an approach, for no other reason than time is of the essence to save lives. However, hierarchical instructional leaders still need to be good at what they do and bring people with them. Even when a command-and-control system is imposed, the sense of sharing the same values and everyone engaging in the same purpose improves outcomes and productivity.

The COVID-19 Inquiry into the UK pandemic has shown that political leadership was often chaotic and did not meet the necessary standards of good leadership (see too the views of Hooper, 2022; Hollington, 2022). As the healthcare system came through the worst of the pandemic, the command approach was clearly not fit for the purpose of repairing a damaged and exhausted health and social care system.

It is unclear why some leaders still cling to an outdated command and control approach. Not one of our interviewees saw merit in this model in the context of partnership and collaborative working. The 2022 Health and Social Care Act makes clear that it is a legal requirement for NHS leaders to collaborate across organisations, and applying fair leadership following a period of command-and-control leadership style is hardly new territory. David Archer and Alex Cameron studied such a transfer of leadership approaches in 2009 and concluded that this was a sensible adaptation required to lead in an environment that is more strongly inter-connected due to innovations in information and communication technology.

More recently, Haskins and Thomas (2022) suggested that amongst the ten attributes of fair leadership are leading an organisation that has a strong sense of shared purpose, where employees feel valued and believe they have a role to play in the organisational success, where there is less hierarchy and more emphasis on teamwork and collaborative networks, where diversity is genuinely appreciated, where people are treated equally, and leaders follow fair and equitable justice in the application of policies and processes within the organisation.

Why Are Fairness and Equity in Decision-Making Important?

Leaders are required by their role to make decisions. They must constantly evaluate different sets of information and advice and analyse these carefully to reach a conclusion which supports the purpose of their work, organisational strategy, and personal values. In a perfect environment there would be time to deliberate, to stress-test models and ideas, to explore in detail the motivations and aims of the differing counsel and advice, and to sometimes change one's mind. But like any organisation, the NHS reality is one where there is a myriad of tasks to complete in too short a time, often not enough support, or resources to do the work to the standard that one would like, and a constant stream of demands and decisions to be made immediately.

Experience and skills are required to maintain the motivation and engagement of colleagues to abide by the decisions the leader makes. Simultaneously, the ability to balance the demands of the role with personal wellbeing and values is constant stressor on decision-making abilities. And this is at all levels of health and social care leadership, whether clinical, corporate, or political.

As our interviews with leaders made clear, the difference with most other organisational leaders is in the impact of decisions in the health and social environments. In the NHS, the clinical decisions save lives, improve, or enhance the life experiences of people with disabilities, chronic pain, or other life-changing conditions, and in the vast majority of cases, effectively treat diseases and illnesses. And the reality is that at worst, when decisions go wrong, people die.

Every day clinical decisions are made about immediate needs, assessments and interventions, diagnostic testing and results, treatment regimes, more interventions, referrals, follow-up consultations, and so on. All our interviewees agreed with the view that executive leaders are expected to provide an environment where all these activities can take place safely and with a high degree of quality standards. Leaders at the board level make decisions which test the merits and quality of the organisation and hold those in senior executive positions (both clinical and managerial), to account for their decisions.

Decision-Making

All types of leaders, whether clinical, corporate, or executive, make decisions which have an impact on people who interact with them and most importantly on patients, users, families, and carers. Decisions in the NHS are not centred on profits, the views of shareholders or even, despite several attempts to market the NHS, on "customers". Rather decisions are centred on safe patient care, skilful assessment, treatment interventions; on wellbeing of the individual and their families; and in public health, on the population. These decisions are often influenced by complex, multi-dimensional aspects of care, from the individual skills of the practitioner to adequate resources, management of budgets, policy implementation, achieving targets and meeting the requirements of policymakers.

Decisions in the NHS directly impact lives and livelihoods in a way that is fundamentally different to many other organisations, and therefore, a strong sense of shared values tends to bring healthcare workers and leaders together in times of challenge. A shared perception that decisions made by leaders are fair and equitable leads to support and engagement with such decisions. The attributes of fair leadership mentioned earlier by Haskins and Thomas (2022) suggests that these are the basis of good decision-making.

Such an approach was potentially expected to be applied post-COVID as many health and social care staff had first-hand experience of these attributes as they faced the challenges of the pandemic. The decisions made by the government as the pandemic lessened are good examples of how an organisational workforce perceives unfair leadership. This was a time when essential workers, including those in health and social care, were publicly applauded during the pandemic, and many felt that there was a shared national sense of purpose. The pandemic was one of those rare historic periods where the government, healthcare staff, and the population generally felt they were pulling together, where the NHS felt valued and there was a firm emphasis on teamwork and a belief that leaders were fair and equitable in the application of national policies and public health programmes.

Almost immediately as the crisis became manageable, health and social care staff were not given, in their view, a fair pay award by the very government which had lauded their efforts. The political rationale for such a decision can be debated, the point here is that the perception of it was viewed as unfair leadership by care staff and it could be argued, was the underlying basis of continuous industrial action in healthcare.

It is hard to comprehend the moral injury suffered by many care workers when they perceived that, irrespective of the views of those outside of direct healthcare, they were devalued and unappreciated by a government which failed to demonstrate Baker and O'Malley's six virtues of fair and kind leadership in organisations: compassion, integrity, gratitude, authenticity, humility, and humour (2008).

Leadership Culture

It is interesting to note that in the COVID-19 inquiry there were consistent examples of a macho, misogynist, masculine-dominated culture inside government at the time which subdued and sometimes openly mocked female leaders. This was not only indefensible but a further example of unfair and poor leadership.

Haskins (2018) surveyed successful women leaders across the public and private sectors and clearly demonstrated that many take the value of fairness seriously, and therefore bring a different and more compassionate approach to leadership. Women leaders saw fairness as a strength in executive and board management because they had learnt through developing their careers in a male-dominated environment, that kindness and fairness led to superior levels of staff engagement, productivity, and wellbeing; something their male peers often missed (Haskins, 2018).

To balance the negative leadership demonstrated by the government, there are several examples of fair leadership in action throughout the NHS. Aaron has an approach which has been found to be useful in everyday leadership decision-making. He takes the view that no problem is so complex that it does not have a root cause, and therefore a solution. Aaron suggests that simplifying the complexity to a level that is understood by all, agreeing on a team approach to the challenge, having realistic objectives, and initiating a plan, allows the measurement of progress.

An example of fair decision-making using this approach can be illustrated in the challenging issue of hospital home care and discharge to assess cases which involve multi-agencies. Aaron and his team recognised the difficulties for each agency to submit adequate resources for partnership working to be effective, and this in turn influenced their involvement both in delivery and in collective decision-making. This was an issue of fairness as decisions impacted on our local population and their access to care facilities. Aaron's team made the decision to commit the Trust to lead the collaboration and provide resource support to partners. This had a beneficial impact on our community but had a negative impact on the Trust finances. The fairness of the decision is seen in the positive impact on population health and an assurance that needs assessments was fair to service users and families.

But was the impact on the Trust finances unfair? This is an example where the emotional intelligence of compassionate leadership is seen in behaviours that could be judged as fair. The question that was deliberated was who, on balance, gained the most positive outcome by such decisions? The alternative was to reduce the impact on the budget at the expense of more efficient and fair access to care provision by our local population. The alternative was judged to be unfair, although others may take a different view. The impact on the budget would be, and subsequently was, ameliorated by actions which took a more sustainable approach to financial recovery.

A second example of fair decision-making was when the executive team was under pressure to respond quickly to a difficult challenge of transforming delivery and introducing new ways of working. Aaron and the leadership team was aware that a fast response would have a quick short-term result but also a negative effect on staff wellbeing as colleagues were in the midst of winter pressures and industrial action and lacked the resources to embed continuous improvement. A decision was reached and conveyed to the board that staff health and wellbeing were of a higher priority, and it was fairer to allow a bit more time for them to address the challenges effectively.

This subsequently proved to be correct as staff had the time, resilience, and motivation to introduce a more effective and sustainable transformation. But it did have an impact on the leadership team who had to repeatedly highlight that supporting staff wellbeing and providing more time to complete change meaningfully were carried out whilst the leaders maintained due scrutiny and accountability regarding pace and speed of change.

These are situations that the leaders interviewed frequently experience and demonstrate how leaders consciously consider issues of fairness and the impact of their decisions.

Compassion in Leadership

All the leaders in discussions with Aaron had a good understanding and recognition of compassionate leadership. They agreed with Michael West's observation that collective leaders are co-dependant on each other and so need to ensure that everyone is equally focused on working across boundaries because the shared goal is to deliver high-quality care (2021). In today's healthcare environment with the increasing number of negative maternity reviews, the terribly tragic impact on families at the Countess of Chester neonatal provision and the subsequent Lucy Letby trial (see the Thirlwall Inquiry, 2023), and the issues of neglect and abuse found in some mental health provision the issue of fair leadership is of the utmost importance.

All the leaders unanimously approached the issues of safe, quality care as priorities in their decision-making, yet also recognised the skills required for them to be able to balance fair decisions with the pressures to meet financial objectives (and they were all aware of how critical financial objectives are to fair decisions), targets, and statutory and regulatory requirements.

They heartedly would agree with West's observation that compassionate and inclusive leaders are needed throughout health and social care today more than ever, and that there is a real need for compassionate behaviours to be consistent and endemic, from political through to local leaders. In many ways their observations chimed with the compassionate values espoused by Baker and O'Malley (see above).

Adaptation and Optimism

The focus on fairness in leadership decisions and the pressures of adapting to compassionate leadership styles are experienced by everyone in their discussions with Aaron. But are they optimistic about the future of the NHS as a fair organisation? Every leader was fully aware of the need to adopt partnerships and collaborations as a way forward in transforming local and regional NHS delivery. They recognised the huge challenges in changing a care culture which has practised competitive market approaches within a decreasing funding envelope for 14 years.

Despite a lingering suspicion by some, none of the leaders believed that there was a planned managed decline of the NHS. Nor did they see any overt planning that suggests the NHS will evolve into a mixed-market health provider, a two-tier health service, or an insurance model introduced by stealth. Rather the decline in real-term year-on-year funding was viewed as political expediency, sudden responses to the political environment (austerity measures, then Brexit for example), and high levels of ministerial changes which prevented ministers from actioning change in a sustainable way.

There is hope and a degree of optimism that a distributive, inclusive leadership style is the right leadership approach to deal with the transformation required to provide high-quality and safe care. Doing more together, across boundaries and agencies is seen as a fairer and more sustainable method of delivering health and social care.

Conclusion

Who Are the Leaders in the NHS?

This is an important question and needs clarification. We would argue that there are roles and responsibilities throughout the NHS which have either overt or covert leadership responsibilities and accountabilities. Some are very transparent and explicitly hierarchical, clearly overt and written into job specifications and salaried roles, for example Integrated Care Directors, National Chief Medical and Nursing Officers, Secretaries of State and Ministers, and the NHS National Executives.

Some are more localised, leading organisations for place such as the executive team of an Acute Trust, Public Health Directors, or Regional NHS executive roles. Others are explicit in the actions of the work itself, for instance the work of the surgeon, general practitioner, consultants, advanced and specialist practitioners, matron, health and safety officers, chaplains, trade union officials, and so on.

But some are more nuanced, and we would argue more covert: the District Nurse doing home visits, locality team managers overseeing the allocation of resources, the professional carer intervening in direct care or leading health promotion, the therapist practising one-to-one work, and the individual professional practitioner at a relatively junior level working unsupervised and providing advice and guidance to patients, families, and carers.

We suggest all are leaders. This is because all influence care to a degree, all have authority within their sphere of influence and therefore, the conclusions regarding fairness and leadership in the NHS are pertinent to whatever role, responsibilities or accountabilities are held. If you hold an overt hierarchical leadership role then you may have different pressures and decision-making responsibilities than clinically based practitioners who often must make independent clinical decisions, but the principles of fairness, compassion, engagement with others, emotional intelligence, and caring are shared and universal aspects of good leadership.

The Importance of Fair Leadership in the NHS

It is undoubtedly a challenging time to be a leader in health and social care. Funding in real terms has declined year on year for nearly 14 years, targets are not being met in many areas, demand continues to rise, a major national structural reorganisation is being embedded, and regulatory regimes are attempting to modernise inspections to be more positive and collaborative in their interactions. Leaders continue to balance local decision-making with regional and national regulatory and statutory requirements. In many ways, this is the environment that attracts talented and motivated leaders, and it is a great credit to the NHS that many such individuals choose to take on this leadership challenge.

As Michael West elegantly writes, for the NHS to continue to survive, the command-and-control model must give way to a collective, shared compassionate leadership approach. West gives several healthcare examples where inclusive leadership has a positive impact on productivity, care outcomes and staff engagement. He found that the instructional, direct management style diluted innovation and damaged the emotional resources of staff, which in turn depleted their abilities to respond effectively to patients. The time is right to disseminate the practices of the many compassionate leaders practising in the NHS, so inclusive values are endemic in the system (West, 2021).

Moving From a Blame to a Learning Culture

It is also time to move beyond the blame and punishment approach when leadership is found to be deficient. NHS leaders do not go about their daily work consciously disrupting the system or the work of colleagues, and there is no evidence that healthcare leaders are engaging in a programme of a "managed decline" in the NHS, in fact the opposite. NHS leaders constantly balance regulatory requirements, resources, staff wellbeing, cultural change, diversity, professional relations, teamwork, accountability, improving organisational performance, and so on. And all with the objective of enhancing the standards of safe patient care. There is a real danger that a "blame the leader" approach will discourage good future leaders from taking on these difficult and complex roles in health and social care.

The current regulatory environment and how "failures" are dealt with both in the media and within the NHS are seen as significant barriers to promoting fair and equitable decision-making. This is also seen as a major risk in encouraging leaders of the future to develop their careers in the sector. There was a general agreement amongst the leaders interviewed that a blame culture is fundamentally about retribution, and not about accountability.

The basis of this approach may, at least in part, be due to the narrative of the last decade about "City fat cats" where leaders are sometimes perceived as chasing their own personal wealth at the expense of customers, quality or ethical behaviours and cause much media coverage. This discourse is easy enough to transfer to public-sector leaders. It is likely that the movement towards punishing leaders is also a consequence of a poorly applied command and control model of leadership and should be seen in the context of a failed systemic leadership model.

Supporting Leaders

An interesting observation from some of the leadership interviews and more general discussions with colleagues on the topic of self-compassion and personal wellbeing indicates frustration with the current support offered to NHS leaders. Very senior leaders at the Board level and system leadership are often "the voice" of compassionate, fair, and equitable leadership values and are rightly expected to pay a high degree of time in this important area. But often their lived experience of how that narrative applies to them in their role is often the opposite.

When things go wrong, problems are encountered within the organisation, or when external agencies are involved, then the compassion and care shown to leaders can be perceived as inadequate, both from within their own organisation and within the wider leadership structures of the NHS and regulatory bodies.

Senior NHS leaders desire and strive to demonstrate that compassionate leadership is demonstrated at all levels, including amongst policymakers and legislators. Yet for some leaders there is a perceived juxtaposition between rhetoric and actions, policies, and practices. Some leaders who have left the NHS hold the view that they were "sacrificed" to demonstrate tough and prompt actions by more senior leaders in the system. Worse, there is a danger that this perception may become more widespread as a norm amongst prospective NHS leaders and more importantly leading to a decline in potentially outstanding leaders choosing a career in health-care leadership.

Training and Development of Leaders

The distributive and inclusive leadership model is more appropriate for modern collaborative healthcare delivery and requires more support so that clinical and care practitioners are empowered to make local decisions within their leadership spheres. Of equal importance is the need to raise the aware-ness of local leaders to the issues that organisational executives wrestle with daily in the context of accountability and governance.

This is an issue that both of us take seriously as there is very little content in most training, educational, and development which prepares staff for executive board issues. In the Morecambe Bay Trust. Like many trusts, we are active in supporting a "Shadow Board" approach where senior local leaders undertake a professional programme as members of a Board which receives and considers the same agenda items and issues as the Trust Board. This enables more insight into governance and accountability issues at the organisational level and allows participants to apply their own decision-making to the same challenges facing the Trust board members and in a safe and supervised setting.

The Complexity of Compassionate and Fair Leadership

Fairness and equity are the outcomes of compassionate leaders, and we would suggest this is the model for the future of NHS leadership. This approach clearly resonates with the collaborative and partnership values of the NHS, as well as demonstrating the values of caring, engagement with population health improvement, and addressing the wellbeing of the nation. In essence we would argue that healthcare is relational, and therefore, the skills of the future leader should be embedded in human relations expertise such as engagement, inclusion, teamwork, partnerships, and collaboration with others.

These relational skills need to be coupled with high levels of analysis, evaluation, technical abilities and the ability to demonstrate fair and equi-table leadership decisions. These are clearly not what some may perceive as "soft" leadership traits, but rather a demonstration of much more com-plex, difficult, challenging, and tougher leadership competencies, yet those that are required in the modern global infrastructure, and most importantly, required to improve patient, user, and staff experiences of the National Health Service.

Recommendations for Future NHS Leadership

Analysing the Evidence

Whilst fairness and equity should be values based on organisational and cultural development, there was broad agreement that policy, planning, and regulatory infrastructure are also needed to "make it something that is measured." Data provide the basis for analysis and evaluation and is seen as essential to effective and efficient decision-making because it allows leaders to see evidence of improvement, identify areas that need further input, and measure and compare across the health sector.

Aaron would argue that what gets measured gets done. NHS organisations are asked to develop annual plans, supported by annual budgets with key measures of success operational, finance and performance driven. This needs to change if the issues of inequity of access, outcomes, and improvements in population health are to be delivered. There should be more emphasis on population health improvement goals that are locally measurable, a clearer framework to demonstrate collaborative cross-boundary and cross-professional working, and a structure which allows the public to understand how and where they can be engaged with place-based collaborations.

Developing Leaders

The current operating environment needs to nationally adopt a more collegiate, distributive, and collaborative leadership approach in the NHS. There is a risk that the serious challenges facing the service will continue to encourage, and celebrate, a breed of more directive, aggressive, performance-management culture, and old-fashioned "hero" leadership approaches. This model is clearly not appropriate when the legislative framework explicitly states that collaboration, partnership, and multi-agency approaches are expected to improve the NHS. Health and Social care requires leaders skilled in distributive and inclusive styles, who recognise the skills and talents that the many can bring to a solution, and where relational and diplomatic skills have a more effective, efficient long-term and sustainable change in delivery.

Accountability

One of the ambiguities surrounding distributive and inclusive leadership approaches is around accountabilities and responsibilities. Who holds these areas within their roles when many are engaged in a collective task? We believe, and so do the leaders interviewed, that distributive leaders should make transparent and explicit the responsibilities and accountabilities of everyone before activities commence. These should then be regularly peer reviewed through a collaborative perspective so team members each know their spheres of responsibilities, accountabilities, and how their actions and decisions contribute to the partnership.

National Frameworks for Support and Intervention

Modern NHS leaders, whether local practitioners or organisational executives, require more robust support mechanisms to allow them to do their job more effectively. The current level of national support for transformation and improvement needs to be strengthened. We have both been engaged with such infrastructure and found it positive in providing extra resources in capacity, capability, governance, and planning terms.

The model should be offered at all levels of the National Outcome Framework (NOF) so that providers can sustain a continuous transformation and improvement programme. The NOF currently grades providers from Outstanding to Requires Support, an outcome of previous one-word judgements but one which has been heavily criticised in the world of education and its use by Ofsted, and so may be altered in due course. The type of support should explicitly include a focus on fair and compassionate support for leaders. One could argue that the dissemination of collaborative and inclusive leadership skills in the NHS would be strengthened if there were joined-up approaches and agreements to support compassionate leaders, including those in government as well as patient-facing practitioners. Such a national approach would also enhance the recruitment of potentially outstanding healthcare leaders.

Inclusion and Diversity

Aaron's discussions with NHS leaders do indicate that a lack of diversity in senior leadership in the NHS (policy making and executive in particular) is a significant issue. We need to focus more purposefully on recruiting, retaining, and developing talent from all areas of our communities, and they need senior decision-making roles to influence a fairer leadership approach to diversity issues.

References

Archer, D. & Cameron, A. (2009) *Collaborative Leadership; How to Succeed in an Interconnected World*. Butterworth-Heinemann, Elsevier.

Baker, W.F. & O'Malley, M. (2008) *Leading with Kindness: How Good People Consistently Get Superior Results.* AMACOM.

Care Quality Commission. (2024) *The New Single Assessment Process Toolkit.* Care Quality Commission.

Department of Health. (1999) *Making a Difference.* Department of Health.

Department of Health. (2000) *NHS Plan.* Department of Health.

Department of Health. (2002) *Liberating the Talents.* Department of Health.

Department of Health. (2004) *Choosing Health.* Department of Health.

Department of Health. (2007) *Our NHS, Our Future.* Department of Health.

Department of Health. (2022) *NHS and Social Care Act.* Department of Health and Social Care.

Department of Health and Social Care. (2012) *Health and Social Care Act.* Department of Health and Social Care.

Gill, A. (2018) Kindness in Sports Performance and Leadership. Chapter 7. In Haskins, G. Thomas, M. & Johri, L. (Eds.), *Kindness in Leadership.* Routledge.

Gorsky, M. (2013) Searching for the People in Charge; Appraising the 1983 Griffiths NHS Management Inquiry. *Journal of Medical History,* 57(910): 87–107. PMCID; PMC3566753.

Haskins, G. (2018) Kindness; Perspectives from Women Leaders. Chapter 5, pp. 85–110. In Haskins, G., Thomas, M. & Johri, L. (Eds.), *Kindness in Leadership.* Routledge.

Haskins, G. & Thomas, M. (2022) In Search of Fairness in Leadership. Chapter 3, pp. 22–37. In Witzel, M. (Ed.), *Post-Pandemic Leadership; Exploring Solutions to a Crisis.* Routledge.

Hollington, S. (2022) Leadership in Crisis; What Lessons Can Be Learned from the NHS Response to the Covid-19 Pandemic in 2020–2021. Chapter 17, pp. 178–191. In Witzel, M. (Ed.), *Post-Pandemic Leadership; Exploring Solutions to a Crisis.* Routledge.

Hooper, A. (2022) Leadership in a National Crisis. Chapter 5, pp. 49–58. In Witzel, M. (Ed.), *Post-Pandemic Leadership; Exploring Solutions to a Crisis.* Routledge.

House of Commons. (2008) *From Citizen's Charter to Public Service Guarantees; Entitlements to Public Services.* HM Stationary Office.

Thirlwall Inquiry (2023) *Building a Picture of the Culture Within NHS Neonatal Units.* Thirlwall. public.inquiry.uk Downloaded 5 March 2024.

Thomas, M. & Rowlands, C. (2018) Fairness and Equity; Should Kindness Have a Place in the Boardroom? Chapter 8, p. 148. In Haskins, G., Thomas, M. & Johri, L. (Eds.), *Kindness in Leadership.* Routledge.

Warner, M. & Zaranko, B. (2023) *Is There Really an NHS Productivity Crisis?* Institute of Fiscal Studies, 17 November. www.Ifs.org.uk.

West, M.A. (2021) *Compassionate Leadership; Sustaining Wisdom, Humanity and Presence in Health and Social Care.* The swirling Leaf Press. www.swirlingleafpress.com

PART THREE

Policy and Skills

7

QUESTIONS OF FAIRNESS IN HEALTH AND SOCIAL CARE POLICY DECISIONS – A SOCRATIC APPROACH

Anthony J Culyer

What Is the Question? *That* Is the Answer!

Making good policy decisions about health and social care would be greatly aided by having a broad set of questions to ponder on one's own or when chairing or participating in collective decision-making, as in a committee or board. What sorts of question might these be? This chapter makes some suggestions.

Rival Visions

There is little agreement amongst people who think or write about fairness or equity[1] in health and social care. Some consider that access to health should be essentially similar, in ethical respects, to access to the other good things of life, like food, shelter and leisure activities, which are part of society's reward system. Through legitimate work or legitimate inheritance, you acquire legitimate income and legitimate wealth which entitle you to purchase a legitimate share of the available marketed good things in society, including health care. So, providing that the starting point is fair, the result, whatever it may be, is also fair (see, e.g., Nozick 1974). Others regard access to health care as a right of citizenship, like access to the ballot box or courts of justice, which should not depend in any way on individual income and wealth, though it will necessarily depend on the income and wealth of society in general: resources are limited and health is not the only good thing,

DOI: 10.4324/9781003410560-10

so health care is only ever going to receive a finite share of the total. On this view (e.g., Tobin 1970), health care is a "primary" good, like rights, liberties, opportunities, income, and wealth, and should be fairly (equally) and cheaply available to all.

THE SOCRATIC METHOD

The Socratic method is a way of teaching attributed by Plato to Socrates (c. 470–399 BC). Socrates himself left no written testimony, but Plato was one of his students and so presumably experienced at first hand his teacher's method. It works through teachers asking searching questions of their students, to clarify students' thinking and expose the reasons for thinking as they do. Through further questions and answers, critical skills are enhanced, mutual understanding strengthened, old beliefs possibly cast aside, and deeper agreements or differences made clear.

For academic analysts like me (an economist with NHS connections) it is not necessary to take sides to be able to offer helpful advice to those who make and implement health and social care policies at whatever level in the NHS[2] (I shall call them decision makers). I propose instead the use of a systematic checklist I term Socratic, because it is cast throughout as a series of questions. The questions are designed to elicit from decision makers answers that enable the creation of a coherent structure for designing, reforming, or managing health care systems. The questions are distributed throughout the chapter and brought together in Appendix A.

I shall also outline some common characteristics of health and health care which bear on fairness. I shall assume that ideas of fairness, being fundamental value judgments that determine both the design and the operation of a health care system, are themselves a product of the system. Specifically, the aims and objectives of health and social care services are set by statutes, precedent, and other conventions of public policy, and by the stated goals of political parties, particularly those of course of the governing party. I thus require the economist, ethicist, epidemiologist, etc., to suppress their own value judgments about what is good for society and do their best to infer the "authentic and authoritative" values as revealed by some combination of the political and constitutional sources. The task for the health policy analyst is to examine the context (Culyer 2018) in which issues of fairness may arise and to explore aspects of the world of health and social care that inhibit implementing the "authentic and authoritative" values of policy makers.

Therefore, structures and processes that are enabling might be invented and implemented.

Starting Points

Useful starting points for a conversation about fairness in health and social care might arise from considering the following general questions:

- *What do I/we consider the health care system to be for?*
- *What do I/we understand by "health", by fairness and unfairness, efficacy and effectiveness, efficiency, and cost-effectiveness?*
- *What do I/we think of some commonly used notions of fairness and unfairness, and some of the conventional measures or indicators of these critical components?*
- *How might my/our own views be effectively disseminated widely throughout the NHS and "owned" not only by the principal decision makers but also by the public whom they serve?*

Great precision or detail is probably not required to structure thinking about efficiency and fairness. However, it may be a useful beginning for decision-makers like managers to answer a few searching questions like these, consider the concepts offered for their practical use, and be armed as decision-makers to interrogate experts from the multidisciplinary and multi-professional health-related world inhabited by physicians, social workers, economists, epidemiologists, statisticians, and ethicists.

"Fairness" attracts the attention of people in many disciplines and professions and may arise as an issue in many practical situations. I shall begin by clarifying the meanings of some terms that I shall use. I shall also characterise the main features of health and social care which may not be familiar to analysts working in other empirical fields.

Clarifying Terms and Distinctions

The most important terms are as follows.

Context. There is a context for all decisions, defined by the culture, history, and traditions of a community, and by the identity of the person doing the deciding, their level of seniority, their degree of discretion, their accountability, the nature of the technologies available, the budget, the interests of multiple stakeholders, and the length of time over which the consequences of the decision will pan out (Culyer 2010). Decision makers' perceptions, values, and professional abilities are three of a multitude of factors, which affect outcomes, costs, expectations, and achievements (Culyer 2018). Changing any of the contextual features is likely to change the decisions that are reached, by whoever is making them. The context may also dictate what may or may not be considered when a decision is being made, which may include fairness, or may impose a specific concept of fairness. The discretion allowed and the constraints imposed are important determinants of how issues of fairness and efficiency can be handled.

For some decision-makers, transparency, and the involvement of (other) stakeholders in a decision-making process, may be regarded as threatening to their status and authority. In what follows, I have tried at to make the questions unthreatening but still searching. The next four are scene-setting:

- *What is the policy context in which a question of fairness has arisen or might arise?*
- *Is there anything in the current context that limits or prescribes how fairness is to be handled?*
- *What types of stakeholders would be useful contributors to a deliberation in the current context?*
- *Can one have a useful deliberation without decision makers' involvement?*

Deliberation. By "deliberation" I include the private, individual, consideration, and weighing of issues as well as group procedures that engage interested stakeholders in the process – including the design of the process itself. Group deliberation is therefore more than mere consultation. It is characterised by the careful, deliberate consideration and discussion of the advantages and disadvantages of various options. The debate is usually informed by evidence (rarely complete), possibly also by expert witnesses (rarely free of all bias) and typically involves all important stakeholders (rarely disempowered voices). There are opportunities for participants both to form and to change their opinions (Culyer 2006, 2020, 2022; Culyer and Lomas 2006; Oortwijn et al. 2022).

- *Are suitable arrangements in place to enable and facilitate deliberation?*
- *Can you judge the validity and credibility of available evidence, or describe the kind of additional research to be commissioned?*

Efficacy. Efficacy is a measure of the maximum benefit of a medical or social intervention under "ideal" conditions. It is indicated by the probability of benefit to individuals in a defined population from a technology under such conditions of use: typically, the conditions are obtained in a research-oriented teaching hospital or primary care practice; or perhaps experimental, as in a clinical trial. More generally, it is the maximum potential effect of a professional intervention in altering the natural history of ill health or social disadvantage for the better (https://www.princeton.edu/~ota/disk3/1978/7805/780504.PDF).

- *Is there credible evidence that the policy instruments under discussion are efficacious?*
- *Is the membership of the decision-making group sufficiently competent to evaluate the quality of the evidence?*

Effectiveness. This is a measure referring to the effect of a particular technology on outcomes when used in *actual* practice. It thus differs from efficacy in that actual practice is a practice as conducted by average professionals working with average resources. Most decisions will require comparisons to be made of the probable consequences of the available options in actual practice. It will sometimes be helpful if a degree of quantification is used – for example, as to "credibility" (low, medium, or high?) or "competence" (years of experience?).

- *Is there credible evidence that the policy instruments under discussion are effective?*
- *Is the membership of the decision-making group sufficiently competent to evaluate the quality of the evidence?*
- *Are ineffective interventions and other proposed changes nonetheless possibly useful from a fairness perspective?*
- *Is it possible to quantify some of the key elements of the foregoing in the current context?*

How Best to Proceed If It Is Not Possible?

Efficiency. The idea of efficiency can be expressed at three different levels:

- *technical efficiency*, where no more resources (doctors, nurses, patients' time, drugs, etc.) are used than are technically necessary to attain a given outcome (there will normally be a variety of different combinations of these arising out of the possibility of substitutability, for example of nurses for doctors, or one drug for another).

- *cost-effectiveness*, where a given outcome is generated using the cheapest technically efficient combination of resources or, conversely, outcomes are maximised for a given level of expenditure (the combinations of resources here will be a subset of those deemed technically efficient).
- *Is there credible evidence that the policy instruments under discussion are cost-effective?*
- *Is the membership of the decision-making group sufficiently competent to evaluate the quality of the evidence?*
- *Is it fair not to provide treatments on the NHS that are cost-ineffective?*
- *Pareto-efficiency*,[3] where the outcome is not only technically efficient and cost-effective but also set at a rate such that an increase in any one resource is not costlier than the additional value generated. The value is usually that perceived by consumers as revealed in their willingness to pay. An adapted version is where the outcome is conceived directly in terms of health. Options are thus considered in terms of their potential for improving people's health. If option A is predicted to generate health Ha, and option B to produce health Hb, then adopting A entails the forgoing of Hb and adopting B entails the forgoing of Ha. Each is the "opportunity cost" of the other.[4] Pareto efficiency exists when neither option dominates the other.
- *Is there credible evidence that the policy instruments under discussion are efficient?*
- *Are the policy instruments under discussion likely to promote or harm the total health or welfare of the community?*
- *Is it fair to give weight to the alternative health gain (opportunity cost) that might have been achieved if a different decision were reached?*
- *Is rectifying an unfairness likely to reduce efficiency in this context?*

Outcome. There is an immense variety of measures of health outcome, some of which are biological and clinical, often specific to a disease or group of diseases (like the presence of cholesterol or sugar in the blood) or more generalised and related to longevity and quality of life. The latter are most relevant to measurements of fairness like indices of inequality, but their construction also raises important ethical questions about how the expectation of life is measured, the importance of age and nearness to death, the dimensions in which quality of life is measured (pain, mobility, etc.), and the degree to which the measures are perceived as adequate measures of "health" (Brazier et al. 2007).

- *Is fairness in the current context to do with outcomes and for whom? What kinds of outcome?*

- *Does the practical measurement or outcomes, for example, as changes in longevity and quality of life, raise issues of fairness?*
- *Are the various components of an outcome measure (relief of pain, increased mobility, reduced confusion, etc.) given fair weights?*

Equity versus equality. Equality is not synonymous with equity. All assertions about equality need to answer the question "equality of what?", answering which will usually unearth obvious exceptions to the idea that equality is always fair. As written earlier, I treat equity and fairness as synonyms, so what is equitable is also fair and what is inequitable, unfair.

- *Is the question at hand to do with equality? If so, equality of what?*
- *Are there issues of fairness in the statistical measures of inequality used to measure distributions?*
- *Are there issues of multiple deprivation, that is, inequalities in many dimensions of the quality of life?*

Horizontal and vertical fairness. Horizontal fairness, or fair equality, requires people with the same ability-to-pay to pay the same amount. Those who are equally deserving, or needy, or have equal ability to pay, are likewise to be treated equally. Vertical fairness is fair inequality. Those with greater deservingness or need should receive greater appropriate treatment or a higher priority. Vertical fairness requires the appropriate different treatment of people with different abilities to pay. Those with greater ability to pay should pay more. The Thatcherite Community Charge (a poll tax) required equal payment from all regardless of ability to pay.[5] It was widely regarded as an unfair equality.

- *Is the distinction between vertical and horizontal fairness likely to be relevant in the current context?*
- *Are some combinations of tax finance, private insurance, and direct payments fairer than others in the current context?*

Stakeholders. In principle, stakeholders include anyone with a substantive interest in the outcome of a decision process. In practice, anyone so designated by a legitimate authority. In health and social care, stakeholders commonly include patients, specific minorities, disempowered voices, informal (often family) caregivers, advocacy groups, clinical and other professional caregivers, pharmacists, care volunteers, health care managers, other community or hospital-based health care workers, manufacturers, researchers, politicians and their advisers, taxpayers, and the public. The categories frequently overlap. Stakeholders may also have conflicting personal and institutional interests. Advocates on behalf of specific patient groups tend to emphasise their needs above those of other patient groups; the interests of known people may be ranked above those of anonymous people; the interests of manufacturers and other commercial stakeholders may conflict with those of health care commissioners. Potential conflicts of interest ought always to be declared but need not debar those declaring them from participation. To be useful in consultations and deliberation, participants need training to understand the procedures in which they are participating and to respect people with whom they may disagree. Competent chairing is essential.

- *Have those involved in the decision-making procedures been fairly chosen and competently trained/briefed?*

System design. This includes the context and structure for policy decisions in systems of public health and social care. "Context and structure" mean the mechanisms (such as laws and regulations), institutions (such as care delivery organisations and public and private agencies), and opportunities available for ordinary people to make choices and express their opinions about the health and care policies that may exist at any levels, national or local, of the system with which they interact. By "ordinary people" I mean to exclude anyone with privileged positions within the system. Such positions may be fairly occupied, but even if judged to be fair they might bias opinions and muddy the distinction between those who are served by the system and those who, in one way or another, operate it.

- *Are there issues to do with opportunities and who has them? Opportunities for what?*
- *Are there fairness issues with processes, for example to access services or to participate in decision making? Are some processes more fair or unfair than others?*
- *What role, if any, exists for ordinary people in planning or operating the system in this context?*

Health Technology Assessment (HTA). This is the critical appraisal of any form of professional intervention intended to improve health or prevent ill health. HTA evaluates medicines, use of diagnostic equipment, surgery, lifestyle

advice, public health measures, and physical adaptation of living and working conditions. Some technologies, like robotics, may be applied in ways
that seem inhuman. Others, like visiting the lonely, may be open to hid-
den abuse. Yet others, like some diagnostic scanning procedures, may scare
patients. Each raises the possibility of unfairness depending, for example, on
the sophistication of the patients and the empathy of the professionals. Care-
less interventions might lead to inadequate diagnoses of needs, failure by
patients to seek help, or failure to comply with treatment regimens.

- *Is it understood by stakeholders and decision makers that HTA is a way of
  evaluating health care interventions of many varied kinds, not just "high tech"
  ones?*
- *Are there any ways in which use of the intervention in question could ameliorate
  unfairness of any kind, or possibly worsen it?*

Unfairness versus misfortune. A misfortune is not necessarily unfair. To be born
with a harelip is a misfortune but not an unfairness. To have access to surgical closure of harelip only if you are white and middle class is, however,
likely to be seen as unfair. Unfairness arises from the actions or inactions
of people. A misfortune arises from nature. Unfairness is thus a social phenomenon, commonly arising inside families, workplaces, and the state. In
this chapter, the focus is on the state. In practice, unfairness and misfortune
may sometimes be hard to separate but what motivates responses to each
will usually differ, with responses to unfairness motivated by the violation
of an ethical principle and responses to misfortune motivated by sympathy
and compassion.

- *Does the current issue concern unfairness or misfortune? Does the distinction
  matter in the current context?*

What Makes Health and Social Care Different? Implications for Fairness

The arrangements made for the financing and delivery of health and social
care are typically responses to a set of characteristics that, collectively, raise
more questions of efficiency and fairness than are to be found in other sectors. To design, reform, or operate, a health and social care system requires
some understanding by decision-makers of the more important of these
characteristics.

Agency

In health and social care, the classic role of a professional lies in determining the user's best interest and acting in a consistent fashion. There is potential unfairness in this agency relationship between principal and agent, where the principal is the patient or client and the agent is the professional (McGuire 2000). Agency arises usually because of asymmetry of information: the professional has expert subject knowledge; and the patient knowledge of their own personal circumstances, attitudes to risk, and preferences. The situation is further complicated by the fact that the professional has an important role in determining the demand for a service as well as its supply. This makes some standard applications of "demand and supply" analysis invalid since supply and demand are no longer independent of one another.

- *In the current context, do professionals face a possible conflict both by advising appropriate procedures for patients and for providing them?*
- *Ought professionals to have a good understanding of the patient's personal circumstances, values, and preferences?*
- *Is the advice given by professionals to decision makers impartial as well as competent?*
- *Are there improvements in the agency relationship that would improve fairness in the current context?*

One possible consequence of imperfect agency is *supplier-induced demand*: the effect that professionals, as providers of services, may have in creating more, or a different, patient demand than if they acted as perfect agents for their patients, particularly if the professional were rewarded by fees, and were a provider as well as an adviser, a dispenser as well as a prescriber (Evans 1974). The asymmetry of information relates not only to judging the amount and type of care but also to the competence of the agent. Inevitably, better-educated and better-informed citizens are more able to detect and avoid false professional claims and incompetent service, which implies that the principal victims of the weak agencies are the less well-off members of society. Policy measures that seek to minimise poor agency include rigorous university training of clinicians, setting standards of care by professional statutory and regulatory agencies like NICE (the National Institute for Health and Social Care), or the Quality Care Commission.

- *Does fairness in the current context require formal guidance for professionals or adjustments in contracts of employment?*

- *Are there fairness issues in NHS staff pay differentials, recruitment and retention that may arise in this context?*

The Gradient

The evidence in the UK and elsewhere is that mortality and morbidity systematically rise as socio-economic status falls (Marmot et al. 1991; Evans et al. 1994; Case et al. 2002; Deaton 2002, 2003; Marmot 2008, 2010, 2015). The rich live longer and better than the poor, and those in the income bracket immediately above live longer and better than those in the bracket later. The differences in both length and quality of life in the UK today are staggering.[6] This phenomenon arises from in-built unfair determinants of a much wider kind – poverty, quality of early parenting, discrimination, poor education, bad housing, and a host of others. Tackling the gradient is the single most important strategy for health equity in the UK, though mostly for other government departments. In health and health care specifically, the major consequence of the gradient is its implication for health insurance (public or private) and for the fair evaluation of the services to be made available in a system like the NHS.

- *How widely across the many determinants of health is the issue likely to range?*
- *Will the policy in question flatten the gradient in health?*

The gradient implies that the need for health care is inversely related to income and wealth. Thus, actuarially calculated insurance premiums will reflect a person's historical usage and will be inversely related to the ability to pay – the poorer will face higher premiums than the richer. This is likely to be regarded as unfair and can be remedied through regulation, for example by requiring insurance companies to use community risk rating rather than individual experience rating, whereby premiums are set according to employer, industry, or regional characteristics. If the resultant premium levels are still regarded as unfair, a subsidy system could be introduced. An ultimate insurance policy solution is to remove health care financing altogether from a premium basis to a tax basis, so that with a broadly proportional tax structure (by which each pays the same fraction of income) or one that is progressive (by which each pays an increasing fraction as income rises) "premiums" are absorbed into a presumptively fairer tax structure.

Health and social care insurance commonly involves some continuing direct payments by patients. Thus, even in the NHS, there are some charges, as for medicines. The removal of all charges, with exceptions deemed not to be unfair, diminishes a potent source of unfair practices, such as extra-billing (McKnight 2007), whereby providers collect from patients the difference between the claim allowed by the insurer and the fee preferred by the provider. It also, however, raises a problem known as "moral hazard" in the form of expanded demands for care that are trivial or ineffective. The state thus becomes the effective insurer and will take on the responsibility for funding service providers. The state (in the shape of NICE in the UK) would also have to decide what services will be made available and to whom, using criteria including assessments of effectiveness and cost-effectiveness, which could perhaps include any likely impact on unfairness in the distribution and availability of resources across regions and disease categories.

- *What insurance and financial issues, if any, are likely to be of concern?*
- *Are there other issues of fairness regarding system funding?*

Externality

Common to concerns about both fairness and efficiency is the impact of what economists call externalities (Buchanan and Stubblebine 1962). These relate to the consequences of an action by one individual or group and their impact on others. They include the impact of the policies of non-health government ministries on health and health care, and vice versa. There may be external costs and external benefits. Some are pecuniary, affecting only the value of other resources (as when a new drug makes a previously available one obsolete and so harms its manufacturer); some are technological, physically affecting other people (communicable disease is a classic example of this type of – negative – externality, antimicrobial resistance is another; herd immunity from vaccination is a positive example); some are utility effects that impinge on the subjective values of others (as when one person feels sympathy and distress at the sickness of another or relief at their recovery). This latter is sometimes known as a caring externality (Culyer 1971a, 1971b). When there are non-pecuniary effects of these kinds, standard economics predicts that the usual market behaviour assumed for individuals will not result in Pareto efficiency. This inefficiency can be addressed by policy interventions such as subsidies to pharmaceutical firms to encourage innovation and to the public to reduce prices and encourage the use of (cost-effective) health and social care services. The caring externality can be seen as a utilitarian description of empathy (Culyer 1971a, 1971b). It can also be captured by some notions of fairness, particularly if the positive externality is generated by greater ease of access to health care for all. "Caringness" is probably best evidenced through qualitative research into public opinion (Jacobsson et al. 2005).

- *Are there any externalities that raise matters of fairness?*
- *Is the fairest policy likely to require collaboration between different sectors and ministries?*
- *Which stakeholders might be especially important in finding a solution?*
- *Are some ways of "internalising" externalities fairer than others in the current context?*

Health Insurance

Unfairness in the availability and cost of insurance was a fundamental political driver for the establishment of the NHS (Webster 1998).

- *Are there issues in the current discussion to do with costs and who bears them?*

Insurance consists of a contract between the client and the insurer such that, when an adverse health event occurs, the insurer will pay defined sums of money either to the insured person or directly to the health service provider. Private health insurance policies are sold either indirectly to consumers in the form of employer-sponsored health insurance (common in the USA) or are directly purchased by consumers. By pooling risks the insurer can select premiums that, after allowances for other expenses, make it worthwhile for the purchaser as well as profitable for the insurance provider. For the insured person, the advantage of insurance is that the possibility of a large financial loss through lost earnings or medical care expenses is exchanged for the certainty of a smaller loss (the payment of a premium). The kinds of benefits provided by insurance policies, public or private, for-profit, or non-profit, are hugely variable and a major topic for health technology assessment (Glassman et al. 2017).

- *Are there issues in the current discussion to do with risks and who bears them?*

All insurance involves a reduction or elimination of charges to the insured individual at the point of use of health care. Libertarian critics of the NHS have for many years regarded the absence of prices at the point of use as a self-evident source of inefficiency (Lees 1960, 1962, 1964; Jewkes and

Jewkes 1962; Buchanan 1964; Goodman 1980). In *both* private and public systems, as well as mixed systems, low or zero prices may generate *moral hazard*. Ex ante moral hazard refers to increases in the probability that the event insured against will occur, for example by insured people taking less care to avoid behaviour hazardous to health. Ex post moral hazard derives from the fact that being insured reduces the price of care to the patient, and hence leads to an increase in demand by insured persons ("over-use") when an event against which one is insured occurs.

While financial incentives or disincentives, like co-payments, can play a role in reducing moral hazard, they tend to offset some of the advantages of being insured in the first place, which limits their effectiveness and can, as already seen, be unfair. Alternatively, direct rationing and quality control measures can be employed, for example by insurance contracts that specify a limited set of procedures for which compensation will be paid, with approved providers contracted to adhere to specific standards of care. There is plainly much scope for unfairness of many kinds to arise in market systems as different providers offer a variety of insurance packages. While these have the advantage of offering choice, the inequalities in coverage and access which arise are likely to be seen as unfair. In the UK, moral hazard is controlled partly through charges (usually with exceptions),[7] partly through managing the types of intervention covered by the NHS, and partly through clinical and other good practice guidelines for health and social care professionals. The latter two processes form the principal tasks of NICE in the UK.

- *Are there fairness issues arising from moral hazard?*
- *Are there issues of "rationing" and the possible consequences of different schemes for allocating health care to regions or individuals?*
- *Are pricing solutions always unfair?*

Unless premiums are regulated, the gradient makes it almost certain that the poorest people in the community will be underinsured or face premiums that are higher than those paid by wealthier people. Even in middle- to high-income countries, a tiered system often exists. For example, in South Africa, there is a private scheme attractive to the relatively well-to-do, a public scheme that is oversubscribed, alongside traditional medicine mainly practised in rural areas. In other countries, like the UK, private insurance schemes operate alongside a public scheme such as the NHS, enabling wealthier patients to access care faster (Zwarenstein 1994). In some countries (Canada is one) a public insurance scheme covering workplace-related causes of illness operates alongside a mainstream public scheme, which again affords faster access to care, earlier return to work, but only for conditions attributable to the working environment (Hurley et al. 2008). Parallel systems frequently facilitate "gaming" strategies through which patients use the main public system for most expensive procedures, thereby facing lower premiums in a private scheme for lesser interventions such as elective surgery, in what is commonly called "queue jumping" – jumps that are not available for the relatively deprived and who are likely to have greater need for care.

- *Is there "parallelism" in the current or proposed arrangements that enables some to have privileged access health care?*
- *Should some groups (workers, the elderly, children) have faster or cheaper access to care than others?*
- *Is it fair for privileged groups to have favoured treatment even though their health gain may be less than the health losses to others arising from their use of a limited resource?*

Efficiency Versus Fairness

Efficiency and fairness in the allocation of resources are sometimes regarded as mutually unsatisfiable criteria for assessing the goodness of social arrangements. There is some truth in this belief but it is easily overdone.

The first two ideas of efficiency described earlier concern the allocation of inputs to outcomes; the third concerns the allocation of outcomes to consumers, clients, or users. It is at the third level that the conflict between efficiency and fairness is most likely to occur.

While it is obvious that unfairness could co-exist with efficient and cost-effective resource allocations, rectifying such unfairness does not necessarily imply any reduction of efficiency or cost-effectiveness, so the oft-claimed conflict may not arise (Culyer and Wagstaff 1993). It nonetheless can appear as an unintended consequence. For example, effective public health education to reduce smoking has a smaller impact on lower socio-economic groups with less impact on behaviour, thereby widening mortality differences from lung diseases (Hill et al. 2014).

At the inter-personal level many distributions of health and social care could be Pareto efficient but fail most tests of fairness. Pareto efficiency can be consistent with the most appalling inequality. The point is that Pareto efficiency takes no account of the fairness of the distribution of outcomes. The fairness or unfairness of arrangements requires criteria other than asking whether they are effective or efficient arrangements. The price mechanism might, in principle, approach a Pareto efficient allocation. Since, however, willingness to pay for outcomes is correlated with ability to pay, which, in turn, depends upon the distribution of purchasing power (income and wealth) which is highly likely to be judged unfair, the unfairness of purchasing power inevitably creates unfairness in the outcomes.

- *Creating greater fairness for some can involve a sacrifice of health and health care for others*

    - *is that likely to be the case here?*

- *What, if any, are the acceptable limits to sacrifices of this sort in this context?*
- *Would enhancing fairness in the current context necessarily involve a reduction in efficiency?*
- *Should some types of unfairness have a higher priority for rectification than others in this context?*

More fundamentally, the individualistic assumptions underlying most "free" market[8] advocacy may be judged inappropriate even if judged to be acceptable in other sectors of the economy.

- *Is there a role for the market to improve fairness in the current context?*
- *Is it fair for people to be able to buy the treatment in question if not available on the NHS?*

An alternative way of thinking about system design can emerge from early brainstorming with policy makers and their advisers. Suppose that the answer to the question "what do they consider the health care system to be for?" is "to maximise the impact of available resources on the nation's health." This will immediately raise the issue of the appropriateness of the market to deliver such an objective and of the fairness of the alternatives.

- *The health and social care systems have many purposes:[9] are some more important than others in the current context?*
- *Would it be fair, for those willing to pay, to "top up" their tax contributions by direct payment to gain access to services deemed insufficiently cost-effective to be offered by the NHS?*

Conclusion

Eliciting the policy values of policy makers and system designers whom the analyst seeks to help, will usually be facilitated by group deliberation

(Chalkidou and Culyer 2019). The various policy makers and managers bring their own culture, knowledge, and experience. So do analysts and advisers. What is regarded as fair may differ according to each sphere of culture and experience (Walzer 1983). The prime purpose of this chapter has been both to offer a checklist of questions to anyone wishing to sort their own views out in a systematic way and to create a framework which decision-makers could use to interrogate experts in the creation and use of an information base for measuring and linking resources to relevant outcomes, and to yield ideas about possible mechanisms for utilising the information to enhance the system's performance. My substantive task has been to create a reasonably comprehensive checklist of fairness-related points to consider. These are drawn together in Appendix A.

My experience with the NHS since the 1970s leads me to believe that introspective questioning, and asking searching questions of all concerned with decisions in the NHS, can result in better and fairer processes and outcomes. That is what the Socratic approach seeks to achieve. Clearer thinking alone is, however, no panacea. Plainly, it is only one element in the business of the NHS's constant reinvention. Nor are the questions I have coined as relevant and complete as they can be. Making them so is for you, the reader, if you submit yourself and your colleagues directly to the Socratic gaze and can think of useful adaptations. The Socratic questions are a collective template for the reader and others to develop further. This is only the end of the beginning. Our final questions include the following:

- *Have you some communications strategies for sharing the results of the deliberation with the various stakeholder groups?*
- *Would it be wise to plan a review at a future date of what has happened following the decision?*

So, let the introspection and the deliberation begin!

Notes

1 I shall take these as synonyms.
2 I shall refer mostly to the NHS but intend to make the scheme applicable to all systems of health care provision and finance.
3 Named after Vilfredo Federico Damaso Pareto (1848–1923), an Italian economist, sociologist, and philosopher. A state of affairs is Pareto-efficient if there is no alternative state that would make someone better off without making anyone worse off.
4 When there are more than two options, the opportunity cost is the forgone value in the health of the best alternative.

5 Margaret Thatcher was Conservative prime minister from 1979 to 1990. The Community Charge was a tax introduced by her government in 1989 (Scotland) and 1990 (England and Wales), replacing domestic rates in funding local authorities. It was a flat-rate, per-capita tax on every adult, at a rate set by the local authority. The charge was replaced by Council Tax in 1993, two years after its abolition was announced.

6 In 2017–19, people living in the least deprived areas could expect to live almost two decades longer in good health than those in the most deprived areas. People in the most deprived areas spend around a third of their lives in poor health, twice the proportion spent by those in the least deprived areas. This means that people in more deprived areas spend, on average, a far greater part of their already far shorter lives in poor health (Williams et al. 2022). See also Love-Koh et al. (2015).

7 For example, prescribed medicines are free for over the 60s, under 16s, 16 to 18s in full-time education, being pregnant, holding various exemption certificates (maternity, disease specific, disability), being an NHS hospital inpatient, being in receipt of specific social benefits.

8 In reality, markets are very far from free – they require a detailed system of private and exchangeable property rights, enforceable at law in the courts, and with elaborate subsystems of payments, payment collection, and monitoring to deter or prevent fraud.

9 Obviously, also to restore and maintain health but also to diagnose, prescribe, inform, advise, comfort and reassure, validate, liaise and guide, authorise time off work.

References

Brazier, J.E., Ratcliffe, J., Tsuchiya, A. and Salomon, J. (2007) *Measuring and Valuing Health Benefits for Economic Evaluation*, Oxford: Oxford University Press.

Buchanan, J.M. (1964) *The Inconsistencies of the NHS*, London: Institute of Economic Affairs.

Buchanan, J.M. and Stubblebine, W.C. (1962) "Externality", *Economica*, 29, 371–84.

Case, A., Lubotsky, D. and Paxson C. (2002) "Economic status and health in childhood: The origins of the gradient", *American Economic Review*, 92, 1308–34.

Chalkidou, K. and Culyer, A.J. (2019) "Deliberative processes in decisions about best buys, wasted buys and contestable buys: Uncertainty and credibility", in Isaranuwatchai, W., Archer, R.A., Teerawattananon, Y. and Culyer, A.J. (eds.), *Non-Communicable Disease Prevention: Best Buys, Wasted Buys, and Contestable Buys*, Cambridge: Open Book Publishers, 147–69.

Culyer, A.J. (1971a) "Medical care and the economics of giving", *Economica*, 38, 295–303.

Culyer, A.J. (1971b) "The nature of the commodity 'health care' and its efficient allocation", *Oxford Economic Papers*, 23, 189–211.

Culyer, A.J. (2006) "NICE's use of cost-effectiveness as an exemplar of a deliberative process", *Health Economics, Policy and Law*, 1, 299–318.

Culyer, A.J. (2010) "Perspective and desire in comparative effectiveness research – the relative unimportance of mere preferences, the central importance of context", *Pharmacoeconomics*, 28, 889–97.

Culyer, A.J. (2018) "Cost, context and decisions in health economics and cost-effectiveness analysis", *International Journal of Technology Assessment in Health Care*, 34, 434–41.

Culyer, A.J. (2020) "Use of evidence-informed deliberative processes – learning by doing: Comment on 'use of evidence-informed deliberative processes by health technology: assessment agencies around the globe'", *International Journal of Health Policy and Management*, 9, 263–5.

Culyer, A.J. (2022) "Reinforcing science and policy, with suggestions for future research; comment on 'evidence-informed deliberative processes for health benefit package design – part II: A practical guide'", *International Journal of Health Policy and Management*, doi: 10.34172/ijhpm.2022.7398.

Culyer, A.J. and Lomas, J. (2006) "Deliberative processes and evidence-informed decision-making in health care – do they work and how might we know?" *Evidence and Policy*, 2, 357–71.

Culyer, A.J. and Wagstaff, A. (1993) "Equity and equality in health and health care", *Journal of Health Economics*, 12, 431–57.

Deaton, A. (2002) "Policy implications of the gradient of health and wealth", *Health Affairs*, 21, 13–30.

Deaton, A. (2003) "Health, inequality, and economic development", *Journal of Economic Literature*, 41, 113–58.

Evans, R.G. (1974) "Supplier-induced demand: some empirical evidence and implications", in Perlman, M. (ed.), *The Economics of Health and Medical Care*, New York: Wiley, 162–73.

Evans, R.G., Barer, M.L. and Marmor, T.R. (eds.) (1994) *Why Are Some People Healthy and Others Not? The Determinants of Health of Populations*, New York: Aldine De Gruyter.

Glassman, A., Giedion, U. and Smith, P.C. (2017) *What's In, What's Out: Designing Benefits for Universal Health Coverage*, Washington, DC: Center for Global Development.

Goodman, J.C. (1980) *National Health Care in Great Britain: Lessons for the USA*, Dallas: Fisher Institute.

Hill, S., Amos, A., Clifford, D. and Platt, S. (2014) "Impact of tobacco control interventions on socioeconomic inequalities in smoking: review of the evidence", *Tobacco Control*, 23, 89–97.

Hurley, J., Pasic, D., Lavis, J., Mustard, C., Culyer, A.J. and Gnam, W. (2008) "Parallel lines do intersect: Interactions between the workers' compensation and provincial publicly financed health care systems in Canada", *HealthCare Policy*, 3, 100–12.

Jacobsson, F., Carstensen, J. and Borgquist, L. (2005) "Caring externalities in health economic evaluation: How are they related to severity of illness?", *Health Policy*, 73, 172–82.

Jewkes, J. and Jewkes, S. (1962) *The Genesis of the British National Health Service*, London: Basil Blackwell.

Lees, D.S. (1960) "The economics of health services", *Lloyds Bank Review*, 56, 26–40.

Lees, D.S. (1962) "The logic of the British national health service", *Journal of Law and Economics*, 5, 111–18.

Lees, D.S. (1964) *Monopoly or Choice in Health Services?* London: Institute of Economic Affairs.

Love-Koh, J., Asaria, M., Cookson, R. and Griffin, S. (2015) "The social distribution of health: estimating quality-adjusted life expectancy in England", *Value in Health* 18.5, 655–62.

Marmot, M.G. (2008) *Closing the Gap in a Generation: Health Equity Through Action on the Social Determinants of Health*, Final Report of the Commission on Social Determinants of Health, Geneva: World Health Organization.

Marmot, M.G. (2010), *Fair Society, Healthy Lives: The Marmot Review: Strategic Review of Health Inequalities in England Post-2010*, London: Department for International Development, ISBN 9780956487001.

Marmot, M.G. (2015) *The Status Syndrome: How Your Place on the Social Gradient Directly Affects Your Health*, London: Bloomsbury.

Marmot, M.G., Smith, G.D., Stansfeld, S. et al. (1991) "Health inequalities among British civil servants: The Whitehall II study", *The Lancet*, 337, 1387–93.

McGuire, T.G. (2000) "Physician agency", in Culyer, A.J. and Newhouse, J.P. (eds), *Handbook of Health Economics*, Amsterdam: Elsevier, 461–536.

McKnight, R. (2007) "Medicare balance billing restrictions: Impacts on physicians and beneficiaries", *Journal of Health Economics*, 26, 326–41.

Nozick, R. (1974) *Anarchy, State, and Utopia*, Oxford: Basil Blackwell.

Oortwijn, W., Husereau, D., Abelson, J. et al. (2022) "Designing and implementing deliberative processes for health technology assessment: A good practices report of a Joint HTAi/ISPOR task force", *Value in Health*, 25, 480–1.

Tobin, J. (1970) "On limiting the domain of inequality", *Journal of Law and Economics*, 13, 263–78.

Walzer, M. (1983) *Spheres of Justice: A Defence of Pluralism and Equality*, Oxford: Martin Roberson.

Webster, C. (1998) *The National Health Service: A Political History*, Oxford: Oxford University Press.

Williams, E., Buck, D., Babalola, G. and Mcguire, D. (2022) *What are Health Inequalities?* London: King's Fund.

Zwarenstein, M. (1994). "The structure of South Africa's health service", *Africa Health*, March, 3–4.

8

FAITH, SPIRITUALITY, AND THE CONCEPT OF FAIRNESS

Ian Dewar and Deborah Wilde

Introduction

Why would anyone be interested in fairness in spirituality and, does it matter anyway?

Fairness is one of those concepts that everyone agrees about and yet struggles to define. It is easy to apply in simple concrete situations but becomes more complex in more nuanced or sophisticated situations.

To highlight this: ten sweets divided between five people is simple enough – two each. But every event has a context. If one person was type 2 diabetic, what would be a fair distribution of sweets? If the person with diabetes needed a sugar boost for potential hypoglycaemia, should some sweets be reserved for them? Even simple examples can swiftly turn complex.

How, then, do you cultivate spiritual fairness? All the major World faiths, and even the growing spirituality movement in Western society, would claim to aspire to it.

This chapter sets out to explore this concept of fairness in the light of religion and spirituality. "Spirituality" feels like "the new kid on the block", it is a word or concept that has grown significantly in usage in recent years and yet, is difficult to pin down. What it does tell us, however, is that this desire for a sense of transcendence will not go away. It keeps coming back in various guises. This is significant.

The first section will provide some understanding of the development of these two concepts in relation to contemporary culture and the relationship

DOI: 10.4324/9781003410560-11

between the two. It will then draw out key themes from religion and spirituality that can be used as positive actions for improvement in the NHS. In particular, it highlights three virtues that can be cultivated to bring a greater sense of fairness to healthcare practice. The second half will apply these critiques to some of the scandals that have affected the NHS, including our own Trust.

Faith and Spirituality

Faith is not simply a question of allocation of resources and language but of values and priorities, as a result, there is no clear "definition". This same difficulty presents itself in relation to spirituality. Is there such a thing as "spiritual fairness"? Societal questions and fairness are inextricably linked.

One place to begin is with the word "Faith". For the purposes of this chapter "Faith" can be understood as a search for meaning or purpose that may or may not be formally articulated. In a healthcare setting, "Faith" or belief in something greater than oneself can surface in the conscious self because of conversation or thoughts shaped by illness and/or uncertainty. It is often understood in a religious context.

Faith is falling from common usage and the direction of travel of contemporary culture means that the word "spirituality" also needs to be considered in the context of faith and fairness.

Spirituality is often perceived as being more encompassing than religion. "Formal religion is a means of expressing an underlying spirituality, but spiritual belief, concerned with the search for the existential or ultimate meaning in life, is a broader concept and may not always be expressed in a religious way." In contrast, religion is seen as a defined set of beliefs and practices to which individuals may or may not subscribe.

The document Religion and Belief Matters, from NHS Scotland, states: "Spiritual care is not necessarily religious; religious care, at its best should always be spiritual".[1]

This distinction is fundamental to understanding the concept of fairness because the growth of spirituality in Western culture has historical roots. This is explored by Sheldrake,[2] who suggests that the latter half of the 19th century saw a cultural change that linked spirituality more to the arts than to religion.

For this reason, spirituality will be understood as an innate desire to stretch beyond the ordinary stresses of life to discover meaning, purpose, and a sense of sacredness.

This concept of spirituality as distinct from religion or, at the very least, not needing formalised religion, continued to grow throughout the 20th century and began to take on a unique life of its own. This point was recognised by the Russian émigré scholar, Fedotov, who noted after the Second World War that: "in our own day a non-Christian, Eastern mysticism, emanating from India is seeping into . . . English literature."[3]

The significance of this is that, generally speaking, people who can afford the time and money for art and literature and are more likely to belong to a body of people who hold positions of influence and decide organisational policies and practices. This is not to say that other classes of people do not make music or appreciate fine architecture, but the emerging middle class of the 19th century took over the ideas from the 18th-century aristocratic "Grand Tour" and began to see art as a way of cultivating the self in contradistinction to normal working life.[4]

As Fedotov also noted: "The term "spirituality" is used in various senses. In the broadest, it defines the loftiest moral and intellectual qualities of man in his relation to God and to nature, to himself and to his fellow men."[5] Spirituality "separated" from "religion" may not be unique; what is novel about the current situation, is that for nearly 1600 years spirituality in Western culture found its source in the Christian religion and no longer does so. Yet, the drive for meaning continues; as Storr points out "the hunger of imagination which drives men to seek new understanding and new connection in the external world is, at the same time, a hunger for unity and integration within."[6]

What Does This Historical Development Mean for the NHS?

The NHS, whether it is commonly acknowledged or not, reflects the cultural mores and aspirations of British culture as shaped by those in positions of power. A government committed to equality and diversity will ensure that these are properly maintained in the NHS.

However, going deeper, if it is true that the 19th century saw the "separation" of spirituality and religion that has continued apace in the 20th century; then that represents a cultural dissonance of which the NHS is a reflection. Fairness in the NHS must be worked out in an institution that is, at one and the same time, a healthcare provider and a bearer of cultural change and challenge.

In this respect, there is a symbiotic relationship between the NHS and wider culture. Take two statements from contrasting politicians:

"Intrinsically the National Health Service is a church. It is the nearest thing to the embodiment of the Good Samaritan that we have in any respect of our public policy."

(Barbara Castle, Labour MP, 1976[7])

"The National Health Service is the closest thing the English have to a religion, with those who practice in it regarding themselves as a priesthood."

(Nigel Lawson, Conservative MP, 1992[8])

There is little evidence to suggest that these two statements do not continue to hold good. So, one cannot talk about justice and fairness in the NHS without talking about justice and fairness in society, and you cannot talk about justice and fairness in society, without trying to understand the thoughts and ideas that water that culture.

To examine fairness in the NHS in relation to spirituality and religion is to open a window on to the values located in the "soul" of British culture.

Religion and Spirituality as a Critique of Healthcare

The next question to ask is what, in concrete terms, can religion and spirituality bring to this need for greater understanding? From our experience as healthcare chaplains, we have identified three "virtues" or "disciplines" amongst many, that can be cultivated to bring a greater sense of justice to healthcare practice and thereby to fairness. These virtues are hospitality, self-reflection, and accountability.

In a frenetic, "industrialised" health care system; all three virtues have the potential to be countercultural and create the space for what Josef Pieper identified in his essay entitled: "Leisure the basis of Culture".[9] That is the relaxed space in which thinking can lead to progress and enrichment in life. These are particularly important in end-of-life scenarios where leisure is a prerequisite for a good death.

Good chaplaincy, in our experience, even in the briefest of encounters, should provide an air of leisure in which a patient, relative or member of staff can engage in an honest conversation on an equal footing, and have the opportunity to *discover meaning, purpose and a sense of sacredness.*[10]

Turning to the three virtues that we have identified; we will look at each in turn and then draw all three together in the concrete example of "death cafés."

For those unfamiliar with this concept, an explanation and examples of usage are given in the section of this chapter entitled, "Taking Stock in Practice."

Hospitality

Hospitality is, or ought to be, a fundamental principle for healthcare in a hospital setting. The word itself, as described by Wikipedia: "Hospitality is the relationship of a host towards a guest, wherein the host receives the guest with some amount of goodwill and welcome."[11]

We will return to the word "guest" in a moment.

Hospitality is fundamental to all major religious traditions. For example, in the Old Testament – a source of religious life for the three main monotheistic religions – it is written that: "The alien living with you must be treated as one of your native born. Love him as you love yourself." (Leviticus 19: 34 NIV). "Alien" from the Latin, "other", carries with it an emphasis on reaching out to the other, so that the other may be known. Therefore, hospitality is not, much as the hospitality industry may like it to be, meeting the needs of a consumer, but, rather, the creation of space to know the stranger cf. also, from a very different tradition: "When abroad behave as though you were receiving an important guest. When employing the services of the common people behave as though you were officiating at an important sacrifice. Do not impose on others what you yourself do not desire." Confucius.[12]

Returning to the word "guest," it is possible to ask important questions from a spiritual and religious point of view about the relationships between staff and patients in a healthcare setting.

Firstly, it is necessary to remember that the healthcare world is based on the premise of professionalism. It cannot be any other way. There must be standards of training, standards of behaviour and codes of conduct. These are criteria/benchmarks against which individuals and organisations can legitimately be measured.

Secondly, however, there is the pressure to care. The word "pressure" is deliberately chosen. Common usage of the word "care" brings with it an emotional element, a sense of sympathy and empathy. But it is quite possible that these can conflict with professional standards. If a person is primarily led by sympathy and empathy, rather than by professional standards, can a person "care" more for one patient rather than another? If so, then that introduces the potential for a lack of fairness.

Thirdly, there is the issue of language itself. The words "clinician" and "patient" describe individual roles, but they also denote a distinct power relationship. The clinician treats the patient. One is active, one is passive. Again, this is legitimate. If you have appendicitis, you don't want to be treated by a dentist, you want a trained and approved clinician. However, at what point does a legitimate power relationship descend into paternalism (or in the case of certain scandals within maternity care settings) maternalism?

Without moving into a long examination of professionalism, pressure, and language, it is possible to posit the concept of hospitality – in its spiritual and religious sense – as a measure of the improvement and maintenance of high-quality healthcare. This can be done by taking the last phrase: "Love him as you love yourself" from the Book of Leviticus. A case study of the absence of hospitality could be the Ely Hospital scandal.

NHS historians have identified the scandal at Ely Hospital as an example of how subsequent scandals would evolve. The Ely Hospital investigation was one of the first documented reports of this nature.

The Committee of Inquiry was set up in 1967 by the Welsh Hospital Board at the request of the Minister of Health, to investigate allegations, made by a nursing assistant employed at the hospital, of ill-treatment of patients and pilfering by staff.[13]

The public outrage at these allegations led to the setting up of a commit-tee of inquiry, chaired by Geoffrey Howe, QC. The eventual publication of its findings would ultimately change the care provided to those with learning difficulties. It was Howe who insisted the inquiry should examine beyond the events at Ely and look at the whole system and the way people with learning difficulties were treated within the 20-year-old NHS systems.

The final transcript of evidence ran to more than 1000 pages. The pic-ture which emerged was of an institution cut off physically from the local community and professionally from the wider world of patient care. One part-time and two full-time doctors were responsible for the care of more than 660 patients. Recruitment was difficult. The hospital's medical officer and junior medical officer had limited experience with other hospitals and received scant professional development after their initial training. This lack of training, development, and networking with similar hospitals was very evident in the report findings.

Historians of medicine and healthcare will not miss the irony that the standard of care at Ely Hospital was below examples of the standards in 19th-century institutions. Diogenes was 12 years old and living inside a tub when delivered to the Royal Albert Hospital, Lancaster. He had mental and physical disabilities. When the Royal Albert was inspected in 1875, it was noted that on admission Diogenes: "Kicked, and swore, and spat, and would not be pacified until his tub was restored to him." Several years later he was making goods, earning money, and viewed the community as his home. "The Royal Albert was commended on its training methods, such as moral treatment and Christian values as the patient had been "surprisingly altered for the better."[14] Spiritual hospitality?

Self-Reflection

The fundamental point of departure for the creation of good quality, fair healthcare is self-knowledge, self-care, or to use older philosophical language – the cultivation of the self. This leads to the second element that spiritual and religious insight and practice can bring – self-reflection. In a system where staff are seriously pressed for time and space away from the frontline, this might seem a luxury, but sometimes a luxury is a necessity in disguise.

Take the well-known phrase attributed to Socrates: "the unexamined life is not worth living". Without wishing to go down the rabbit hole of a philosophy tutorial, the phrase can usefully be translated into: "Why do you get out of bed in a morning?" This is not an idle question. People need a reason for living. It is also valid because it sheds light on what might be one of the main causes of difficulty in healthcare and in the NHS in particular, the dissonance between "management speak" and praxis.

The NHS is not exempt from management cliches that seem to say one thing, whilst delivering something else.

Orwell's character, Winston, in *1984*, under pressure from his torturer O'Brien, must realise that sometimes 2 + 2 is 4, sometimes it is 5, sometimes it is 3, and, sometimes, it is all of them at once.[15] The, at times, unremitting issuing of NHS statements/slogans/management speak (delete as appropriate) can create confusion as to what 2 + 2 actually is. There is only one answer to this dilemma and that is to have the courage to stop, to hold up a mirror and look. How well do we know ourselves?

Taking this advice, is NHS managerialism any different to Orwell's O'Brien? It doesn't torture, but its incessant messaging and restructuring of values wear down people into submission. Perhaps the NHS is more *Brave New World*[16] than *1984*[17] but at what point does managerialism become a "spirituality" in its own right and how does that impact on fairness? Does the shape of managerialism kill genuine compassion?

If these are legitimate questions, then they have implications in all sorts of areas for justice and fairness. Justice and fairness do not begin at the bedside, they begin in the very structures of the caring organisation with the organisation of its resources and in the training, support and expectations of its staff. They begin in the society in which we live and with the politicians we appoint.

One of the most salient recent reports that highlights this principle has been the Ockenden Report, in response to the maternity services scandal at Shrewsbury and Telford NHS Trust. The report concludes that 201 babies and nine mothers might have survived if they had received better care and raises serious questions about how avoidable deaths and injuries to so many mothers and babies could have happened. As noted by Vize, there is a need for "deep soul searching by clinical and managerial leaders throughout the health service" to understand the recurrence of the same problems.[18]

The Ockenden Report concludes that the failings were caused by a "toxic mix." Staffing pressures, training gaps, and overstretched rotas all contributed. At the same time there was a failure to follow clinical guidelines or to investigate and learn from mistakes. Staff did not listen to patient experience, women were blamed or held responsible for poor outcomes, even death, and there was a lack of compassion in the treatment of, and response to, patients. Inadequate leadership and a bullying culture left staff feeling unable to raise concerns or escalate problems.

What space then is there in our institutions for self-reflection, cultivation of the self? It is worth pausing to reflect on a point of connection between religion and spirituality that can be used to deepen this critique. Spirituality is seen as personal self-development, so may be good for individuals, but not institutions: whereas religion is seen as more structural, more organisational. Yet both would advocate self-knowledge and, the cultivation of the self as a way forward. Can the two support each other? Yes, they can. It is one of the geniuses of English Law, that it treats organisations as persons, you can sue a company. This opens the door to a very intriguing concept that does not get enough serious debate – organisations have personalities.

Self-reflection is a critique that can be applied to a healthcare setting to both the organisation's (from directors to porters) and the organisation per se.

Fundamental to every spiritual journey is: "How far along the path am I?" "What is good?" "What needs to be looked at?" "Am I moving or am I being driven?"

When was the last time our organisations were encouraged, and our staff supported, in taking time to self-reflect? This does not, and should not, mean some kind of management or administrative tick list. It means having the courage to be silent, to stand in front of the mirror and allow the truth to reveal itself. Because that, in essence, is what religious and spiritual self-reflection is. It is not possible to have a "target" in the spiritual life. It is not possible to say that: "By next Tuesday, I will be 20% nicer." Character cannot be cultivated like that. But it is possible to have an aim, to have a purpose.

Targets are helpful, useful tools but if used as an ultimate aim, they are at best bad masters and at worst, tyrants. A healthcare service driven by targets will be one of these things, and it is by becoming one of these things that the door is open to mistakes and corruption.

Of course, that can sound fanciful: "So, what you are saying is that in an over worked, under pressure, resource strapped organisation, you want people to down tools and self-reflect?" Yes, that is precisely what is being proposed. Because at this present time; pressure is increasing, burnout is common, waiting lists are getting longer, frustration and staffing turnover are higher and that show little or no sign of changing. In the frenetic treadmill of activity and demand, the chances of mistakes, corner-cutting, neglect and corruption increase – bad soil produces bad plants. No justice and fairness there. The answer being suggested, is not, yet another "initiative" but the rediscovery of the ancient tradition of self-reflection.

Accountability

Accountability flows from self-reflection. The reason for this is simple. Self-reflection is a form of discovery. By self-reflecting, as an individual and/or as an organisation, it is possible to create the conditions for learning things that wouldn't otherwise be learnt. Accountability arises when the question is asked: "What do I do about what I now know?"

In all religious traditions there is the concept of apprenticeship. The words may vary, but be they: pilgrim, disciple, follower, pupil – or even, if you are a Star Wars fan, padawan,[19] the essence is the same. There is a process of growth, usually under the guidance of a more seasoned traveller, but, without exception, growth under the tutelage of accountability. The individual is responsible for their own growth and development. If it is true that organisations have personalities, then it is possible to speculate that organisations have a responsibility to be accountable that goes beyond simply getting the accounts in on time and keeping the Department of Health happy.

Accountability requires more than lip service. Organisations are quick to promote the view that they want to know what staff think but as the executive summary of the Francis report states:

> We heard contradictory accounts of some cases from those with different perspectives. There is nevertheless a remarkable consistency in the pattern of reactions described by staff who told of bad experiences. Whistleblowers have provided convincing evidence that they raised serious concerns which were not only rejected but were met with a response which focused on disciplinary action against them rather than any effective attempt to address the issue they raised.[20]

Compare this to the Ockenden report which stated that staff still felt unable to speak out, they were afraid of reprisals[21] even though promised anonymity.

To say that an individual or organisation is accountable is simply a statement. If an individual or organisation does or says something in response to a sense of accountability, that is simply to supply information. The key question is: "how do you create accountability?" This is a very difficult question to address: accountability, self-reflection, and the courage to create hospitality are all character traits of mature human beings and mature organisations and so to ask the question is to ask the question of NHS Trusts, are they mature organisations?

Why is this so important? As has been highlighted, these three critiques can be applied to scandals that have shaken the status of the NHS. In all these scandals, it is frequently the absence of the mature characteristics that have allowed a degradation of service to come into being.

So, how can accountability be created? The beginning of the process is to invert the order of the three disciplines. Accountability begins, when self-reflection takes place and self-reflection takes place when hospitality is created. In short, the courage to stop and take stock.

Taking Stock in Practice

An unusual, but powerful, example that incorporates all these three virtues is the use of death cafés.

A death café is simply the creation of space in which people come together, are given refreshments, a set of introductory questions and the freedom to discuss in small groups their responses to those questions. These questions can range from: "What is your most important item and life and who would you leave it to." "Have you ever seen a dead body?" "What is your earliest memory of death?" Groups are free to initiate their own questions and pursue their line of thinking as there is no specific, intended outcome. Cafés normally last for approximately an hour and individuals and groups are invited to give feedback at the end.

Death cafés have been used by chaplaincy at UHMBT as a point of engagement with junior doctors, nursing staff, student nurses, the wider public, and school sixth formers alongside being an element in bereavement training days.

The essence of a death café is to talk about death, but its potency lies in the ancillary questions and conversations that it provokes. For example, junior doctors frequently talk about personal philosophy and beliefs in relation to their work because they can talk without the pressure to pass an examination, and without the need to get the "right" answer. The education department at the Trust frequently comments on the highly positive feedback from the junior doctors.

Other members of staff have reported going home and making wills, having conversations with family, and loved ones about what is important to them. Members of the public have expressed appreciation about the opportunity to talk freely in relation to a taboo topic and, fascinatingly, sixth formers have used them to reveal to school staff that they have recently undergone a bereavement about which the staff were unaware and in one illuminating case, one pupil who was set on a career in the armed forces recognised that they may need to take someone's life and therefore used the café as a means of exploring their own thoughts and feelings around this issue.

It is worth noting at this point, that chaplains themselves must create places of hospitality, self-reflection, and accountability: this can take a variety of forms, from something as simple as engaging with nature through wild swimming, maintaining quality study, or finding a spiritual director. The Chaplaincy Department itself must also reflect these principles in its layout and sense of welcome. It should also be a place where chaplains and chaplaincy volunteers can find the space to reflect after deep or intense encounters. The structure, shape, and pattern of chaplaincy work and resources should be a mirror to chaplains themselves of the need to maintain hospitality, self-reflection, and accountability.

The Relationship Between the NHS and Society

This is far easier said than done. To return to an earlier point, there is a symbiotic relationship between the NHS and society. Society does not stop. It is 24/7 news, views, and entertainment. It is possible to order a takeaway, book a flight, and put your requests for an ideal partner on a dating app all at two o'clock in the morning. Life is instantaneous. Results are (or are expected to be) immediate. The NHS behaves as society behaves and society behaves as the NHS behaves (or seeks to behave) – target-driven, turnover-focused, crisis-ridden. The NHS and society mirror each other.

There is, at play here, a fundamental dishonesty. The NHS, in its current configuration, cannot operate as society wants. Its operating software is 1948 and yet, at the time of writing, it is 2023. Somebody, somewhere has to shout "stop!" There is between society and the NHS, a collusion in self-deception.

The public have unrealistic expectations of what the NHS can and should deliver and the NHS unrealistically acts (and believes?) that it can and should deliver these things – in short, the unrealistic expectation that it can meet unrealistic expectations. Is there a way out of this malaise?

The Kirkup Report

We will refer to the Kirkup report from our own Trust.

The Morecambe Bay Investigation was established by the Secretary of State for Health in September 2013 following concerns over serious incidents in the maternity department at Furness General Hospital (FGH).[22] The consequential report covering the period from January 2004 to June 2013 concluded that the maternity department at FGH was dysfunctional and identified serious problems in five areas.

It is less than surprising that the observed themes resonated with issues surrounding serious incidents in other Trusts.[23] The five domains were clinical competence, poor working relationships, the over-powering influence of some clinical leads, failures of risk assessment and care planning, grossly inadequate response from clinicians to serious incidents with repeated failure to investigate properly and learn lessons.

Taking the Executive Summary of the Kirkup report[24] the three spiritual critiques we have highlighted can be applied to its Executive Summary.

In terms of hospitality: "There were failures of risk assessment and care planning that resulted in inappropriate and unsafe care" (para 4). "Led to the unnecessary deaths of mothers and babies" (para 5).

In respect of self-reflection: "Between 2004 and the end of 2008 there was a series of missed opportunities to identify problem in the unit . . . investigations followed the same inadequate process and failed to identify problems" (para 7).

"By the early part of 2009, there was clearly knowledge of the dysfunctional nature of the FGH maternity unit at Trust level, but the response was flawed" (para 12).

Taking an organisational example of accountability: "At the same time, in early 2009, the Trust was heavily focused on achieving Foundation Trust (FT) status, and this played a significant part in what transpired" (para 13). Because of a specific corporate target, basic operational standards of care were overlooked or neglected, especially those of hospitality, self-reflection, and accountability.

Conclusion

The purpose of this chapter was to explore faith and fairness in the NHS. It has highlighted that fairness is not a simple commodity for distribution. It has drawn attention to the change in the religious and spiritual landscape of British society but found common threads of value and practice. It has suggested that three key practices can contribute in a critical manner, to improvements in standards and consequentially care. It has sought to highlight that the NHS debate is a societal debate. National reviews have considered the inequalities in care provision that discriminate against those in rural, isolated, high deprivation, or difficult-to-recruit areas.[25]

What is sobering is that investigations regarding serious failings in NHS care have chequered its history and, despite the "lessons have been learnt" language, the repetition of such errors is obvious.[26] In an article focusing on the Independent Review of Maternity Services at the Shrewsbury and Telford NHS Trust[27], a leading nurse academic, professor of patients' safety and healthcare quality, described the similarity and frequency of these major investigations as "telling" and "sobering". Jones comments on earlier and more recent malpractice within Trusts, "You can cut and paste recommendations from that (Ely, Cardiff) into every subsequent report around the failures of the NHS." That is a sobering message. There is an endemic, historical, repetitive nature of these reports.[28]

What then is the best way forward? It is a common religious and spiritual practice, when problems are encountered, to go back to the origins of belief, identify key principles and ask how they relate to current challenges. In the case of the NHS, it seems to us those basic principles centre on the fact that following the Second World War people wanted a fairer society and healthcare was a key component of this desire. Despite the difficulties encountered in establishing the NHS, it reflected a wider desire for a fairer society. This was encapsulated in the rallying cry "Free at the point of use".[29] This principle still holds true, but the question is, where is the point of need?

In a society with an ageing population, many of whom have multiple illnesses, with increasing pressure on a large, costly, and unwieldy organisation, the point of need cannot be the point at which people enter the healthcare system, because the need cannot be met adequately. The point of need must be earlier in a prospective patient's journey, and this means Population Health. To deal with health at this level would be to reduce some of the chronic pressure on the current system and allow more time for hospitality, self-reflection, and accountability.

The NHS is not alone in this predicament. As far back in 1994, Charles Handy in his book "The Empty Raincoat",[30] brought into organisational thinking the concept of the sigmoid curve. Figure 8.1 is adapted from his thinking. In essence it is a letter "s" laid on its side, creating a line on which you can trace the struggle to establish something (the post-war NHS), its growth and success (the spread of health care for all and its impact on overall health and wellbeing) and the top of the curve at which decline begins to set in (the 1980's, the 1990's, 2000's?). Figure 8.1 is adapted from his thinking.

Figure 8.1: Sigmoid Curve of the Development of the NHS

Normally decline leads to demise and collapse. But the NHS – like the banks –is too big to fail, it cannot be allowed to, so instead we have "propped up" decline. With each successive government promising reform, but happy to keep the show on the road. Perhaps, in the end, the NHS will not collapse, it will just burn out.

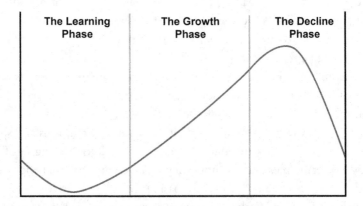

FIGURE 8.1 Sigmoid Curve of the Development of the NHS.
Source: Adapted by the Authors from Charles Handy's discussion of the Sigmoid Curve, The Empty Raincoat pages 49–64, Hutchinson, 1994 with the permission of Charles and Scott Handy

But if Charles Handy's concept is useful, it is possible for an organisation to start a second sigmoid curve.

To achieve this would require taking the bold step of removing the NHS from the realm of party politics. This can be done. Universal Credit, although at times controversial, was and remains a cross-party initiative. "We actually agree with the concept behind Universal Credit (UC), which was to bring six different benefits together into a unified system of support. That is the right thing to have done."[31] If it was the right thing to do there, why not Health? This would be challenging and require a level of self-reflection going back to the origins of the NHS and the willingness for political hospitality to allow open and honest critique and an agreement of accountability for healthcare that is more sophisticated than crude waiting lists.

Organisations in a decline phase can become defensive. A critique of this very issue was found in the Times Weekend Essay, "The NHS is stuck in a cover-up culture – there is a better way".[32] Defensiveness can only be challenged by hospitality that creates openness, self-reflection that allows for honesty and accountability that finds common territory.

In the confines of this chapter, we have glanced at some of the more well-known scandals in care within the NHS in recent years. We will close with a final reference to the Ockenden report. The last incidences occurred between 2000 and 2019 and what is poignant, and alarming is that in the review's final stages staff withdrew from participation and their accounts were removed.

If we do not want such incidences to be a continuing feature of the NHS, causing pain and undermining its work, then we need to have the courage to return to its founding principles which can be done by incorporating the virtues of hospitality, self-reflection, and accountability.

Notes

1. Referenced in: Religion and Belief Matter: An Information Resource for Healthcare Staff, Fair For All – Religion/Belief Project. The Scottish Inter Faith Council. 2007, p8.
2. Sheldrake, P. 2012. *A Short Introduction to Spirituality*, Oxford University Press.
3. Fedotov, G. P. 1952. *A Treasury of Russian Spirituality*, Seed and Ward, Preface.
4. See Hughes, K. Conspicuous Consumption. In *The Middle Classes: Etiquette and Upward Mobility*. Online Reference: https://brewminate.com/the-middle-classes-in-the-19th-century-etiquette-and-upward-mobility/The British Library (bl.uk)
5. Fedotov Op cit.
6. Storr, A. 1997. *Solitude*, Harper Collins, p124.
7. Delamothe, T. 2008, July 5. A fairly happy birthday. *British Medical Journal* 337(7660): 25–29. NHS at 60. See link: https://www.ncbi.nlm.nih.gov/pmc/articles/PMC 2443550/#:~:text=%E2%80%9CIntrinsically%20the%20National%20Health%20

Service,respect%20of%20our%20public%20policy.%E2%80%9D&text=%E2%80%9C
The%20National%20Health%20Service%20is,regarding%20themselves%20as%20a%20
priesthood.

8. Ibid.
9. Pieper, J. 2009. *Leisure, the Basis of Culture*, Ignatius Press.
10. Author's emphasis.
11. https://en.wikipedia.org/wiki/Hospitality.
12. The Analects. 1979. *Confucius*, Penguin Classics, Book XII.2, p112.
13. Ely Hospital, Cardiff: Inquiry Findings HL Deb, 1969, March 27, vol 300 cc1384–93.
14. Barnard, L. 2016–2017. *To What Extent Did the Royal Albert Asylum Portray Societal Notions of 'Idiots' and 'Imbeciles' Within the Victorian Era?* HI6100 – History Dissertation, University of Chester.
15. Orwell, G. 2021. *1984*, Harper Collins.
16. Huxley, A. 2007. *Brave New World*, Vintage Books.
17. Ibid.
18. Vize, R. doi:10.1136/bmj.o860; https://www.bmj.com/content/376/bmj.o860.
19. Just to be clear, neither author places themself in this category.
20. Francis Report Executive Summary 2015.
21. https://www.gov.uk/government/publications/final-report-of-the-ockenden-review/ockenden-review-summary-of-findings-conclusions-and-essential-actions.
22. Kirkup, B. 2015. *The Report of the Morecambe Bay Investigation*, HMSO.
23. Learning not blaming: Response to three reports on patient safety Government response to the Public Administration Select Committee report on clinical incidents, and the Morecambe Bay Investigation published 16 July 2015.
24. Morecambe Bay Investigation Report published 16 July 2015. Independent investigation into maternity and neonatal services in Morecambe Bay makes far-reaching recommendations to prevent future unnecessary deaths. Morecambe Bay Investigation published 3 March 2015.
25. The Kings Fund. 2022, June 17. *What are Health Inequalities?* The Kings Fund.
26. Similarity of NHS care scandals 'sobering'. R. Gilroy. 2019, November 20. *Nursing Times*.
27. Final report of the Ockenden review. Findings, conclusions, and essential actions from the independent review of maternity services at the Shrewsbury and Telford Hospital NHS Trust. Department of Health and Social Care, 2022, March 30.
28. Jones 2019 Similarity of NHS care scandals 'sobering', says nurse academic. *Nursing Times*.
29. The founding of the NHS: 75 years on - History of government (blog.gov.uk)
30. Handy, C. 1994. *The Empty Raincoat*, Hutchinson.
31. Labour will "fundamentally reform" UC to "simplify" the system, Ashworth says – Labour List.
32. The Times Weekend Essay 'The NHS is stuck in a cover-up culture – there is a better way.'

PART FOUR

Access, Equity and Fairness of Delivery

9

CONTEMPORARY SPECIALIST PROVISION

Access, Equity, and Fairness of Delivery in the NHS

Mike Thomas

Introduction

This chapter focuses on five areas that provide common yet "specialist services" within the NHS: Community Care, Emergency Care, Cancer Care, Stroke Care, and Child and Adolescent Mental Health Care. While there are many other spheres involved in healthcare, these five areas are commonly found in many NHS providers and are experienced frequently by members of the public. In addition, they all have government "targets" placed on them, for example, reduced waiting times or pre-set time periods for access to diagnosis, referral, and treatment, and all undergo punitive actions if such targets are consistently "breached". I have gathered the views of clinicians in these areas through individual interviews and discussion, and I have also spent time in some of the specialist areas and observed practices and contextualised my deliberations around the values of fairness and equity.

Since its inception the NHS has always adapted to change, whether structural or procedural, and has assimilated a myriad of statutory and policy developments in line with different political strategies. It has always survived, even through years of "austerity" measures, a global pandemic, and constant technological and pharmaceutical advances. The NHS endures. I would argue that its original principles of equal access to care, and fairness underpinning where provision is delivered still apply. But what do front line clinicians think? Are they aware of such values in their busy clinical lives?

DOI: 10.4324/9781003410560-13

Do they still adhere to, and put these principles into practice? And are they important to them?

The interviewees were Jane McNichols (JM), Consultant Breast Surgeon, Oncologist and Chief Medical Officer, Rachael Broadley (RB), Clinical Manager, Stroke Unit, Terry Drake (TD), Clinical Transformation Lead, Child and Adolescent Mental Health Services, Pauline Preston (PP), Senior Manager, Community Care. I would also like to thank those clinical practitioners who made me welcome when I visited and observed their work in emergency departments. Each had a different emphasis yet also had many shared approaches, and each speciality gave insight into the complexity of healthcare delivery, the underlying compassion in practice, and the importance of value-based principles of care.

Discussion Points

Performance Targets

There are several interesting issues regarding fairness and equity that arise from the views of experienced clinicians. For some, setting mandatory targets appears to be accepted as having some merit in the context of fairness and equity. In stroke care in particular the focus on meeting targets (and avoiding negative responses when targets are breached) seems to create a system whereby patients are assessed and treated within a fixed period, whoever they are.

As Rachael points out,

> *The intervention pathway is full of examples. In stroke care there are set minimum targets for all stages of interventions, from diagnostic tests to rehabilitation. Very often these targets are based on time, the time that must be given to take and analyse blood enzyme levels for example. So, it doesn't matter who the patient is, or what background they have, everyone must be seen in the same way. The targets in their way regulate fairness and equity of access and treatment.*
> *(RB)*

In cancer care there is a similar approach, and it is not surprising that the political administration adopts target-driven strategies to care. Jane observed that targets dominate the care delivery,

> *There are several important issues that could be addressed differently. Services in oncology are stretched and staff haven't the time to push more on access*

issues that are not measured. Everyone concentrates on targets, so if it's not a target.

(JM)

But a more nuanced examination reveals a more complex picture. As Terry mentions, in Child and Adolescent Mental Health Services (CAMHS), the access to assessment is itself problematic.

There is a difference between equity and fairness in the system. Everyone can access . . . based on clinical need, and that seems equitable. Within the system there is an interesting issue of fairness. If you have ADHD (Attention Deficit/ Hyperactivity Disorder) for example, then you may have to wait a number of months to start a treatment support programme. Yet we know that . . . any delay in treatment increases the chances of problems in later life. But prioritisation is based solely on acute need and imminent risk . . . is that fair?

(TD)

Terry's point regarding neurodevelopmental presentations is further reflected in The Independent newspaper which cites charities the Donaldson Trust, the Brain Charity, and community health provider CHS Healthcare as showing 190,000 patients expected to be waiting for autism diagnosis by 2024. In 2023, there were 130,000 waiting to be seen and 67,600 waiting more than a year (NHS Providers Today's Health News, 2023).

A similar point can be found in cancer care, as Jane succinctly points out, *"Another view is that having target standards is fair, but only if people access treatment and that is affected by background, education, culture, age, and other socioeconomic factors"* (JM). The fact that access to assessment and treatment has targets does not address the clear evidence demonstrating that better-educated, higher-income, middle-class people are more likely to access cancer screening services quicker and receive treatment earlier whereas those with fewer life opportunities or chances to access care when their cancer has developed further and require more complex (and more expensive) interventions (UK Parliament Health Committee, 2021). This is a real health issue for the UK, data up to 2019 shows there were 167,142 deaths from cancers in the UK despite an increase in survival rates (nearly 50% survived for ten years or more and 38% of cancers were preventable, Cancer Research UK, 2019). But since the pandemic the demand for cancer care has risen and in 2023, the number of those waiting more than 62 days for treatment, a cancer target, had doubled (NHS Confederation, 2023).

Targets are a reality and in specialised services a mandatory requirement, for some the approach does appear to have merit; Rachael is clear that *"In stroke care the requirement to meet set targets does ensure fairness, no matter who the person is"* (RB). Targets seem to work in certain condition-specific contexts where short timescales have an impact on an individual's overall outcome, and urgent treatment is required. In a different context where time can provide consideration over a longer basis, and a more cross-disciplinary team outside of one service approach is required, then the issue of targets can be perceived in other ways. Terry observed that

> *It's important, [for the individual], that there is more fairness about access to multi-disciplinary services whose earlier intervention would be beneficial. I guess it's less to do with centralised targets and meeting pre-designated standards, and more to do with enabling more localised approaches to care, and more clinical decision-making that are specific to individualised needs.*
>
> (TD)

Targets have their place; they can be important levellers in terms of fairness to access and equity of interventions. They are also important in building and maintaining trust and confidence amongst patients, users, and carers. Gay Haskins (2018) and colleagues demonstrated how important it is for health and social care organisations to build trust-based relationships, both inside and outside the system. But they are a subtle policy tool, used in the right context they are valuable and do seem to demonstrate fairness and equity. But used crudely and bluntly, they lose their value, not just in moral and ethical terms but also in driving up gaming behaviours (the practice of returning data which shows compliance due to deviations in definitions from the required target), slowly normalising lowered standards of care, and decreasing innovation and creative thinking. For policymakers applying targets is a subtle skill and requires a rationale that clinicians can support. Rachael comments, *"So, it doesn't matter who the patient is, or what background they have, everyone must be seen in the same way, the targets in their way regulate fairness and equity of access and treatment"* (RB).

Education, Housing, and Employment

Public health messaging has developed hugely since the years of government "instructional" programmes, but nevertheless, there is much more to do to make care fairer and more equal. Terry observes that *"more focus on the whole person, which means closer integration with schools, social care, housing and so on"* (TD).

In many ways healthcare acts as a mirror to the wellbeing and security of the country at large. A lack of effective interventions in areas such as infant development, education, employment, housing, and the environment really does inhibit the life opportunities of individuals and creates situations where the individual has a higher chance of becoming unwell or chronically ill. Jane notes, *"having target standards is fair, but only if people access treatment and that is affected by background, education, culture, age, and other socioeconomic factors"* (JM). This is an important point and covers a range of different health risks. Examples include serious cardiovascular issues experienced by long-term drug use to manage enduring and chronic mental health conditions (MIND, 2023) or the rise in morbid obesity amongst the general population (before the pandemic over 25% of adults in England were obese and nearly 40% overweight), clinically contributing to various poor health conditions (Obesity statistics from the House of Commons Library, 2021).

Public health messaging does have an impact, for example the level of the population accessing screening is much improved, but this increase can cause further pressures, particularly on personal finances. Jane comments in reference to cancer services,

> *Screening services have a better history regarding access and equity but having cancer brings its own inequalities. A good example is the economic impact on the person experiencing cancer, on their income, expenditure, sick pay and so on. Taken in proportionality, there is undoubtedly inequality here.*
>
> *(JM)*

Could there be a different approach to providing care, moving more towards a whole person and whole service approach? Terry has a particular view which highlights not only the opportunities for collaborative approaches but also the frustrations with the current NHS structure, a view widely held by many in mental health care,

> *The support that we provide can become the basis of a young person's life, how they learn, enjoy experiences, get a job, form future relationships and so on. It's important for that individual that there is more fairness about access to multidisciplinary services that can intervene early enough.*
>
> *(TD)*

The NHS should not be expected to carry the burden of intervening when the root cause of many illnesses can be traced to life's opportunities and lifestyle choices (or lack of either). More early interventions and policy interventions that create real collaborative action between education, housing, employment, and health would lead to less need for acute specialist interventions, or at the very least a reduction in complex, expensive treatments. As Pauline notes, *"Partnership discussions and maintaining relationships . . . to make them stick. You just have to keep going because it's the right thing to do"* (PP).

The Individual . . . Not the "Condition"

It is rather disappointing, when one considers the advances made in labelling and stereotyping (The Prisma, 2022), that conditions rather than the person still dominate approaches to care. Central NHS planning looks at "stroke", "cancer", etc. There is still no whole-person service that provides approaches to both physical and mental health simultaneously. This is a form of unfairness. Terry states,

> *Mental health encompasses so many elements of a person's life . . . we have to see the whole of a person's life, and often who they share it with. We don't just respond to 'diagnosis', we respond to the person.*
>
> *(TD)*

In other words, care often involves seeing the person in the entirety of their lives, not whether someone has mental, or physical, conditions or how they progress within their treatment programmes. This is in line with the World Health Organization's (2010) definition that mental health is a state of well-being in which the individual realises his or her own abilities, can cope with the normal stressors of life, work productively and fruitfully, and is able to contribute to his or her community. In many ways mental health is ahead of other fields of care, particularly those involved in physical interventions. Collins, Drake, and Deacon (2013), had outlined this position a decade ago, and it is interesting that ten years later there is still no text that complements their work, for example raising issues of mental health conditions amongst individuals who access acute medical care.

For many years healthcare providers have stressed the need for practitioners to see the person rather than their condition, and whilst it is true that these days clinicians rarely refer to the "kidney in bed four", nevertheless treatment pathways are based on specialisms. There has been an incremental growth in clinical specialists and advanced practitioners, and whilst there is an argument for specialisms because they provide enhanced care to patients with specific conditions, these evolutions in care pathways prevent the development of a whole-person approach to care.

As well as being unfair it is inequitable. Most practitioners understand individuals experiencing mental health conditions may also have physical disorders, and most individuals with physical disorders require mental health support. Yet the structural organisations and delivery of care remain stubbornly separate, to the detriment of the individual, the economic costs of care, and opportunities for better preventive population health strategies. Advocates for more collaborative working have been saying this for many years, for example Archer and Cameron's work on collaborative leadership was written in 2009. The last word from Terry again, "*children and adolescent mental health services are really about life opportunities, not diagnosis or treatment . . ., we don't 'treat' conditions. We're there to support better futures for children and young people*" (TD).

Boundaries

The NHS structure prevents opportunities for genuine collaboration with social care which results in an inequitable and unfair system. Pauline has many years of community experience, "*Organisational boundaries, they still exist, everyone knows collaboration is better than co-location . . . but barriers still exist. It's not about money*" (PP).

Take another example; "out of borough" care, the practice of outsourcing patients to care units geographically distant from their homes, which not only is practically inconvenient for the patient and their families but adds to the expenditure of care delivery. It is commonly found in mental health care,

> *We have geographical teams, we have specialist intervention teams, and we have acute residential provision. . . . Unfortunately, the demand is high and . . . some children have to be referred away from where they live, sometimes quite some distance.*
>
> *(TD)*

Such referrals are due to resource shortages, or organisational boundaries, that inhibit true collaboration. Yet they can be overcome. Pauline observed,

> *In Adult Social Care . . . part of the issue is the budget being held in in one department, so access is via a queue system. I worked with our community team and implemented a training programme, so colleagues were able to carry out the same assessment as adult social care staff, (who supervised the community staff). It used to take eight to twelve weeks to access assessment, now it's done in one day, it's just a different process and structure completely.*
>
> *(PP)*

Providers strictly adhere to commissioned contracts. Multiple health and social care practitioners see a patient because each holds separate "contracts", when one practitioner could provide most of the care. The political introduction of commissioning caused unfairness and inequity due to the lack of flexibility to adapt commissioning to encourage broader partnership approaches. The Clinical Commissioning Groups, brought in under the 2012 Health and Social Care Act, have been swept aside and replaced with a new Integrated Care System (ICS), under the 2022 Health and Care Act, and it is too early to deduce whether such structural unfairness will be addressed. However, where work has been done there is cause for optimism, "*Another example is more agile working, bedside at home, which works well with Primary Care and delivers both preventable interventions and faster treatment*" (PP).

The new ICSs (Integrated Care Systems) have oversight of geographical health provision and will work closely with designated localities (often termed "place"). Inflexible boundaries will be addressed with opportunities for more delivery across different organisations. Practitioners have a degree of hope that the new system will work, "*Well now we have the ICS, we should be ashamed if we can't make a difference*" (PP).

Technology

Of importance when considering crossing boundaries and working collaboratively is the pace of change in innovative technology. Advances such as e-prescriptions, shared electronic patient records, devices for remote monitoring purposes, and shared diagnostic data across care providers are all having an impact on collaborative working. There is a sense of inevitability that health and social care will eventually be combined into one structure and delivery. Whether local authorities or local health providers are best placed to be the single provider is a decision to be made, but e-administration, record-keeping, diagnostic datasets and monitoring data will influence the decision.

Alongside the technological advances in corporate data collection are innovations such as home monitoring via CCTV, handheld devices, and other communication sources which can remotely assess an individual's balance, mobility, hygiene, blood pressure, heart rate, glucose levels, diet, concentration levels, confusion, and so on, and alert the person and care providers when preventive interventions are necessary. In due course, there will be electronic "companions" which will converse with the individual and provide social friendship, health prompts, and collect health data, as well as engage in actions which will reduce the advances of specific deteriorating conditions.

In primary care, there will be more digitalised and remote General Practice advice, consultations, and treatment. The days of face-to-face meetings with a human GP are slowly ending, and the individual will instead be supported by a range of practitioner skills, some provided through technology and some by a highly dual or multi-trained individual able to provide different skills, rather than the current inefficient model of different skills being delivered by different people.

In acute settings, there will be more use of robotic interventions in surgery and invasive techniques used for diagnostic purposes. Some elements of hospital-based care will be delivered in the person's home due to innovative developments in monitoring, which will also lead to less reliance on acute and emergency services.

Social Background

After years of government-imposed austerity (from 2010), social background remains a form of inequity. As Jane notes on oncology outcomes, *"having target standards is fair, but only if people access treatment and that is affected by background, education, culture, age, and other socioeconomic factors" (JM)*. Inequity due to background is a recurring UK problem. The work carried out by Kynaston in 2008 on the post-war years can be compared with The Black Report (1982), and Whitehead's work in 1988, and Hutton's work in 1995. Yet despite attempts at levelling up there has been no real breakthrough.

The political principle of a smaller public sector and less state intervention has demonstrably not succeeded. General wealth has not been distributed to most of the population (Equality Trust, 2020), the UK is poorer (House of Commons Library, 2023), population health has deteriorated (BMJ, 2023), and people are dying earlier (The Health Foundation, 2022). Jane again, *"the economic impact on the person experiencing cancer, on*

their income, expenditure, sick pay and so on. Taken in proportionality, there is
undoubtedly inequality here" (JM).

The lack of coherent health strategies bringing together housing, education, and economic planning has had a severe impact. Government departments remain in separate silos, the Treasury continues to dominate policies,
and attempts at "levelling up" have not had any measurable positive impact.
More people are developing serious conditions, and dying earlier, because
they lack the infrastructure to improve their health.

As Jane points out,

> *Inequalities often lie in geographical distribution . . . where treatment centres are*
> *located or even how an organisation's referral system works. Access is not inequal-*
> *ity, BUT time and travel are. People may not always be able to access transport, or*
> *cover the costs of public transport, parking fees, or time from work or home commit-*
> *ments . . . other issues such as the financial costs of ambulance travel between sites, or*
> *the fact that some hospitals have better supported research trials or funding than others.*
>
> *(JM)*

It has already been mentioned that the middle classes are more likely to see
their GP earlier, be referred quicker, be more compliant with treatment, and
have much better outcomes. Those from less affluent backgrounds have the
opposite experience (and at a higher cost to the taxpayer). The NHS should
be praised for continuing to deliver care in such circumstances and continue
to confront barriers.

The NHS is not the same healthcare provider of pre-pandemic times;
never mind earlier years, it has evolved to reflect society's influences and
current needs for a contemporary lifesaving and life-enhancing network.
And yet, for all its commendable adaptability and flexibility as a healthcare
provider, so much still depends on the individual, their awareness of their
own health, and their motivation to access services in the first place.

Historical and Financial Comparisons

At its heart the practical application of politics is about choice. Governments
choose to lower, or raise taxation, spend on specific projects, drive policy
in certain directions, and respond to crisis in a particular way. In the United
Kingdom, the political choice for over a decade has been to reduce spending
on public service and raise taxation in covert ways. Healthcare strategies have
been financially based and this has dominated all discourse.

Jane provides an interesting insight on the discourse on comparing the financial costs of treatment in the NHS over many years (inevitably showing annual increase), but

> *Drugs and surgical techniques have been major breakthroughs regarding recovery and longevity. A lot of people now live much longer and have meaningful lives who would have died earlier many years ago. Advances now come so quickly that they are faster than the period for training staff.*
>
> *(JM)*

The NHS has not remained static since its inception, it evolves, changes, and adapts, so past comparisons are difficult. Jane argues that comparing year-on-year cost of oncology treatment should not be reductive;

> *Expenditure increases all the time and people don't always understand the reasons . . . it's standard practice for patients to be scanned before surgery today, fifty years ago the approach would have been an x-ray, some anti-biotics and pain relief medication.*
>
> *(JM)*

Treatment outcomes are so much better today because of technical advances, new screening, drug, and radiotherapy interventions. The options for clinical interventions are so complex that a simplistic expenditure comparison is meaningless. Yet debates about future healthcare, population health, and resource allocation continue to rely on past expenditure comparators. Each decade brings new advances and social developments, and it is a complex exercise to analyse the past with the present, so any conclusions must be taken with caution.

Compassion

It is clear from the interviews and my observations of clinical practice that values do influence day-to-day practices. Terry states they are "*Self-evidently important, we could not do our jobs effectively without being fair and equal.*" (TD), while Pauline comments

> *I'm consistently consciously aware of fairness and equity in community care. You must be honest with staff, be open, visible, and available. You have to be consistent and clear, for example this is the plan so work to the plan. Community care is brilliant at delivering plans . . . not just reciting plans but delivering on them.*
>
> *(PP)*

This emphasis on honesty as a moral precept and that on authentic leadership are important compassionate approaches (West, 2021) and Johri, Corich, and Haskins (2023).

Values are upheld in clinical specialities and supported across the NHS, Rachael notes that fairness and equity are *"Very important . . . but that would be the same in all areas of the NHS,"* (RB), a view supported by Terry, *"they belong to the workforce and when implemented they make a difference to the lives of service users, their families, and our staff."* (TD). I observed a tender act of kindness in a busy emergency department when a doctor took time to talk to an elderly woman lying on a corridor trolley. Later, I asked why he did so, he had noticed that no one had talked to the patient for 20 minutes, and he thought she could do with a "chat". These little compassionate acts, often unnoticed, drive value-based care, a point often noted by West (2021) when he examined how carers managed within their work environments.

Despite austerity measures, a global pandemic, industrial unrest, winter pressures, regulatory burdens, and structural changes, NHS clinicians and managers remain influenced by fairness and equity values. It is not uncommon to observe fatigue, a level of scepticism and a simmering anger, about a system that can be difficult to deliver at times. Terry observes that

> *if you have ADHD for example, there is often a significant delay in gaining a diagnosis and starting a treatment programme. Is that fair when we know that early intervention . . . can have a dramatic and beneficial impact on a young person and that any delay increases the chances of wide-ranging issues in later life.*
> *(TD)*

Moreover, Jane comments *"Inequalities often lie in geographical distribution. What I mean is issues such as where treatment centres are located or even how an organisation's referral system works. Access is not inequality, BUT time and travel are."* (JM).

Underlying these emotions and perceptions are genuine levels of authentic and deeply held personal values and conscious awareness of fairness and equity. Clinicians do not practice with emotional non-engagement or amoral values, they apply their personal sense of caring and professionalism and measure themselves against their own internal standards and those of their colleagues. Where frustrations do spill over, in the context of fairness and equity of care, it is often because there is nowhere within the system for their frustrations to vent. Take for example recruitment, most observers know this is an issue that directly impacts on how services could be delivered to a higher standard. There are already 154,000 fewer staff and this could rise to 571,000 by the mid-2030s (The Guardian, 2023). Yet pleas to increase the workforce are often judged by financial rather than care considerations. How then should clinicians respond when they know that having more colleagues would improve care, and are aware that everyone else knows too, yet nothing improves?

It is a testament to NHS practitioners and leaders that they continue to apply values of compassion and kindness whilst constantly being aware that care could be fairer and more equitable. And the reason seems to be based on purpose. As Haskins and Thomas (2022) point out, a strong sense of purpose provides the "why" for doing things, while values, those guiding principles, complement the purpose. In the case of NHS staff, the purpose is caring, with all the underlying values that it entails. The last word to Pauline, perhaps an observation that neatly sums up the core issue at the heart of the modern NHS, *"it's always about people . . . you just have to never give up"* (PP).

Recruitment

Recruitment and training are a constant source of concern. The issue of new workers was mentioned by Rachael when asked what would improve fairness and equity in stroke care, *"Resources. Mainly employed qualified staff, (rather than a reliance on agency staff)." (RB).* And having regularly employed staff has an impact, *"they have been focusing on recruiting nurses who can be employed by the Trust to lessen reliance on agency staff, and that obviously is having an improved effect on consistency of staffing and care given." (RB).* Short-staffing ranges across the NHS and is not restricted to any geographical areas or specialities of care. In mental health Terry notes the shortages of skilled practitioners,

> there is a degree of equity of access but the issue of fairness . . . is a real one for lots of families. So much depends on the skills and awareness of the practitioner carrying out the assessment and then having access to the appropriate intervention in a more timely manner, rather than referral to another waiting list.
>
> (TD)

Each practitioner has their own aspirations for recruiting staff, Rachael wants

> More emphasis on stroke care and the specialist skills in pre-registration nurse education. It's difficult to recruit nurses anyway, and they must be trained as they

join the stroke team. It would be helpful if they had more understanding of the skills and techniques of stroke care beforehand.

(RB)

While Pauline would like *"recruitment of people with values is integral to fairness and equity"* (PP).

One of the most stressful issues faced by clinical staff is the financial control of access to healthcare careers. Professionally registered student intakes are tightly controlled by the government, and not unusual for numbers to be cut due to financial constraints. A lesson painfully experienced when just five years after the Health Secretary substantially cut student numbers, there were insufficient NHS professionals to tackle the impact of the pandemic. Even a hasty increase in response to specific healthcare requirements will not benefit the patient until at least three to five years and is acutely felt by frontline staff. Jane notes,

Oncology is difficult to recruit to as a speciality. Drugs and surgical techniques have been major breakthroughs regarding recovery and longevity. . . . Patients now live much longer and have meaningful lives. . . . Advances now come so quickly that they are faster than the period for training staff.

(JM)

Clinicians know it will be several years before more recruits arrive and do the best they can whilst they wait.

Conclusion

Practitioners are consciously aware of the values of fairness and equity, and these are important on both a personal and professional level. Pauline comments *"I can't emphasise enough how important"* (PP). And Jane reflects on fairness and equity in her daily work, *"Yes, always considered"* (JM). Their strong commitment to compassion and the values of fairness and equity reflects the finding of West (2021), who gave many examples of NHS staff applying kindness as a core element of their day-to-day work. West also notes that most health and social care staff dedicate their lives to caring for others, so it should be no surprise to find that values are so intrinsic to their care.

Practitioners are acutely aware that the NHS could be better, fairer, and more equitable, and they often display sophisticated thinking, underpinned by frontline experience and skills, on how to make their care structures and systems better. If the clinicians and leaders I observed and interviewed are representative of the NHS in general, and I believe they are, then the original values-based premise for establishing the NHS remains alive and passionately held by NHS staff. The demonstrations of anger and frustration by frontline staff since the pandemic are because they perceive that their values of caring, compassion and fairness are being attacked and undermined to a degree that requires more robust responses. The current industrial action is fundamentally about upholding the values of fairness and equity that many feel are increasingly difficult to apply.

For the interviewees, national NHS leaders are perceived as supporting the values of fairness and equity but current structures and processes prevent better collaborative and cross-boundary workings, and anyway, many leaders and managers are constantly engaged in providing more with declining resources. The interviewees have risen through the system, and they sometimes have points of disagreement with managers, but in the main, frontline clinical staff believe that their organisational ethos, and their leaders, share the same values and ambitions for a fairer and more equitable NHS.

Lessons Learned

Firstly, NHS strategic planners and policymakers need to be aware that for frontline staff, values of fairness and equity are constant, conscious drivers for caring. Interventions, commissioning, or policies that ignore such important ethical dimensions of practice will be difficult to implement effectively or efficiently.

Secondly, experienced, and skilled staff have a clear understanding of NHS challenges and can articulate solutions, particularly at the local level.

There should be a forum within the NHS where clinical staff can be represented, be supported to engage in strategies, and their proposals heard at the national planning level. Rachael knows what she is doing,

> Just doing my job really, everyone in the team has to input different skills and knowledge, the team works well together, and I see my role as ensuring we not only meet the targets but also improve care, and that never stops.
>
> (RB)

Terry suggests that "*being aware and conscious of our values . . . continuing to push the argument that individualised care packages, provided early, can make a big impact on a child's development and life chances.*" (TD). And Jane proposes that

"Encouraging and supporting more linear accelerator units, for example local radio-therapy services really seem to be making a difference. . . What would improve the services would be things like shared single waiting lists, centralised services for referrals and access." (JM).

Thirdly, some reflective questions for the reader. Does the NHS reflect the society within which it operates? Are its core values of caring, compassion and fairness a reflection of wider UK values? If your answer is yes, then what will you do to reduce the challenges faced by the NHS? If the answer is no, then what alternative societal values do you think are held? And where will that lead the NHS? It has already been discussed earlier that governments choose the paths they wish the country to take. The resources and strategies required by a national health system to meet the needs of its population in a fair and equitable way are therefore about choice too. What will you do to uphold the values of fairness and equity of healthcare?

Finally, the NHS does not operate in isolation from other elements of society. Good education, housing, employment, and locality play important roles in improving population health and politicians understand these issues. Yet councils, housing, education, health, and employment continue to be organised and funded within separate governmental departments and the Treasury dominates thinking towards economic reductionism. Early intervention, educational opportunities, housing, and employment prospects alongside joint health and social care interventions improve the health of the population and reduce the burden on the NHS.

There should be more emphasis on closer integration between the NHS and early years parenting, education, housing, employment, and social care at the place level and nationally. More think tanks and policymakers should explore the societal benefits of such an approach, and politicians need to be more courageous in legislating for closer collaboration between agencies and organisations to ensure an improved approach to healthcare.

References

Archer, D. & Cameron, A. (2009) *Collaborative Leadership – How to Succeed in an Interconnected World*. Butterworth-Heinemann, Elsevier. Oxford.

The Black Report (1982) *Inequalities in Health*. Townsend, P. & Davidson, N. (Eds). Penguin Books. Middlesex.

British Medical Journal (2023) *International Comparisons Expose the UK's Poor Performance on Health*. https://www.bmj.com/content/bmj. 14 July 2023.

Cancer Research UK. (2019) *Cancer Statistics for the UK*. www.cancerresearchuk. 22 July 2023 11.20am.

Collins, E., Drake, M. & Deacon, M. (2013) *The Physical Care of People with Mental Health Problems – A Guide for Best Practice.* Sage Pub. Ltd. London.

The Equality Trust. (2020) *The Scale of Economic Inequality in the UK.* https://equalitytrust.org.uk

The Guardian Newspaper. (2023) *NHS Staff Shortages in England Could Exceed 570,000.* https://www.theguardian.com. 26 March 2023.

Haskins, G. & Thomas, M. (2022) In Search of Fairness in Leadership. Chapter 3, pp 22–37. In Witzel, M. (Ed). *Post-Pandemic Leadership – Exploring Solutions to a Crisis.* Routledge. Abingdon, Oxon.

Haskins, G., Thomas, M., Bennett, D., Gibb, A., Gibb, Y., Gill, A., Johri, L., Murray, C. & Rowland, C. (2018). Conclusions – Bringing Kindness to the Fore. Chapter 10, pp 185–198. In Haskins, G., Thomas, M. & Johri, L. (Eds). *Kindness in Leadership.* Routledge. Abingdon, Oxon.

Health and Care Act. (2022) www.legislation.gov.uk.

Health and Social Care Act. (2012) www.legislation.gov.uk.

The Health Foundation. (2022) *International Comparisons of Life Expectancy.* https://www.health.org.uk/international. 17 April 2022.

The House of Commons Library. (2023) *GDP – International Comparisons; Key Economic Indicators.* https://commonslibrary.parliament.uk.

Hutton, W. (1995) *The State We're In.* Vintage. London.

Johri, L., Corich, K. & Haskins, G. (2023) *Mastering the Power of You – Empowered by Leaders Insights.* Routledge. Abingdon, Oxon.

Kynaston, D. (2008) *Austerity Britain, 1945–1951.* Bloomsbury Publishing. London.

MIND. (2023) *Side Effects of Antipsychotics.* https://www.mind.org.uk. 30 July 2023 11.30am.

NHS Confederation. (2023) *What the Latest Data Tells Us About Progress Against Targets.* www.nhsconfed.org. 22 July 2023 11.30am.

NHS Providers Today's Health News. (2023) *Independent Newspaper Coverage.* https://www.hugedomains.com/domain_profile.cfm?d=nhsproviders.com 13 April 2023.

Obesity Statistics. (2021) *Adult Obesity in England.* https://commonslibrary.parliament.uk.

The Prisma. (2022) *Labelling Identities – Comment in Focus,* 15 May 2022. www.theprisma.co.uk 30 July 2022 11.50am.

UK Parliament Health Committee. (2021) *Cancer in the UK 2020: Socioeconomic Deprivation.* https://committteees.parliament.uk 23 July 2023 11.40am.

West, M.A. (2021) *Compassionate Leadership – Sustaining Wisdom, Humanity and Presence in Health and Social Care.* The Swirling Leaf Press. https://swirlingleafpress.com

Whitehead, M. (1988) *The Health Divide.* Townsend, P. & Davidson, N. (Eds). Penguin Books. Middlesex.

World Health Organization. (2010) *Mental Health Definition.* WHO. Geneva.

10

FAIRNESS IN THE NHS

Patient and Employee Perspectives: April 2023

Clare Murray

Introduction

This chapter is focused on the most important element of the NHS: people. In particular, what are the perceptions and experiences of patients/service users and NHS employees relating to fairness in the NHS? This chapter was written in 2023. I would like to thank all of those who invested their time to take part in the research and for their invaluable insights.

Background: NHS in 2023

Hilary Cottam (2019) highlights how the NHS functions much like a factory, where patients enter the system when they get ill, are treated, and then are either cured or die. Cottam argues that this system worked very well in the 20th century, "when we suffered from episodic illnesses like polio, pneumonia or whooping cough, diseases that responded well to medicine and/ or hospitalization." However, she goes on to argue that we are now facing different problems as modern diseases are often chronic and cannot be cured. Conditions such as obesity, diabetes, and cancer account for 70 % of health expenditure (Department of Health, 2012).

As a case in point, let me introduce you to Terry, one of the patients we spoke to. Terry is 87.5 years old and has lived on his own in Cornwall for the past 25 years. Previously very healthy, in 2010, at the age of 75 years, Terry was diagnosed with early-stage chronic kidney disease. He started under the care of his renal consultant, attending regular six monthly appointments,

DOI: 10.4324/9781003410560-14

where his kidney function was consistently monitored through routine blood tests. His consultant prepared him for the fact that in 10 years' time he would most likely require kidney dialysis.

As time went on, and as expected, Terry's kidney function slowly deteriorated. His appointments with his consultant became more regular every three months. He was also assigned regular appointments with the dietician and had regular appointments with a dialysis nurse who would provide important information about starting dialysis. Over this time, these three people – Terry's renal consultant, the dietician, and the dialysis nurse – provided not only clinical care and information but also consistent psychological support.

In early 2017, Terry suffered a series of recurrent chest infections, which left him with a chronic respiratory condition. His GP referred him to a respiratory consultant, who prescribed him an ongoing low dose of steroids, which he is still taking.

By October 2020, Terry's kidney function had deteriorated and hit the threshold for requiring dialysis: 7%. Two weeks later, Terry had to start 3 x a week kidney dialysis at West Cornwall Hospital.

As you may imagine, despite knowing that this was inevitable it was nevertheless a huge transition for Terry, both physically and psychologically. He also had to accept the reality that dialysis was keeping him alive and that he would need this for the rest of his life. Were it not for the care and kindness of his renal consultant, dialysis nurse and dietician leading up to Terry starting dialysis and the care and kindness of the renal unit team when he began treatment, this significant transition would have been even harder for him to navigate.

In October 2021, almost one year on from starting dialysis, Terry became severely anaemic. His renal consultant referred him to a consultant haematologist, who arranged for several diagnostic tests, including a bone density scan, CT scan, and PET scan. The results, sadly, led to Terry being diagnosed with multiple myeloma (cancer of the plasma cells) in January 2022.

Terry's renal consultant liaised with the consultant haematologist, and they worked together to develop an appropriate treatment protocol (a combination of steroids and chemotherapy) for the myeloma that Terry could tolerate given that he was on dialysis.

From April 2022 until July 2022, Terry embarked on treatment for the myeloma: 4 × 5 weeks of weekly chemotherapy injections.

From July 2022 until November 2022, except for one five-day period and one eight-day period at home, Terry was unfortunately in hospital with various chemo-related infections including pneumonia, sepsis, e-coli, and cellulitis.

Terry rallied round and arrived home on 1 November 2022. However, his long stay in hospital had left him more physically frail and he was discharged with a care package in place, which meant he had 3× day care visits to help him.

By Christmas 2022 however, Terry was slowly going downhill again and on 27 December he was admitted to hospital with another bout of pneumonia and then developed sepsis. Having cleared these infections (and now affectionately referred to by his family as "Lazarus"), Terry was moved to his local hospital for rehabilitation with the physiotherapist to build his physical strength back up. After returning to the ward following one dialysis session, Terry had a fall and fractured his hip. This required surgery three days later, where he needed half a hip replacement. He spent five days in the trauma ward before being moved to a local nurse-led community hospital at the end of January 2023, ostensibly to receive more frequent and intense physiotherapy to help him regain some mobility after his hip surgery and the next step towards getting him home.

By April 2023, Terry was deemed medically fit for discharge and the process began to secure him a 4× day care package to enable him to return home. Two weeks later, whilst still in hospital, he developed pneumonia and sepsis again so was transferred back up to the main hospital for treatment and recovery. Having rallied round once more Terry is now back at his local hospital and the process of securing him a care package starts again.

Terry is a good example of the kind of patient that Cottam (2019) refers to – his Chronic Kidney Disease has been monitored and treated over the past 13 years and he now in 2023 requires dialysis to keep him alive. Similarly, his multiple myeloma needs frequent monitoring and treatment when it becomes active. Both his conditions are chronic and incurable.

Patients like Terry are increasing in number, which adds to the workload of all clinicians involved in his care. Not only that, his multiple chronic conditions mean that there is more need for clinicians with different areas of expertise to collaborate and work together to create appropriate treatment protocols, which requires more of their time.

Despite these modern challenges for the NHS, the UK government's austerity agenda over the past 12 years has meant lower levels of NHS funding and NHS Trusts are largely running a financial deficit (Robertson et al., 2017). There is some research to show that this is having a direct impact on employee wellbeing and acting as a barrier toward access to services and care provided to patients (NHS England. NHS Staff Health & Wellbeing, 2016) and is the context within which the current study was conducted.

The Study

The aim of the study was *to establish how fair patients/service users and NHS employees perceive the NHS in relation to:* (1) overall perceptions of fairness (patients/service users and NHS employees), (2) behaviours that show fairness in relation to access to NHS services (patients/service users), (3) what fairness looks like in terms of behaviours at work and at the broader level of organisational culture (NHS employees), (4) what fairness looks like in terms of behaviours relating to the quality of care (NHS patients/service users and employees), and (5) Perceptions of barriers to fairness (NHS patients/service users and employees).

For this study, fairness was defined as "treating people impartially" (Oxford English Dictionary, 2023). Data were gathered from 20 patients/service users and 10 NHS employees through a combination of interviews and an online survey. NHS employees included a range of roles: ward managers, nurses, doctors, and physiotherapists who had worked in the NHS for between 2 and 23 years. All respondents were based in England.

The survey included a combination of scaled questions (on a scale of 1–10, where 1 = "very unfair" to 10 = "extremely fair") and open-ended, verbatim questions. Patients/service users were asked about their overall experience of the following services: GP, out-patient services, and in-patient services (i.e., hospital stays) and NHS employees were asked about their particular NHS organisation and culture. The interviews adopted the same format as the survey questions but were conducted either face-to-face or virtually with 11 patients/service users and six NHS employees.

Overall Perceptions of Fairness

Patients/Service Users

First of all patients/service users were asked to rate their overall perceptions of fairness of the different NHS services (i.e., GP, out-patient services, and in-patient services) they had used in the last two years.

Overall, perceptions of fairness across the different NHS services were generally positive. In terms of out-patient services (i.e., day/minor surgery, diagnostic tests such as a CT scan, PET scan) 90% of respondents rated their experience as "extremely fair".

A third (33%) of the patients/service users who participated in the study had had experience with NHS in-patient services (i.e., a stay in hospital). Their perceptions of fairness in relation to these services were overwhelmingly positive, with all rating their experience as "extremely fair."

This highlights the fact that, despite the financial deficits and challenges with resources and staffing that the NHS is currently facing, when it comes to patients' experiences in the hospital, either as an outpatient or inpatient, those working at the frontline of patient care are doing so in a way that patients perceive as fair.

Perhaps not surprisingly the biggest variation in perceptions of fairness was in relation to GP services. Whilst 75% of patients rated their experience of their GP services as "fair" to "extremely fair, 25% had a more negative experience, rating their experience as "not at all fair" to "somewhat fair", and gave the following reasons for their score:

> "*Poor service. Complaints are followed up somewhat superficially, clearly ticking a box − nothing actually changes*"
> "*It's so hard to get an appointment and even trying generally to get through to make an appointment is a nightmare*"

Terry also rated his experience of his GP service as "somewhat fair". His score was related to the fact that he often found it difficult to get an appointment as well as the fact that his GP practice had been forced to use locum GPs due to an inability to recruit permanent GPs, so he would never see the same doctor. For Terry, consistency of GP was important for making him feel safe and being able to trust that links were made between his symptoms (which would mean a quicker referral to a specialist) rather than treating them as a "one off."

Interestingly, the mostly positive experience of fairness in relation to GP services reported in this study somewhat contradicts the findings from the most recent national GP patient survey that found approximately one in seven patients did not get an appointment when they tried to book one (*The Times*, 24 March 2023). This has been linked to an increasingly ageing population with multiple, complex medical needs (like Terry), which places significant demands in terms of workload and time on GPs as well as a national shortage of GPs. However, the findings reported here suggest that there are pockets of GP services across England that patients perceive to provide a fair service.

NHS Employees

All NHS employees rated their particular NHS organisation as "fair" to "extremely fair". The reasons for their score generally related to the care provided to patients, that is, *"we're treating everyone with respect and kindness, like we would like to be treated."* Slightly lower scores reflected less fairness in relation to workload and pay.

We then wanted to explore in more detail the views of patients/service users regarding the specific behaviours they observed that show fairness in the context of access to NHS services and quality of care.

Fairness in Relation to Access to NHS Services/Treatment

Patients/Service Users

In terms of access to NHS services and treatment, the behaviours patients/services mentioned tended to fall into one of two general themes:

i) Treating all Patients the Same

First of all were behaviours relating to treating every patient the same, regardless of age, gender, and socio-economic status in terms of access to NHS services and treatment. Linked to this was the observation that clinical staff were inclusive and non-judgmental, as the following quotes demonstrate:

> *"Treating all patients the same irrespective of their behaviour or status"*
> *"Treat everyone the same, regardless of age, gender, etc."*
> *"Being inclusive, non-judgmental"*

One patient/service user also made the important point that fair access to service is also seen at the broader level of the organisation (i.e., organisational culture), which may vary according to geographical area:

> *"Fair access to service given to individuals without socio-economic bias on a day to day basis but also as an organization. I believe that some geographical areas have better access to services and treatment"*

ii) Respect

The second theme to emerge focused on the behaviours that show respect to patients, which in this instance is defined as "having due regard for someone's wishes, feelings or rights" (Oxford English Dictionary, 2023). Some patients/service users mentioned behaviours such as active listening and effective communication that help to show respect to patients, as the following quotes demonstrate:

> *"Active listening. Respect"*
> *" Treating people with dignity and respect as individuals"*
> *" On my visits to outpatients sections and during a short stay in hospital I witnessed courtesy and respect to all visitors and patients"*
> *"They communicate well and listen well explaining why response is slow at present"*

What is interesting here is that patients' responses relating to questions about fairness in terms of *access* to NHS services all focused on how they were treated, that is, in the interaction between patients and NHS staff.

In terms of the perceptions of NHS employees, what behaviours do they see that show fairness in their organization?

Fairness in the Workplace: NHS Employees

When asked to describe the behaviours that show fairness in their NHS organisation, one employee mentioned *"equal opportunities* for staff. However, most responses focused on how patients are treated, rather than how the organisation treats employees, as the following quotes show:

> *"We go above and beyond to help all our patients wherever we can"*
> *"All patients are treated equally without discrimination"*

Drawing on what is known about the impact of organisational culture, set by the behaviour of leaders, and how that affects employee's behaviour at work, NHS employees were asked whether they believed the culture of their NHS organisation affects fairness at work. All respondents strongly agreed that it did, as one employee said:

> *"Culture has a big impact"*

Exploring their responses in more detail, again the main theme focused on respect, kindness, and compassion shown to others as well as the equal opportunity for employees to attend training and other organisational benefits, as the following quotes show:

> "You have to have an open and honest approach and give everyone the opportunity to partake in training or other things the organisation offers. You also have to respect and show compassion for others, which my organisation does"
>
> "We have a very kind and helpful team (GPs, nurses, health care assistants and reception team)"

For NHS employees, fairness at work is mostly shown by the respect, compassion, and kindness in the interaction between patients and employees and between employees, and the quality of care provided to patients.

Fairness in Relation to Quality of Care: Patients/Service users

Then, we were also interested to find out from patients/service users themselves about behaviours they have observed that show fairness in the context of the quality of care that they have received. The findings show that these tended to fall into one of three general themes:

i) Treating People the Same

Interestingly, the theme of "treating people the same", which emerged in relation to access to NHS services, was also a theme in relation to quality of care:

> "Treating people the same in spite of anything listed in the next box"
>
> "NHS staff seem to provide consistent services to people from a range of different backgrounds"
>
> "The NHS is broken, albeit the staff are absolutely amazing and I feel we cannot fault anything they do"

ii) Openness/Communication

Taking time to explain aspects of care and treatment as well as NHS employees' general openness in communication with patients also emerged as a theme:

> "Quality of care must include openness and readiness to explain symptoms, treatments, procedures and likely consequences"

iii)   Empathy and Kindness

Empathy and kindness also emerged as a theme in relation to fairness in terms of quality of care. Terry, in particular, had a lot to say on this issue, as he explains later:

> *"Nurses show an understanding of what it is like being in hospital. . . . I couldn't wish for better quality of care [by West Cornwall renal unit staff]. They are all kind, understanding and very helpful, which is a lot to do with Christine [Christine Davies, Renal Unit Sister, West Cornwall Hospital]. I've noticed that she gets involved in the same way that all the other nursing staff do, like Frank [Frank Scuito, Unit Manager] at Treliske Renal Unit"*

Terry also highlighted another aspect of fairness in relation to quality of care and that is patients' observations of the interactions between the different levels of clinical staff, as Terry explains:

> *"The way Dr P [Terry's renal consultant] treats his staff – he treats everyone equally and seeing that as a patient relaxes you. He treats all the staff on the same level, doesn't use his consultant position, and listens to and respects their opinion. Staff perform better as a result and he is liked and respected so patients get the benefit"*

This provides further support to the view of all NHS employees in this study that the culture of the organisation has a significant impact on their perceptions of fairness in their NHS organisation. However, it also shows how much patients benefit, that is, a positive working environment created by the clinicians at the top level of the organisation, shown by the way they treat their staff, makes staff feel more respected and valued which then enhances the sense of psychological safety that patients feel as a result.

It's Not All About the Patient

Finally, although it was only Terry and one other patient who mentioned this point in the study, it is worth highlighting as it reflects what patients/ service users and their families can sometimes forget: that NHS staff are human beings too.

Whilst being sick and in hospital often means patients are scared and vulnerable (and therefore sometimes angry and frustrated) and their families are also scared and distressed, treating all staff involved in a person's care with reciprocal respect and (where appropriate) humour just enhances the experience for both patients, their families and staff. As Terry says:

> *Their [the West Cornwall renal unit team] attitude – they're relaxed, joking and talk to you, which makes me feel relaxed. I ask about their family, how their children are getting on. It's not all about the patient, it shouldn't be. They have feelings too!*

Having explored patients/service users and NHS employees' perceptions of fairness and the behaviours that show fairness in relation to access to NHS services and quality of care, what do these two groups believe to be the main barriers to fairness in the NHS?

Main Barriers to Fairness in the NHS

Patients/Service Users

From the perspective of patients/service users, barriers to fairness almost all tended to focus on one theme: lack of funding and undervaluing of employees, as the following quotes show:

> *"Insufficient resources and staff in areas with high levels of population"*
> *"Availability of fully qualified and experienced staff"*
> *"Underfunding across the organization, undervaluing of employees in terms of pay, lack of employee support"*

One patient also raised the same issue as Terry with regard to how patients and relatives treat staff, again emphasising the need to treat staff with respect:

> *"[The] attitude of patients and relatives who are unappreciative and rude"*

NHS Employees

Perhaps not surprisingly, similar themes in relation to barriers to fairness also emerged from the responses of NHS employees and also included aspects such as organisational structure and planning:

Limited Resources and Working Conditions

Most NHS employees cited limited resources, which affect pay, working conditions and staffing as barriers to fairness:

> *"Lack of resource in high demand areas"*
> *"Pay is unfair"*
> *"Working conditions, lack of workforce planning, understaffed"*

Organisational Structure

Other employees cited organisational structure as a barrier to fairness as one person says:

> *"NHS is too top, heavy. Needs more people on the floor and less managers"*

Conclusion

The aim of this study was to hear from patients/service users and NHS employees in their own words about their experience and perceptions of fairness in the NHS.

Relationships Are Key

What is striking is that both patients and employees all focused on aspects relating to the interaction between patients and those caring for them, which highlights the importance of relationships in a health care context. In particular, relationships between NHS employees and between staff and patients that are characterised by respect, kindness, and empathy, are critical for patients to feel psychologically safe, which has a positive impact on their recovery.

It is clear from both an employee and patient perspective that organisational culture plays an important role in helping to create the right environment for these relationships to develop and flourish. Specifically, as Terry articulates so well, when senior clinicians are seen to treat their teams with respect this enhances patients' feelings of safety and the quality of care patients receive from the broader clinical team.

The study also highlighted another important fact, which is perhaps less often cited, which is that it is not just how patients are treated but also how patients and their family treat the people who are caring for them. It is so important to remember that these people are human beings too.

This point is best brought to life by another example from Terry: during one emergency trip to the hospital, he entertained the paramedics by asking one of them, Helen, to marry him. He made such an impression that the next morning, when Terry was still in a bed in A&E waiting to be admitted to the ward, Helen was back on shift and came to look for him. When she found him, she fetched him a cup of tea. Terry was over the moon. It is these small acts of kindness that make such a difference.

The fact that barriers to fairness cited by both patients/service users and NHS employees are strikingly similar highlights the impact of chronic underfunding of the NHS on both staff and the patient experience. It also suggests that were these barriers to become more entrenched and widespread (as is becoming the case), this is likely to affect patient–staff relationships and, in particular, the quality of care staff provide and patients receive. The significant increase in mental health issues amongst employees across all areas of the NHS (Rimmer, 2018; NHS Employers. Stress and Its Impact on the Workplace, 2020) is a warning that cannot be ignored and is a manifestation of the impact of consistently "having to do more with less" and of being underpaid and undervalued.

An increasingly ageing population of people with multiple, complex medical needs serves to add to the workload and levels of stress NHS employees are exposed to. As Dame Clare Gerada, head of the Royal College of General Practitioners, said on a recent BBC Question Time programme specifically devoted to the NHS (19 January 2023): "If we can't treat our employees with kindness and compassion, how can we expect them to treat patients with kindness and compassion?" Ensuring NHS employees have access to adequate professional and psychological support is important to help them navigate this very challenging landscape.

It needs to be pointed out that there was a relatively small sample size of NHS employees and patients/service users included in this study. As such the situation relating to fairness in the NHS is likely to be more complex than outlined here. However, the findings show that despite the serious challenges facing the NHS, the overwhelmingly positive experiences of patients/service users in this study regarding access to and quality of care tell us that the core values (i.e., respect, empathy, and kindness) and key motivational drivers (i.e., helping and caring for others) of those working in the NHS still have a significant, positive impact on patients and their recovery.

What is clear is that at the heart of any change/ reform needs to be the consideration of the relationship between patients and clinicians/care providers as well as between NHS employees. The need for psychological safety, trust, respect, kindness, empathy, and (where appropriate) humour help patients, their families, and employees cope with often distressing and fearful situations.

It's probably time to let you know that Terry is my Dad. I have been on this journey with him almost every day for the last three years and have witnessed the experiences he has described first hand. I would like to take this opportunity to thank every single person who has been involved in Terry's care, particularly everyone at West Cornwall Hospital Renal Unit, his renal consultant, all the staff in Grenville Ward and the Duchy Renal Unit at Treliske Hospital, as well as the staff on Medical Ward 2 at West Cornwall Hospital. Without them all, Terry and I and the rest of our family could not have made it through the last two years.

Finally, in the words of Aneurin Bevan, one of the original architects of the NHS: "The NHS will last as long as there are folk left with faith to fight for it." It is clear that the NHS is currently in crisis but, even in crisis, you can still see the NHS at its very best: superior care, kindness, and empathy. If that's not worth fighting for, I don't know what is.

References

Cottam, H. (2019). *Radical Help: How We Can Remake the Relationships Between Us and Revolutionise the Welfare State*. Virago Press.

Department of Health (2012). *Report: Long-Term Conditions Compendium of Information*, 3rd edition. Department of Health.

NHS Employers. *Stress and Its Impact on the Workplace*. Available online: https://www.nhsemployers.org/retention-and-staff-experience/health-and-wellbeing/taking-a-targeted-approach/taking-a-targetedapproach/stress-and-its-impact-on-the-workplace (accessed on 1 September 2020).

NHS England. (2016). *NHS Staff Health & Wellbeing: CQUIN Supplementary Guidance*. Quarry House. Available online: https://www.england.nhs.uk/publication/nhs-staff-health-and-wellbeing-cquinsupplementary-guidance/ (accessed on 23 July 2019).

Rimmer, A. (2018). Staff Stress Levels Reflect Rising Pressure on NHS, Says NHS Leaders. *BMJ*, 360, k1074.

Robertson, R., Wenzel, L., Thompson, J., and Charles, A. (2017). *Understanding NHS Financial Pressures: How Are They Affecting Patient Care*, 1st edition. The King's Fund. Available online: https://www.kingsfund.org.uk/sites/default/files/field/field_publication_file/UnderstandingNHSfinancialpressures-fullreport.pdf.

PART FIVE
Conclusion

11

FAIRNESS IN THE NHS

Mike Thomas and Gay Haskins

Introduction

As we write this final chapter on 7 July 2024, the Conservative party led by Rishi Sunak has lost the UK General Election of July 4th. The UK has elected its government for the next five years: a new Labour administration led by a new Prime Minister. The future direction of the NHS is in new hands and is viewed as of critical importance. In his opening speech, Sir Keir vowed, *"Have no doubt – that we will rebuild Britain. . . . With wealth created in every community. Our NHS back on its feet, facing the future."* (Starmer, 2024)

As a result, the issues of fairness in the NHS covered within this book have relevance and urgency, for policymakers, healthcare workers, the population's health and wellbeing, and most importantly, the millions of individuals who rely on the NHS for their care.

This chapter examines what this study of fairness and equity in the UK National Health Service has demonstrated, and what can be learned from the various chapters, experts, and contributors. It identifies 12 recurring themes, reaches conclusions, and makes recommendations regarding the future of the National Health Service.

Our Unequal Health

The NHS is still regarded as a crown jewel of the British Institution around the world. The enjoyment of good health is considered basic to our happiness, harmony, and security. Our understanding of health as a state of complete physical,

DOI: 10.4324/9781003410560-16

mental, and social well-being and not merely the absence of disease of infirmity; as one of the fundamental rights of every human being without distinction of race, religion, political belief, economic or social condition has largely been the principle behind the creation of the Welfare State, especially after the Second World War.

These are the words of Dr Sakthi Karunanithi, clinician and Director of Public Health for Lancashire in the opening chapter of this book. Yet Sakthi's chapter goes on to describe and decry the fact that there are big variations in the health status of individuals from differing socio-economic, cultural, and environmental backgrounds in the UK and that these are the building blocks of significant health inequalities. Geographical location also plays a key role in health disparities with those living in the North of England frequently showing patterns of lower life expectancy, higher infant mortality rates and worse health and wellbeing than in the South. Examples cited in Sakthi's chapter include the fact that male disability-free life expectancy at birth in the most deprived areas was 17.6 years fewer than in the least deprived areas from 2018 to 2020, for females it was 16.8 years fewer. And these health inequalities are worsening. Doesn't this seem unfair?

In the second chapter, Ian Gregory, whose work has been in the fields of Philosophy and the Philosophy of Law, emphasises health inequalities. Ian makes a fundamental point when he states that since the inception of the NHS in 1948, no major political party has seriously and openly voiced an alternative system of healthcare delivery for the UK. Need continues to be a fundamental principle of the NHS, and it continues to provide free healthcare at the point of access to those in need. Yet health inequalities have grown in the last 40 years, as have arguments that wealth equals choice and opportunities and could be the determinant of access to healthcare.

This is not to say that there have been no attempts to address health inequalities. There have been many investigations into the issue (the Whitehead Report in 1987, the Acheson Report in 1998 and The Marmot Review and update in 2010 and 2020, for instance). And levelling up is a stated priority. But the debate and actions on healthcare inequalities have seemed at times to be lost in the noise of economic austerity, political principles, and a government which believes in less State intervention and which, through different guises, has been in power for nearly a decade and a half.

Conclusion: Health care inequalities in the UK are huge and multifaceted. They require urgent attention. Our government should grasp the opportunity to address them.

Recommendations: The new UK government should consider the establishment of a No 10, Fairer Society Unit to report on actions to reduce inequalities on an annual basis to Parliament. Every local authority should publish a Health Inequalities Covenant, similar to their Local Plan, identifying local development and investment opportunities, to describe how they will narrow their health inequalities. The impacts of their decisions should subsequently be monitored and the process should continue.

The Value of Fairness

Personal values and ethical principles are deeply embedded in NHS professions, many feel their work is vocational and for the greater good. The NHS Constitution and the values of free healthcare are ingrained in the values held by many NHS staff. In chapter nine on contemporary specialist provision, Rachael Broadley, Terry Drake, Jane McNichols, and Pauline Preston (all experts in their clinical fields) clearly articulated that fairness and equity were principles which they held dear and which needed protection on a regular basis, otherwise causing frustrations in their practices.

In Chapter 10, Consultant Organisational Psychologist, Dr Clare Murray provides a moving account of how values linked closely with fairness, like empathy, kindness, respect, dignity, and compassion impact directly patient care and support for relatives. She highlights the importance of relationships in hospital patient care, "*relationships between NHS employees and between staff and patients that are characterised by respect, kindness, and empathy, are critical for patients to feel psychologically safe, which has a positive impact on their recovery.*"

Andrew Corbett-Nolan, Chief Executive of the Good Governance Institute, underlines the importance of fairness to Boards in chapter three; not just as a virtuous end, but as a crucial element of success. In chapter four, Advisor Ann Highton demonstrates that ethics and fairness are intrinsically linked to governance and accountability in the NHS with the aim of providing transparency around the quality of healthcare delivery, patient safety, and equity of care amongst others. Good governance reflects good practices of social justice, equality, and equity.

However, Foundation Trust CEO, Aaron Cummins in his examination of leadership in chapter six, found that many NHS CEOs felt that their organisations were disproportionately focused on policies, procedures, and targets instead of on prioritising fairness of access, delivery, equality and diversity, and staff needs. This is a perspective found throughout the book and one impact of a top-down hierarchical leadership is the way such leadership and organisational approaches create an adherence to organisational targets and processes. These create pressures and challenges for front line staff who must manage resources and productivity in such environments.

The impact of austerity measures, a global pandemic and post-pandemic financial planning cause a degree of frustration, and sometimes anger, for front line staff who feel short-changed as they are compelled to do more with decreasing resources. The public too feel frustrated by growing waiting lists, long periods between referrals, and their experiences of a standard of care resource that they see as lacking in the quality they expect in their time of need. Chaplains Ian Dewar and Deborah Wilde suggest that the social and psychological contract between staff who struggle to meet demand and wish to maintain high values of fairness and equity, and the public who demand immediate access to world-class quality of care when they are often most vulnerable and scared, can barely continue unless there is a more honest debate about realistic expectations.

Conclusion: Despite the challenges summarised earlier and the challenge of inequality of provision discussed in the previous section, our conclusion is that the values linked to fairness remain fundamental principles of the NHS. Fairness as a value has continued through many difficult periods for the NHS for the last 75 years, is embedded in delivery, is highly valued as a personal ethic by many NHS staff, and is held in high esteem by the people who use the NHS. The public expect fairness to be the basis for NHS provision and delivery, and this view has not changed since 1945.

Recommendations: Every effort must be made to ensure that the values of fairness, and the qualities linked to it, continue to be fundamental to the operations of the NHS. As a result, cultures of respect, trust, kindness, and empathy can continue to be nourished within the Service. Attention must be paid to the considerable focus on policies, procedures, and targets at the expense of fairness, respect, and kindness.

Faith, Spirituality and the Virtues of Hospitality, Self-Reflection, and Accountability

Alongside values and personal ethics, we found that faith and, increasingly, spirituality play an important part in healthcare delivery. Chaplains Ian Dewar and Deborah Wilde see spirituality as an innate desire to stretch beyond the ordinary stressors of life to discover meaning, purpose, and a sense of sacredness. Other contributors who are practising clinicians view their clinical work as essentially vocational, and not primarily for personal gain. We propose that many who work in the NHS share this deep sense of meaning and purpose in the caring sector.

Ian and Deborah point out that the NHS reflects the cultural norms and aspirations of UK culture as shaped by governments and those in power. We would suggest that this is causing a challenge to those who hold a spiritual, vocational element towards their caring profession and practice when faced with the more instrumental and less altruistic demands of increasing productivity, spending less time with patients, working with reduced resources and meeting targets, the biggest issue being time, or lack of time, to care adequately.

Conclusion: Those in power in government and in policy making positions within the NHS need to re-examine the effect that their often highly managerial policies are having on all those who work daily within the Service and to re-consider what is needed for staff to have the time to give adequate care both to themselves and to their patients.

Recommendation: Ian and Deborah propose that the three virtues of hospitality, self-reflection, and accountability can offer a model which provides those essential resources of time and space for self-reflection and sharing concerns with others. We endorse this proposal. In addition, their example of the Death Café (a creation of space in which people come together and are given the freedom to discuss experiences and anxieties about life and death) is life-affirming and would strengthen self-reflection within organisations. This would support a closer alliance between the practitioners' sense of purpose and meaning with their capacity, with support, to meet the challenges of contemporary healthcare delivery.

Wealth Versus Need

The word "need" and the phrase "at the point of need" occur frequently in this book. In Chapter 2, Ian Gregory writes that arguably, the most fundamental notion informing the ambitions of the NHS is "Need." The NHS was established because of a belief and commitment to put in place health care provisions that allow all those in need to be healthier and live better lives. A system of universal health care is therefore required.

We support Ian's view that the argument that wealth is a determination of access to healthcare can be much diminished when all political parties agree that need is the determinant of access, and that equity should remain a core principle of the NHS Constitution, irrespective of wealth, gender, sexual orientation, ethnicity, colour, or age.

Nonetheless, there is evidence of a growing number of people turning to private health insurance to meet their demands: particularly for more speedy diagnosis and hospital appointments. Wealth versus need as determinants of access has gained some traction. The existence of private independent healthcare providers, insurance schemes, and individual payment for certain health services and products is more common and increasing, yet most of the population still expects, and receives, free access at the point of need in the NHS.

However, it is hard to deny that, since 1950, the original principle of free healthcare has been gradually eroded, with salami-slicing of "free" healthcare into payments for certain aspects of the original National Health Service, for example ophthalmic care (spectacles), dentistry, and many pharmacy prescriptions and healthcare products (note the differences in country approaches to prescription charges between Scotland, Wales, England, and Northern Ireland).

These early reversals from "free" health provision were accelerated through the reforms of the conservative government led by Margaret Thatcher in the 1980s. Today, following this slow drift away from the original NHS principle of free care, we often read the phrase "*free access at the point of need.*" Everything outside this definition is therefore open to market forces, and payment.

But where is the point of need currently? Should it be shifted? Should it be earlier, in preventive and population health activities and would this in fact lessen the crisis? Should services like free dentistry be reconsidered? The NHS cannot cope with the present and increasing demand for access at the point of need, which now frequently seems to mean at the point of crisis.

Conclusion: The growing number of people turning to private healthcare provision as well as the general drift to fee-based access at the point of need is a cause for concern. In addition, the growing emphasis on the point of need, why it has occurred, what it means and where it is in the overall map of healthcare needs, needs urgent consideration. A discussion of whether all needs are equally worthy of our attention should also take place and, if not, how to determine and manage a fair prioritisation.

Recommendation: We recommend, whichever government is in power, measures are taken to analyse the impact of the contemporary definition of free access at the point of need, particularly focusing on social justice principles, socio-economic circumstances, and health outcomes, to determine whether the current system of NHS delivery meets the public expectation of fairness and equity of access at the point of need.

Patient and Staff Perspectives

In chapter ten, Dr Clare Murray provides a moving account of the experience of her father over a long period suffering from chronic kidney disease. The story is one of the NHS at its best: characterised by different specialists working together and treating both their teams and their patients with respect, and by patients who treat those caring for them with care, respect, and good humour. It is a story of the importance of fair and mutually respectful relationships and of acts of kindness that really make a difference.

But Clare's chapter also cites barriers that prevent these staff/patient relationships from flourishing: limited financial resources which affect pay, working conditions, and recruitment; perceptions of a top-heavy structure; a lack of availability of fully qualified and experienced staff; too many demands and too little time. These barriers were emphasised by both staff and patients in Clare's study and were found to be strikingly similar whether mentioned by staff or patients.

The clinicians interviewed in Chapter 9 on Contemporary Specialist Provision cite a further complexity. It seems that once seen and on track for attention, patients are likely to be well looked after. But the access to assessment can be very problematic and troublesome. This is particularly the case with access to Mental Health Services. Terry Drake, who works in Child and Adolescent Mental Health Services highlights the fact that everyone can access the system based on clinical need. He continues, *Within the system there is an interesting issue of fairness. If you have ADHD (Attention Deficit/ Hyperactivity Disorder) for example, then you may have to wait a number of months to start a treatment support programme.* Moreover, he cites those waiting for autism diagnosis by 2024 as 190,000.

Conclusion: With sufficient funding and staffing the NHS can flourish. Just like Clare's father, there are countless others who have the good fortune to experience the NHS at its very best: superior care, kindness, and empathy. We echo Clare's words at the end of the last chapter, *If that's not worth fighting for, I don't know what is.*

Recommendation: We must not give up on the NHS. In the weeks before the last election took place, the NHS was in the top three concerns in most polls, and clearly remains important for millions of citizens.

It may be difficult to acknowledge at a time when the cost of living is negatively impacting on so many, but the government must invest more in the NHS. It is currently in dire need of more capital funding, requires more clinical professionals, needs to embrace technology, new ways of working, and more pace with higher productivity. This cannot be achieved without planned and adequate funding. The public expects it, we would argue even want this approach, and politicians who continue to ignore the required funding of the NHS do so at the risk of losing votes.

Governance

In Chapter 3, on Fairness in Boards and Governance, Andrew Corbett-Nolan contends that fair organisations work better, have more impact, and create longer-term, sustainable value. He lists seven principles (or virtues) that guide the behaviours of leaders who hold public office: selflessness; integrity; objectivity; accountability; openness; honesty; and leadership.

But if accountability is so important, what does it imply? For Ian Dewar and Deborah Wilde, it flows from self-reflection and arises when the question is asked, "What do I do about what I know?" It involves the courage to stop and take stock. It involves the courage to be scrutinised. As Andrew Corbett-Nolan writes, *"Holders of public office are accountable to the public for their decisions and actions and must submit themselves to the scrutiny necessary to ensure this."*

The ambiguity around clear expectations of accountability and governance in the NHS is a recurring theme. Ann Highton, Strategic Advisor, Radar Healthcare at the Good Governance Institute, and author of Chapter 4, calls for greater clarity around an agreed series of definitions for specific contexts and circumstances, whilst in Chapter 6, Aaron Cummins found a level of leadership frustration with the blurring of managerial risk management with legal rather than policy definitions and applications of legal definitions of responsibilities and accountabilities.

Ian Gregory suggests in Chapter 2, that the challenges of allocating scarce resources by government departments create a lack of clarity around responsibilities in delivery and reaching targets. In Chapter 7, on Fairness in Health and Social Care Policy Decisions, Emeritus Professor of Economics, Anthony J Culyer offers a stimulating Socratic approach for decision-makers to use to understand fairness in policy decisions at all levels in health and social care. His Appendix, "Fairness in Health and Social Care Policy: Socratic Questions'", is designed to assist decision makers in answering a series of questions, enabling the creation of a coherent structure for the design, reform, or management of health care systems. It could also be utilised as a tool for planning and delivering collaborative and partnership working, and evidence for governance and assurance purposes. He offers a comprehensive range of questions that all those engaged in policy decisions should review, discuss, and reflect upon, in both private consideration and group deliberation.

Conclusion: Our conclusion is that all those involved in the governance of the NHS should regularly reflect on the principles that Andrew Corbett-Nolan has listed and ensure that they understand their implications for those involved in public office in terms of both decision-making and action. They should also use questions such as those Anthony J Culyer has listed for periodic review, discussion, and reflection. Attention should also be paid to the perception that there is too much regulatory oversight from too many bodies. This adds to the lack of clarity regarding agreed, shared definitions of accountability and governance, particularly in cross-boundary collaborations and partnerships between different organisations.

Recommendation: We recommend a clearer, agreed, and shared definition of governance terms such as integrity, accountability, openness, selflessness, and responsibility amongst Professional, Statutory, and Regulatory Bodies (PSRBs) and that the NHS executive should lead this process with PSRBs, local authorities, patient representatives, and the charity, voluntary, faith, and enterprise sector.

Collaborative Care Delivery

The NHS is currently expected to deliver care in a much more collaborative way than has been expected in the last decade. There is more emphasis on partnerships and cross-boundary working and less demarcation between community, primary, and acute care. The NHS is now also expected to work with local authorities and social care providers as well as the third sector. Yet a theme in this book is the lack of support for leadership and staff development to work in this new environment and move away from competition, the growth of one's own organisation at the expense of others, and the practice of other market forces when implementing strategies and care provision.

Many leaders and staff are struggling to work in an integrated system: there is a lack of cohesion between community, primary and acute care, and local authority social care providers are not playing a full role in planning and delivery locally. As Senior Manager of Community Care, Pauline Preston noted, demarcation and boundary barriers are resistant to change, and CEO Aaron Cummins found that leaders want to apply new skills of emotional intelligence, diplomacy, and negotiations. Finance Director, Chris Adcock, and Trust Chair, Mike Thomas, found tension in accountability and auditing systems when resources needed to be shared across boundaries and autonomous legal organisations.

Conclusion: Much more needs to be done to develop existing NHS and social care staff in the principles and practices of collaborative care delivery. This should include the development of existing leaders to acquire the skills of emotional intelligence and system working. There is a sense of urgency as integrated systems have been in place for two years at the time of writing and there is a continuing lack of pace and activities which transform existing health care provision to better meet the needs of the population.

Recommendations: We recommend a regional (not central), oversight of staff development strategies explicitly focusing on working collaboratively. By "oversight", we mean that bodies such as the Integrated Care Boards, Local Authorities, and Provider Collaborative Boards work together with education providers to implement local strategies to transform and enhance collaborative health and social care delivery. This should correlate and demonstrate staff development and support with evidence-based local changes in integrated delivery within a fixed time frame agreed by all parties.

Funding should be provided through combined health and social care budgets, Health Education England, and NHSE education and training funds.

Reforms, Reviews, and Interference

The high number of review that the NHS and its staff have endured, and the growing number of policy initiatives is a recurring theme. A quick look down the Chronology provided at the beginning of this book reveals how policies seem to change with every change of government. Many perceive these as burdensome and a constraint to delivery and increases lower productivity. Moreover, as emphasised by Aaron Cummins and Mike Thomas, these centrally directed operational plans mean that the NHS Executive is therefore under pressure to deliver political objectives. This flows down the hierarchy with regional and local leaders expected to adapt their plans accordingly.

The rationale for arguing for the NHS to have a non-partisan status, to be in essence above political differences, is due to the societal benefits of good healthcare. Our study of the NHS shows a constant, unremitting political interference in healthcare delivery.

The Coalition government of the Conservative and Liberal Democrat parties ushered in the age of austerity in 2010, which has had a real-term negative impact on public service funding. It remains unclear whether the Liberal Democrat side of the Coalition government signed up to the conservative philosophical principles of a smaller state and fewer government interventions, or whether they believed they were being pragmatic in their approach to the economy following the financial debacle of 2008. Whatever their beliefs the two parties applied fiscal constraints on the NHS which ill-prepared the country for the pandemic in 2020. Today the NHS is playing catch-up while challenged by a shortage of clinical staff, a growing demand for its services, an unresolved reform of social care, and continual financial pressures. It is difficult not to conclude that the short-termism of much of UK political actions in the last decade has had a real and negative impact on people's wellbeing and health, and austerity measures did not work.

Funding of the NHS, or any other parts of governmental responsibility, fundamentally comes down to political choice. For the NHS, the government chooses how much should be invested in the health and wellbeing of the population, and how resources should be distributed.

Conclusion: Central political control leads to ever-increasing interference and a lack of time for policies to be embedded, measured, and analysed. A centrally controlled large organisation like the NHS is susceptible to regular political interference. This has bedevilled and prevented progress in UK healthcare and population health improvements (see the Chronology at the commencement of this book). It is unfair organisationally and strategically and impacts negatively on people's health and wellbeing.

The NHS has so much administration and bureaucracy put on it that attempts to transform care have led to a reduction in the resources available at the point of need. Many clinicians are taken away from patient care to attend meetings, carry out administrative duties, travel, and so on.

Recommendations: we recommend that the NHS should have a period free from central policy reforms and changes. We support the recommendation made by Ian Dewar and Deborah Wilde that a review of current healthcare strategies, provision and delivery should be put under a Royal Commission. This should build on the current NHS Long Term Plan and NHS People Plan by achieving cross-party agreement on its recommendations and implementation. It should pay particular attention to the use of technology and Artificial Intelligence and the role these can play in reducing the load on clinicians and administration. Once in process, time should be given for the recommendations to be embedded and evaluated without the political interference of introducing new or different policies in the same fields.

We recommend a move away from constant "reforms" towards oversight at the regional level, with space for local, place-based NHS experts and the public to work together on local strategies with pre-determined success outcomes with a minimum of a three-year financial plan. We would argue that this approach would provide more stability, certainty and evidence of impact that would benefit the health of the population.

Regulatory and Statutory Oversight

Caring for people is an inherently risky endeavour. Done well and the quality of life of the person receiving care is improved, done poorly and the individual experiences increased suffering, and at worst, death. It is morally right, responsible, and fair to have a process of oversight of care, to have agreed minimum standards, and support to continuously enhance and improve. Equally staff development and support are essential for compliance with regulatory requirements and to transform clinical practices. This seems to be a view supported by the findings of this study on fairness in the NHS.

Regulators such as the Care Quality Commission (CQC) are viewed similarly to Ofsted in the education sector, an inspectorate that arrives on site without prior notice and delivers one-word judgements which do not reflect the complexity of healthcare delivery. It is too early to conclude whether the recent narrative approach adopted by the CQC will alter such perceptions but a more supportive, joint interventionist approach to improving standards and quality of care is highly appreciated by NHS staff. The work of System Improvement Teams/Boards (SIBs), which work within and alongside staff identifying areas for improvement and providing guidance and reflections on outcomes, appears to have more acceptability and support than that found for the CQC.

The NHS needs regulatory and statutory oversight. The NHS has had several scandals and several commissioned reports and public inquiries with the aim of learning lessons, preventing recurrence and primarily to ensure patient safety. Such reports often identify those who are responsible and accountable, and who are subsequently asked to give testimony and evidence. There are contemporary developments which are blurring public-sector responsibility and accountability. For example, online narratives and media coverage frequently focus on blame and retribution.

Public anger is understandable, and repeated failures increase frustrations, anxieties, and outcries that "The NHS is broken." However, the potential consequences of this blame approach can be that individuals may be reluctant to tell the truth due to fear of retribution. Moreover, skilled and talented leaders may decide not to seek a career in the NHS. It is also not good governance to blur the distinctions between responsibility, account-ability, blame and retribution.

Within this book we are conscious we have not covered the issues of fairness in several regulatory bodies (examples include the General Medi-cal Council, Health Professions Council, and the Nursing and Midwifery Council) or guidance organisations such as the National Institute for Health and Care Excellence (NICE). However, we presume the same principles of governance and accountabilities apply.

Conclusion: The crux appears to be the method of oversight and the application of governance and accountability. This can be divided into two areas; agreed and shared definitions of responsibility and accountability; and more transparent evidence that those who regulate and inspect understand and consider the real-life pressures for staff working with decreasing resources and increased demand. For example, in Chapter 4, Ann Highton found dis-sonance between staff and managerial approaches to regulatory adherence which was often based on different perceptions of governance and account-ability. Moreover, Chapter 9, on specialist services, suggests that there is a commonly held view amongst clinicians that policymakers and regulators do not often understand the stressors of delivering healthcare with diminishing resources and increasing demand.

The regulatory oversight provided by the CQC may be in question given the existence of the National System Improvement Board (SIB) which appear to have more staff confidence and trust. The SIB system works nationally and collaborates with providers in enhancing care and where necessary transforming the method and processes of delivery to better meet patient and user needs. The SIB teams, working within and alongside organisa-tional staff, constantly monitor the progress and pace of change and provide objective reports to various oversight groups to ensure good governance and accountability. Although it does not have the "Inspectorate" responsibility of the CQC it appears to be more supported by NHS staff due to its practice of working with, rather than carrying out inspections of, organisations and staff. It may be that the SIB may develop from its existing framework of sup-porting providers, to taking on the responsibilities of the CQC itself, which we would argue has more contextual relevance with regard to overall patient safety and care.

In addition, current systems of internal regulatory oversights and govern-ance such as whistleblowing policies, freedom to speak up and complaints processes are not robust enough to support learning, increase patient safety, quality of care, or fairness to those who speak up.

Recommendations: We recommend that consideration is given to the replacement of the Care Quality Commission (CQC) with the System Improvement processes. The system improvement teams should work within and alongside providers over a period sufficient to meet pre-engagement criteria for improvements. This could be a more effective method of health care improvement than the CQC inspection regime, and arguably more salient to protect patient safety and improve quality of care.

The System Improvement Teams/Boards (SIT/B's) should work with all health care providers, not just those identified as needing interventions.

The current system of "scoring" providers with single-word judgements such as "outstanding, good, requires improvement or inadequate" should be replaced with designations, which can provide more detailed information regarding the areas undergoing improvement, the stated goals and evidence of achievement and applied to all providers to demonstrate continuous improvement.

We recommend an overhaul of the whistleblowing system to identify genuine cases, rather than differences of opinions, grievances, or personal pursuits which can clog up processes for learning and are unfair to those that speak up for patient safety and quality issues. Whistleblowing processes should clearly signpost how to follow normal complaints, arbitration, or grievance processes and only when these have demonstrably been exhausted or failed should the category of whistleblowing be applied. We would suggest a wider application of restorative justice processes to enhance this process (see Parkinson, 2023).

We would also recommend that the Complaints Ombudsman Office, on a regional or local level, should provide guidance and regularly review organisational compliance regarding dealing with complaints and supporting genuine whistleblowers.

Freedom to speak up processes should have national guidelines which encourage anonymous submissions to provide enough information for complaints to be investigated, and signposts are clearly provided so that staff are aware of how to access the organisational and staff representatives' processes, which may be more appropriate.

Targets and Goals

Targets and goals appear to have support when they demonstrate benefits to patients and resources. In chapter nine, Clinical Manager, Stroke Unit, Rachael Broadley found a degree of fairness in the way clinical expectations are correlated with targets in stroke care. In children and adolescent mental health and oncology respectively, Terry Drake and Jane McNicoll see the benefits of targets when they are realistic and paired with adequate resources and health inequalities strategies. That same issue, explored in earlier chapters by Ian Gregory in an ethical context and Sakthi Karunanithi in a public health context, concluded that need, rather than wealth, education or social status should be the determinants of access to healthcare.

A further recurring theme lay in the imposition of targets without an understanding of consequences. A good example was provided by Clinical Transfer Leader, Child and Adolescent Mental Health Services, Terry Drake, in chapter nine on Contemporary Specialist Provision. Terry noted that a referral for assessment was not the same as referral for treatment, and the waiting list continues to grow:

> *Within the system there is an interesting issue of fairness. For example, if you are a child with acute clinical needs then you will be seen quickly and rightly so. But if you have ADHD for example, then you may start a treatment support programme months after accessing the system. And is that fair? We know that early intervention, family support and multi-agency work can have a dramatic and beneficial impact on a young person's life, any delay increases the chances of later life problems. Yet the system is geared towards acute need, I think that this does create an unfairness for those families wishing to have earlier intervention but are deemed to have less acute needs.*

Another example would be the rising levels of patients in acute care who are staying too long in hospitals due to not meeting the criteria to reside elsewhere. This impacts patients in urgent and emergency care who must wait longer for beds. As Senior Manager, Community Care, Pauline Preston observed, the acute hospital providers cannot solve this issue without collaboration with community care services, primary care, and social care providers.

Conclusion: Our conclusion, which may be deemed controversial, is that targets are useful. They allow organisations to know if they are performing to required standards, and target data helps with comparative analysis (how well one organisation is doing compared to peer groups). However, great caution should be used when setting and applying targets. They need to be set by organisations at the appropriate levels (national, regional, or local) and in collaboration with patient representatives and healthcare providers.

Recommendations: We recommend a move away from national centralised targets towards those set at regional levels. Objectives should be based on local strategies for health improvement, good use of resources, and within Integrated Care Boards (ICBs), commissioning contracts expectations. Wherever possible targets should be collaboratively set and implemented by healthcare providers in the community and primary care, acute services, and social care departments, particularly within mental health, autism, and learning disabilities services. They should also adhere to some collaboratively determined shared values and processes.

A Tax-Funded National Health Service?

In many ways, fairness is a utilitarian act. In this philosophy, everyone is counted equally. For example, at its base, one human is the same as another, neither more nor less, and decisions are made on the basis of consequences. In utilitarianism, decisions relate to the most unifying consequences for others or alternatively avoid consequences, which cause disunity. Utilitarianism also regards the consequence on an individual to be of less moral importance than the impact on the majority; in other words, decisions and consequences have a societal impact. (Bird, 2006; Smith, 1929; Russell, 2000) Utilitarianism would view the greatest benefit for the majority as measured in overall happiness, living standards, and health (Bezhanyan, 2017).

These concepts are clearly within the responsibilities of governments, whether one's political beliefs promote a smaller state, with emphasis on personal responsibility for oneself, or for more state intervention and support for those whose circumstances prevent opportunities to improve their lives. Politically, there will always be a dilemma regarding fairness when implementing policies which aim to improve living standards and population health due to the consequences of allocating resources on whether to raise or lower taxes.

Fairness is wrapped within moral and ethical principles, which involve decision-making on equity and social justice. People reach a judgement on whether certain behaviours, attitudes or actions are unbiased and demonstrate respect for people and situations, and whether these are viewed as morally right or wrong.

Much of any government's income is spent on defence, public services such as health, welfare and education, its physical infrastructure such as roads, rivers, and ports, and on supporting businesses and organisations which produce food and goods for the benefit of society. By government income, we mean taxation and its explicit use to support societal good, such as its healthcare services.

For the past 75 years, the UK government has funded the National Health Service through central taxation, with each administration spending more or less (in real terms) than the preceding government due to its underlying political philosophy (for example, a belief in smaller or larger State intervention). More of the population benefits from a stronger, well-resourced NHS, and more of the population have fewer benefits from a weak, under-resourced NHS. And not just in terms of personal health outcomes, but in life's opportunities for increased engagement with education, employment, cultural activities, and living a better life longer. The allocation of central resources, as Ian Gregory highlights in the second chapter, is an ethical as well as political choice.

Yet successive governments, and the public, have evaded any large-scale social discourse on the fairness of paying tax and consequent benefits. CFO, Chris Adcock, and colleagues note, in chapter five on Fairness and Finance, that the social and political narrative around the fairness of a national, centralised resource for the good of the UK population is often simplified: low tax, good and high tax, bad, for instance. But we would argue that there is a moral responsibility in taxation and in the fairness of proportionate taxes for the benefit of the population. This needs an honest, public debate so that people fully understand the reasons for paying taxes, their use, and the consequences for their overall happiness, health, and living standards.

Conclusion: the issues around a tax-funded national health service should not be reduced to economic criteria. This is a particular narrative in the UK where the cost of public services and personal taxation is seen as a burden and dominates the debate. Rather, the debate should focus on the personal responsibility of contributing to the communal good and the consequent benefits such as improved defence, security, health, and living standards. Our scrutiny of fairness in the NHS shows the lack of mid or long-term consistency in its funding policies and strategies and a growing public awareness of the impact of political decisions on their own and their families' health outcomes.

Recommendation: There should be an open, honest public debate about personal tax thresholds and the use of public taxation in the UK with an emphasis on the greatest societal good rather than on political principles or personal wealth. The discussions should not be based on *how much* a person pays in taxation, but on *how responsible* is it for an individual to contribute to the societal benefits. Such a debate should give emphasis to the benefits of a healthier and happier population and the consequent resource and cost requirements to provide both a preventive and intervention healthcare system in the UK.

The time seems right to decide the fairness of a tax-based NHS provision and, if the present system is desired, then for political parties, if they have the courage, to allocate the NHS the status of a non-partisan public service with a minimum of a ten-year funding plan supported by politicians across the spectrum.

Funding

Accepting the tax-based funding for the NHS leads us to the theme of funding issues and challenges which have been imposed by various governments. Whilst overall spending on the NHS has increased substantially since its inception in 1948, this spending has not been consistent and has varied both in real terms (taking away inflationary costs) and in the percentage of GDP. Great care must be taken in analysing the financial data as figures are often presented out of context or do not consider extraneous circumstances. For example, spending did increase from 2020 to 2022, but that was during the COVID-19 pandemic when the NHS was operating on what could be termed a wartime, or national emergency footing. Since that period spending has only increased by 1% in real terms for 2024/25 (The Kings Fund, 2024).

In Chapter 5 on fairness and finance in the NHS, both Bill Boa experienced NHS finance director and independent finance leader, and Stephen Downes, Director of Strategic Finance for Lancashire and South Cumbria Integrated Care Board, noted that the NHS has been operating at 100% capacity for many years and therefore the flexibility needed to deal with issues such as the pandemic were simply not available. This may have added to the costs required to adapt quickly to this global event.

Pace and speed of change is an interesting issue when engaged in financial planning. The relatively recent approaches of ongoing annual planning cycles have had a detrimental impact on the capacity and abilities to make required transformative changes in healthcare. Bill Boa talks about the complexity of adapting to fast-changing advances with the requirement to adjust financial plans accordingly.

In Chapter 5 on Fairness and Finance, a wider view held by healthcare finance experts is presented. This is because longer term planning cycles would benefit the NHS because they would allow pace and adjustment to be more considered and achievable, as well as provide a degree of certainty regarding income and expenditure.

A longer period of financial planning cycles would, we believe, have a positive impact on preventing the industrial disputes which have beset the

NHS since the pandemic ended. It is understood that NHS workers are fighting not only for better salaries but also for improved working conditions, more resources, and a period of stability within their work environments. In addition, the government needs to approach industrial disputes with a more collaborative mindset than sometimes appears to have been demonstrated by governments in the recent past; the costs of strikes are huge and successful collaboration and discussion is critical.

Conclusion: One of the problems with NHS funding is the lack of cross-political agreement on its worth to the nation and its populace. The NHS continues to be held in huge affection by many people and, as stated earlier, is consistently cited as a top priority in current pre-election opinion polls, yet political differences appear to prevent a non-partisan approach to one of the UK's real assets (see the conclusions regarding a tax-based system above). Furthermore, despite the growing budget for the NHS, there is inconsistency in short-term financial planning which is influenced by annual political goals, rather than a needed longer-term certainty in commissioned services and funding.

Recommendation: We recommend, although we recognise the bravery required to do so, a cross-party agreement for longer term funding cycles for the NHS, of at least three years.

The Future Then?

The National Health Service has survived 75 years of turbulence and major global challenges and continues to deliver healthcare free at the point of need. It remains important to the public. This has been clearly demonstrated in pre-election polls where it is consistently in the top three concerns for voters. It also has value, meaning, and purpose for many who work within it. It has coped with too many reforms and policy interventions, rising demand and a global pandemic. The NHS has survived.

Our view of the future is one of NHS continuity. We conclude that the NHS will continue to survive and adapt to more challenges. In addition, a major transformation will occur through the growing use of technological advances.

We see hugely impactful transformation brought about by remote diagnosis, robotic surgery, e-prescribing, hospital at home, remote monitoring of symptoms and electronic administration, not least a shared system of electronic patient records: these advances will improve healthcare and reduce cost and resource use.

We recognise that many technological resources require renewal, replacement and updating and that procurement and purchasing will require funding. However, the overall cost of technology will decrease and the impact on preventive healthcare, population health approaches and a reduction in both demand and stay in acute settings will support the variances of funding and commissioning streams.

We also conclude that staffing requirements in the NHS will change, sometimes like technology, quite rapidly. We envisage more dual-qualified healthcare workers employed in the NHS. Practitioners trained and qualified in areas such as simultaneous mental health with child health, social work with mental health and learning disabilities, urgent and emergency medicine with mental health, and dual training in acute care with care of frail neurologically impaired individuals.

We appreciate that current Professional, Statutory, and Regulatory Bodies (PSRBs) will find these transformations difficult, some will struggle to establish adequate oversight without falling into the position of protecting their profession's identity as their first and most important priority. We believe this would be detrimental to patient safety and quality of care. Some PSRBs must accept they will have to relinquish their current dominance and authority. Politicians need to be confident enough to legislate for the oversight and regulation of new types of professions where necessary.

This is because different working arrangements will transform health care delivery and access. For example, general practice with specialities working in both the community and acute hospital settings, a combined midwifery, infant, and family expert, and more movement as a normal expectation between community and hospital-based staff, with both working across local settings rather than in one environment separate from others.

This will have huge benefits for patients and will bring the inevitable closer union between health and social care into a more effective structure. It will also reduce the financial burden with skilled staff more able to work within current differing specialities and boundaries. Our view is that generalist care staff are of more value to patients and quality of care than the constrained care pathways implemented when staff are too specialised and need to continuously refer to other specialities.

Such an approach will lead to a decrease in the demarcation between social care and healthcare provision with closer integration and funding of joint health and social care teams, more involvement of patients and families in care regimes and more utilisation of the third sector in delivery. This is an exciting and dynamic development and provides an approach that will bridge the gap. We see the future as health and social care with no demarcation, whether structurally or financially, but working as one organisation for the benefit of users and patients and families and carers.

The drive for productivity and better use of health and social care resources will mean more acute trust mergers and potentially more localised group-type organisations spanning across acute, community, primary and social care, but under one overall executive leadership team and board.

Resource use and productivity will also lead to fewer central interventions and a rise in locality–place leadership of the NHS with more local accountability and community involvement in strategy and planning decisions.

The future of the NHS is one of hope, dynamism, of transformation and improved health and social care outcomes for the population and we reject the negative discourse which suggests the NHS is broken beyond repair. We believe in the values of fairness and kindness which are the bedrock of caring and are expounded by practitioners and users of the NHS in this book. We have discovered that the principles of the NHS are alive and well, and continue to be believed, held and applied by NHS staff. That alone is a testament to the courage and commitment of NHS staff.

The Past and Present

We thank everyone who has contributed to this book, our co-authors, expert commentators, those who kindly participated in many discussions and interviews, and the patients, families, and carers who experience the NHS when they need it most. Their experiences and views have provided a sense of optimism and hope in the context of fairness and kindness in the NHS. We do not underestimate the huge challenges facing the NHS, or the efforts that are needed to improve and transform health and social care delivery. But we are heartened by the dedication of staff, who keep going in a difficult environment, and by the patients and users, who continue to understand and appreciate that care is free at the point of access in the National Health Service.

We end with gratitude and thanks to all those who have worked within the NHS over the years and continue to do so. The work done and being done today within the UK National Health Service is unique in the world. The bravery and dedication demonstrated by many during the pandemic, and in the recovery work afterwards, is a testament to their values and principles, and the practical application of fairness and kindness.

The NHS is adaptable, flexible, and will transform to meet the demands placed upon it. Long may it continue.

References

Bezhanyan, R. (2017) *Utilitarianism and Tax Policies*. Master of Arts Submission, American University of Armenia. Yerevan.

Bird, C. (2006) *An Introduction to Political Philosophy*. Cambridge University Press. New York.

Keir, S. (July 4, 2024) *Opening Speech on Becoming Prime Minister*. https://www.gov.uk/government/speeches/keir-starmers-first-speech-as-prime-minister-5-july-2024.

The Kings Fund. (2024) *The NHS Budget and How It Has Changed; What Is the NHS Budget and How Is It Funded?* https://www.kingsfund.org.uk/insight-and-analsysis/data-and-charts/nhs-budget-nutshell (downloaded 15th May 2024).

Parkinson, L. (2023) *Restorative Practice at Work; Six Habits for Improving Relationships in Health-care Settings*. Crown House Publishing. Carmarthen.

Russell, B. (2000) *History of Western Philosophy*. Routledge. London.

Smith, N.K. (1929) *Immanuel Kant's Critique of Pure Reason*. Macmillan Press. London.

APPENDIX A

Fairness in Health and Social Care Policy Decisions: Socratic Questions – Designed by Anthony J Culyer

Broad Contextual Questions

- *What do I/we consider the health care system to be for?*
- *What do I/we understand by "health", by fairness and unfairness, efficacy and effectiveness, efficiency, and cost-effectiveness?*
- *What do I/we think of some commonly used notions of fairness and unfairness, and some of the conventional measures or indicators of these critical components?*
- *How might my/our own views be effectively disseminated widely throughout the NHS and "owned" not only by the principal decision makers but also by the public whom they serve?*

Specific Context

What is the policy context in which a question of fairness has arisen or might arise?

- *Is there anything in the current context that limits or prescribes how fairness is to be handled?*
- *Are suitable arrangements in place to enable and facilitate deliberation?*
- *Is it understood by stakeholders and decision makers that HTA is a way of evaluating health care interventions of many varied kinds, not just "high tech"?*
- *Are there any ways in which use of in question could ameliorate unfairness of any kind, or possibly worsen it?*
- *What types of stakeholder would be useful contributors to a deliberation in the current context?*
- *Can one have a useful deliberation without decision makers' involvement?*

- *Have those involved in the decision-making procedures been fairly chosen and competently trained/briefed?*

Questions About Fairness as A Concept

- *Does the current issue concern unfairness or misfortune? Does the distinction matter in the current context?*
- *Is the question at hand to do with equality? If so, equality of what?*
- *Is fairness in the current context to do with outcomes and for whom? What kinds of outcome?*
- *Are there issues to do with opportunities and who has them? Opportunities for what?*
- *Are there issues of multiple deprivation, that is, inequalities in many dimensions of the quality of life?*
- *Are there issues to do with costs and who bears them?*
- *Are there issues to do with risks and who bears them?*
- *Are there fairness issues with processes, for example to access services or to participate in decision making? Are some processes more fair or unfair than others?*
- *Are there issues of fairness regarding system funding?*
- *Are some combinations of tax finance, private insurance, and direct payments fairer than others in the current context?*
- *Are there issues of "rationing" and the possible consequences of different schemes for allocating health care to regions or individuals?*
- *Are there fairness issues arising from moral hazard?*
- *Is there "parallelism" in the current or proposed arrangements that enables some to have privileged access health care?*
- *Should some groups (workers, the elderly, children, those with "orphan" diseases?) have faster or cheaper access to care than others?*

Some Technical Questions

- *Is the distinction between vertical and horizontal fairness likely to be relevant in the current context? Does the practical measurement or outcomes, for example, as changes in longevity and quality of life, raise issues of fairness?*
- *Are the various components of an outcome measure (relief of pain, increased mobility, reduced confusion, etc.) given fair weights?*
- *Can you judge the validity and credibility of available evidence, or describe the kind of additional research to be commissioned?*

- *Are there issues of fairness in the statistical measures of inequality used to measure distributions?*

Epidemiological and Public Health Questions

- *How widely across the many determinants of health is the issue likely to range?*
- *Is there credible evidence that the policy instruments under discussion are efficacious?*
- *Is the membership of the decision-making group sufficiently competent to evaluate the quality of the evidence?*
- *Is there credible evidence that the policy instruments under discussion are effective?*
- *Is there credible evidence that the policy instruments under discussion are efficient?*
- *Are the policy instruments under discussion likely to promote or harm the total health or welfare of the community?*
- *Is there credible evidence that the policy instruments under discussion are cost-effective?*
- *Will the policy in question flatten the gradient in health?*
- *The health and social care systems have many purposes; are some more important than others in the current context?*
- *Is it possible to quantify some of the key elements of the foregoing in the current context? How best to proceed if it is not possible?*

Questions About Conflicts and Trade-Offs

- *Creating greater fairness for some can involve a sacrifice of health and health care for others – is that likely to be the case here?*
- *What, if any, are the acceptable limits to sacrifices of this sort in this context?*
- *Would enhancing fairness in the current context necessarily involve a reduction in efficiency?*
- *Is it fair to give weight to the alternative health gain (opportunity cost) that might have been achieved if a different decision were reached?*
- *Are ineffective interventions and other proposed changes nonetheless possibly useful from a fairness perspective?*
- *Is it fair not to provide treatments on the NHS that are cost-ineffective?*
- *Is it fair for people to be able to buy the treatment in question if it's not available on the NHS?*
- *Would it be fair, for those willing to pay, to "top up" their tax contributions by direct payment to gain access to services deemed insufficiently cost-effective to be offered by the NHS?*

- *Is rectifying an unfairness likely to reduce efficiency in this context?*
- *Is the advice given by professionals to decision makers impartial as well as competent?*
- *Ought professionals to have a good understanding of the patient's personal circumstances, values, and preferences?*
- *In the current context, do professionals face a possible conflict by both advising appropriate procedures for patients and for providing them?*
- *Are there fairness issues in NHS staff pay differentials, recruitment and retention that may arise in this context?*
- *Are there any externalities that raise matters of fairness?*
- *Which stakeholders might be especially important in finding a solution?*
- *Are some ways of "internalising" externalities fairer than others in the current context?*
- *Is the fairest policy likely to require collaboration between different sectors and ministries?*
- *Should some types of unfairness have a higher priority for rectification than others in this context?*
- *Is it fair for privileged groups to have favoured treatment even though their health gain may be less than the health losses to others arising from their use of a limited resource?*
- *Is it possible to quantify some of the key elements of all the foregoing in the current context? How best to proceed if it is not possible?*

Questions About Implementation

- *What insurance and financial issues, if any, are likely to be of concern?*
- *Is there a role for the market to improve fairness in the current context?*
- *Are pricing solutions always unfair?*
- *Are there improvements in the agency relationship that would improve fairness in the current context?*
- *What role, if any, exists for ordinary people in planning or operating the system in this context?*
- *Does fairness in the current context require formal guidance for professionals or adjustments in contracts of employment?*
- *Have you some communications strategies for sharing the results of the deliberation with the various stakeholder groups?*
- *Would it be wise to plan a review at a future date of what has happened following the decision?*

INDEX

Note: Page numbers in *italic* indicate a figure on the corresponding page.

Abelson, J. 102
access 137–138, 150–151; boundaries 143–144; compassion 147–149; education, housing, and employment 140–142; fairness in relation to 159–160; historical and financial comparisons 146–147; the individual and the condition 142–143; lessons learned 151–152; performance targets 138–140; recruitment 149–150; social background 145–146; technology 144–145
accountability 47, 94–95, 127–128, 172–173
Acheson Report 11–12, 170
adaptation 89–90
Adcock, Chris 64, 177, 185
agency 108–109
Agenda for Change (AFC) 60–61
Ajayi, Foluke 78
Albert Hospital, Royal 124–125
allocation: of funding 75–76; of resources 25–27
Amos, A. 113
apathy 60
Archer, D. 85, 143
Artificial Intelligence 179
Asaria, M. 116
assurance 38
Attlee, Clement 21, 64–65
austerity 67–68

Babalola, G. 118
Baker, W.F. 87, 89
Barer, M.L. 109
barriers 58–59, 163
Bennett, D. 140
Bevan, Aneurin 21, 64–65, 166
Beveridge, William xv, 12
Bezhanyan, R. 184
Bird, C. 184
Black, Douglas 11
Black Report 11, 145
Blair, Tony 67–68, 73, 79–80
blame culture 91–92
Boa, Bill 64, 68–71, 75, 186
boards 37, 48; definitions 38–39; director 46–47; historical context 39–41; linguistic insights 41–42; public-sector bodies 44–46; stakeholders 42–46
Book of Leviticus 123, 124
Borgquist, L. 117
boundaries 143–144
Bowden, Julie-Ann 50
Brazier, J.E. 104
Brexit 90
British Medical Association (BMA) 32
British Red Cross 9
Broadley, Rachael 138, 140, 148–151, 171
Brown, G. 67, 75
Brown, T. 70

Buchanan, J.M. 110, 112
Buck, D.118

Cameron, A. 85, 143
Cameron, David 67
Cancer Research UK 139
Care Quality Commission (CQC) 55, 58, 80, 180–182
Carstensen, J. 111
Case, A. 109
Castle, Barbara 122
Chalkidou, K.116
change: positive change is possible 12–13
Charles, A. 156
Chartered Governance Institute 38
Child and Adolescent Mental Health Services 138–139, 175, 183
chronology xvi–xxix
Citizen's Charter 79
Clifford, D. 113
Clinical Commissioning Groups (CCGs) 41, 81
collaborative care delivery 177–178
Collins, E. 142
command leadership 84–85
communication 161
compassion 147–149
compassionate leadership 84–85, 89; complexity of 93
compensation 60–61
complexity: compassionate and fair leadership 93
conditions 142–143
conflicts 193–194
Confucius 123
Connor, Steve 51
context 73, 101–102, 191–192
conversations 62
Cookson, R. 117
Corbett-Nolan, Andrew 37, 171, 176–177
Corich, K. 148
Cottam, Hilary 154, 156
"Covenant for Health" report 14–15
COVID-19 pandemic 6–8, 68, 75, 82–87, 186; COVID-19 Inquiry 75, 82, 84, 87
culture: blame 91–92; ethical 38–39; just 56–58; leadership 87–88; learning 91–92
Culyer, A.J. 99–102, 110, 113, 114, 117, 176–177, 191
Cummins, A. 78, 87–89, 94–95, 171, 176–178

Davies, Christine 162
Deacon, M. 142

death cafés 122, 128–129, 173
Deaton, A. 109
Debtors' Act (1869) 40
decisions/decision-making 86–87; agency 108–109, 114–115; efficiency versus fairness 113–114; externality 110–111; fairness and equity in 85–86; gradient 109–110; health insurance 111–113; rival visions 99–101; Socratic questions 191–194; starting points 101; terms and distinctions 101–107
deliberation 102
delivery 137–138, 150–151; boundaries 143–144; collaborative care 177–178; compassion 147–149; education, housing, and employment 140–142; historical and financial comparisons 146–147; the individual and the condition 142–143; lessons learned 151–152; performance targets 138–140; recruitment 149–150; social background 145–146; technology 144–145
Department of Health 16, 127, 154
development of leaders 93, 94
Dewar, I. 119, 172–173, 176, 179
director 46–47
diversity 95
Dodge, H. 43
Dodge, J. 43
Downes, S. 186
Drake, M. 142
Drake, Terry 138–143, 147–149, 151–152, 171, 175, 183
Duchy Renal Unit 166

economic imperative 9
education 140–142
effectiveness 103; effective control 39
efficacy 102–103
efficiency 103–104; versus fairness 113–114
Elizabethan Poor Law 12
Ely Hospital 124
empathy 162
employee perspectives 163–166, 175–176; background 154–157; fairness in relation to access to services/treatment 159–160; fairness in relation to quality of care 161–162; fairness in the workplace 160–161; main barriers to fairness 163; overall perceptions of fairness 157–159
employment 140–142
Environmental, Social, and Governance (ESG) movement 44

epidemiological questions 193
Equality Law 20, 22, 31
Equality Trust 145
equality versus equity 105
equity xvi–xxix, 70, 137–138, 150–151;
    boundaries 143–144; compassion
    147–149; in decision-making 85–86;
    education, housing, and employment
    140–142; versus equality 105; historical
    and financial comparisons 146–147; the
    individual and the condition 142–143;
    lessons learned 151–152; performance
    targets 138–140; recruitment 149–150;
    social background 145–146; technology
    144–145
ethics 21–22, 32–33; allocation of resources
    25–27; determining priorities 27–30;
    ethical culture 38–39; fairness in the
    workplace 30–32; importance of need
    23–25; increasing inequalities 23; origins
    and development of NHS 20–21
Evans, R.G. 108, 109
externality 110–111

Fairclough, Norman 41
fairness 187–190; in boards and governance
    37–48; collaborative care delivery
    177–178; of delivery in NHS 137–151;
    ethical pointers 20–33; and faith and
    spirituality 119–133, 172–173; and
    finance 64–76; funding 184–187; in
    governance 50–63, 176–177; and
    organisational leadership 78–95; patient
    and employee perspectives 154–166,
    175–176; in policy decisions 99–115;
    reforms, reviews, and interference
    178–180; regulatory and statutory
    oversight 180–182; Socratic questions
    191–194; targets and goals 182–184;
    and unequal health 169–171; value of
    171–172; wealth versus need 173–174
faith 119–122, 131–133, 132, 172–173;
    and accountability 127–128; as
    critique of healthcare 122–123; and
    death cafés 128–129; and hospitality
    123–125; Kirkup report 130–131; and
    self-reflection 125–127; and society
    129–130
Fedotov, G.P. 121
finance: allocation of funding 75–76;
    contemporary impact of funding
    policies 68–70; contemporary specialist
    provision 146–147; context 73; different
    approaches to planning 72–73; fairness

and equity 70; fairness and politics
    73–75; history of funding policies
    64–68; public confidence 75; reform
    70–72
Finnegan, Caroline 51
Ford, Henry 43
Ford Motor Company 43
Francis Report 128
Freedom to Speak Up Guardian 54
Friedman, Milton 43
fundamental values of society 9–10
funding 186–190; allocation of 75–76;
    policies 66–67, 68–70

Garrity, Julie 51
George, Andrew 46–47
Gerada, Dame Clare 165
Gibb, A. 140
Gibb, Y. 140
Giedion, U. 111
Gill, A. 83, 140
Glasby, J. 67
Glassman, A. 111
Gnam, W. 117
goals 182–184
Good Governance Institute (GGI) 41, 171,
    176
Goodman, J.C. 112
Gorsky, M. 79
Gove, Michael 75
governance 37, 48, 50–51, 176–177; and
    apathy 60; barriers to 58–59; definitions
    38–39, 51–54, 53; director 46–47;
    fair compensation 60–61; historical
    context 39–41; a just culture 56–58;
    and leadership 59–60; linguistic insights
    41–42; linking fairness and 55–56; and
    nursing care 61; procedural document
    processes 54; public-sector bodies 44–46;
    relationship between fairness and 53–54;
    speaking up 54–55; staff opinion of
    fairness 58; stakeholders 42–46; working
    differently 62–63
gradient 109–110
Gregory, I. 20, 170, 176, 183, 185
Griffin, S. 117
Griffiths, Roy 79

Ham, Chris 71–72
Handy, C. 132–133
Hanson, Jackie 78
Haskins, G. 85, 86, 87, 140, 148, 149
health xvi–xxix, 3–8, 4–5, 14–17,
    169–171; economic imperative 9;

imperative to uphold fundamental
values of society 9–10; lessons from
history 10–12, 13–14; moral imperative
8; policy imperative 8–9; and positive
change 12–13
Health and Care Act (2022) 45–46, 69,
81, 144
Health and Social Care Act (2012) 81, 144
Health and Social Care Act (2022) 81, 84
healthcare: agency 108–109, 114–115;
efficiency versus fairness 113–114;
externality 110–111; gradient 109–110;
health insurance 111–113; religion
and spirituality as critique of 122–123;
rival visions 99–101; Socratic questions
191–194; starting points 101; terms and
distinctions 101–107
Health Education England 178
Health Foundation, The 9, 145
health insurance 111–113
Health Technology Assessment (HTA)
106–107, 191
Hewitt Review 9
Highton, Ann 50, 171, 176
Hill, S. 113
history xvi–xxix, 10–12, 13–14;
contemporary specialist provision
146–147; fairness and governance
39–41; spirituality and religion
121–122
Holden, Sue 78
Hollington, S. 84
honesty 47
Hooper, A. 84
horizontal fairness 105
hospitality 123–125; virtues of 172–173
House of Commons 79
housing 140–142
Howe, Geoffrey 124
Hurley, J. 117
Husereau, D. 102
Hutton, Will 66, 145

implementation 194
inclusion 95
inequalities 3–8, 4–5, 14–17, 23, 169–171;
economic imperative 9; imperative to
uphold fundamental values of society
9–10; lessons from history 10–12,
13–14; moral imperative 8; policy
imperative 8–9; and positive change
12–13
Institute for Fiscal Studies (IFS) Deaton Review
9, 15

insurance *see* health insurance
Integrated Care Boards (ICBs) 45–46, 69,
78, 178, 184, 186
Integrated Care Systems (ICSs) 144
integrity 47
interference 178–180
interventions 179–180, 182–189;
contemporary specialist provision
138–145, 147–148, 151–152; finance
74–75; organisational leadership 95;
Socratic approach 101, 102–103,
106–107, 112–113

Jacobsson, F. 111
Jewkes, J. 111–112
Jewkes, S. 111–112
Johri, L. 140, 148
Joint Stock Companies Act (1844) 39–40
just culture 56–58
"Just Culture Guide, A" 57

Karunanithi, S. 3, 170, 183
Kawachi, I. 8
Keating, Caroline 50
Keir (Sir) 169
Kennedy, John F. 57
kindness 162
King, Mervyn 38, 44, 48
Kings Fund 68, 70, 186
King IV report 38–39
Kirkup report 130–131
Kynaston, D. 65, 145

Lavery, Kevin 78
Lavis, J. 117
Lawson, Nigel 122
leadership 38, 47, 59–60, 78–79,
82–84; adaptation and optimism
89–90; command leadership 84–85;
compassionate leadership 84–85,
89, 93; contemporary operating and
political environment 81–82; culture
of 87–88; decision-making 85–87;
development of 79–81; importance of
fairness and equity 85–86, 91; moving
from blame to learning culture 91–92;
recommendations 94–95; supporting
leaders 92–93; training and
development 93
learning culture 91–92
Lees, D.S. 111
legislation xvi–xxix
legitimacy 39
Lester, H. 67

Letby, Lucy 59, 81
Levelling Up and Regeneration Act 8
Levy, David, Dr 78
life expectancy xvi–xxix
Limited Liability Act (1855) 39–40
linguistic insights: governance and fairness 41–42
listening 62–63
Lister, J. 69
Lomas, J. 102
Love-Koh, J. 116
LSE 65
Lubotsky, D. 109

Mackey, John 83
Major, John 79, 80
Marmor, T.R. 109
Marmot, M.G. 109
Marmot Review Report 8–9, 12, 23, 170
Martin, Tracey 51
Mcguire, D. 118
McGuire, T.G. 108
McKnight, R. 110
McNichols, Jane 138–139, 141, 145–148, 150–152, 171, 177
misfortune 107
mission/vision 38
moral imperative 8
Morecambe Bay Investigation 130
Morecambe Bay NHS Foundation Trust 64, 93
Murray, C. 140, 154, 171, 175
Murray, Terry 154–156, 158, 162–166
Mustard, C. 117

national frameworks for support and intervention 95
National institute for Health and Care Excellence (NICE) 4, 5, 116, 181
National Outcome Framework 95
need 23–25, 173–174
NHS 187–190; access, equity, and fairness of delivery in 137–151; collaborative care delivery 177–178; ethical pointers 20–33; and faith and spirituality 172–173; finance in 64–76; funding 184–187; governance 50–63, 176–177; history of xvi–xxix; and organisational leadership 78–95; patient and employee perspectives 154–166, 175–176; reforms, reviews, and interference 178–180; regulatory and statutory oversight 180–182; relationship between society and 129–130; targets and goals 182–184; and unequal health 169–171; value of fairness 171–172; wealth versus need 173–174
NHS Confederation 139
NHS Constitution 21–23, 26, 27, 29, 29, 131, 171, 173
NHS Employees 154, 157, 159, 160–165
NHS Employers 60, 165
NHS England 9, 41, 45, 57, 157
NHS Resolutions 57, 63
NHS Staff Health & Wellbeing 157
NHS Staff Survey 54, 57–58
No. 10 Fairer Society Unit 16–17, 170–171
Nolan Principles 37, 47
Nozick, R. 99
nursing care 61

objectivity 47
Obodai-Payne, Siobhan 51
Ockenden Report 126, 128, 133
Office of National Statistics (ONS) 6, 16, 70
OFSTED 80, 95
Oliver, Chris 78
O'Malley, M. 87, 89
Oortwijn, W. 102
openness 47, 161
operating environment (NHS) 81–82
opinion 58
optimism 89–90
organisational leadership 78–79, 82–84; adaptation and optimism 89–90; command leadership 84–85; compassionate leadership 84–85, 89, 93; contemporary operating and political environment 81–82; culture of 87–88; decision-making 85–87; development of 79–81; importance of fairness and equity 85–86, 91; moving from blame to learning culture 91–92; recommendations 94–95; supporting leaders 92–93; training and development 93
organisations: and fairness 46–47; structure 164; see also organisational leadership
Orwell, G. 125
outcome 104–105
Oxford English Dictionary 157, 160

Pareto efficiency 104, 110, 113
Parkinson, L. 182
Pasic, D. 117
Patient's Charter 79

patient/service user perspectives 175–176; background 154–157; barriers to fairness 163; relationships are key 164–166; the study 157–162
Paxson, C. 109
performance targets 138–140
Pieper, Josef 122
Pilgrim, D. 66
planning 72–73
Platt, S. 113
policies xvi–xxix; agency 108–109, 114–115; efficiency versus fairness 113–114; externality 110–111; funding 66–67, 68–70; gradient 109–110; health insurance 111–113; policy imperative 8–9; rival visions 99–101; Socratic questions 191–194; starting points 101; terms and distinctions 101–107
politics 73–75; NHS political environment 81–82
Poor Law 12
Portillo, M. 65
Preston, Pauline 138, 142–144, 147, 149–150, 171, 177, 183
Primary Care Trusts (PCTs) 67, 81
priorities 27–30
procedural document processes 54
Provider Collaborative Board 178
public confidence 75
Public Health Act (1872) 11
Public Health Act (1875) 11
public health questions 193
public-sector bodies 44–46
public service 47

quality of care 161–162
questions: agency 108–109, 114–115; efficiency versus fairness 113–114; externality 110–111; gradient 109–110; health insurance 111–113; rival visions 99–101; Socratic 191–194; starting points 101; terms and distinctions 101–107

Ratcliffe, J. 104
Reason, James 54
recruitment 149–150
reflection points 73
reform 70–72, 178–180
regulatory oversight 180–182
regulatory requirements xvi–xxix
relationships 164–166
religion 119–127, 131
Religion and Belief Matters 120

resources: allocation of 25–27; limited 164
respect 47, 159–160
reviews 178–180
Richards, Len 50
Rimmer, A. 165
Robertson, R. 156
Rogers, A. 66
Rowlands, C. 83, 140
Royal Charter 40
Russell, B. 184

Salomon, J. 104
Satz, D. 9
Scattergood, Jane 78
Scuito, Frank 162
Second World War 3, 10, 13–15, 121, 131, 170
selflessness 47
self-reflection 125–127, 172–173
services/treatment: fairness in relation to access to 159–160
Sheldrake, P. 120
Sisodia, Raj 83
Slave Compensation Act (1837) 40
Smith, G.D. 109
Smith, N.K. 184
Smith, P.C. 111
social background 145–146
social care xvi–xxix; agency 108–109, 114–115; efficiency versus fairness 113–114; externality 110–111; gradient 109–110; health insurance 111–113; rival visions 99–101; Socratic questions 191–194; starting points 101; terms and distinctions 101–107
Socratic approach 101; agency 108–109, 114–115; efficiency versus fairness 113–114; externality 110–111; gradient 109–110; health insurance 111–113; questions 191–194; rival visions 99–101; Socratic Method 100; starting points 101; terms and distinctions 101–107
speaking up 54–55
specialist provision 137–138, 150–151; boundaries 143–144; compassion 147–149; education, housing, and employment 140–142; historical and financial comparisons 146–147; the individual and the condition 142–143; lessons learned 151–152; performance targets 138–140; recruitment 149–150; social background 145–146; technology 144–145

spirituality 119–122, 131–133, *132*,
  172–173; and accountability 127–128;
  as critique of healthcare 122–123; and
  death cafés 128–129; and hospitality
  123–125; Kirkup report 130–131; and
  self-reflection 125–127; and society
  129–130
staff opinion 58
staff perspectives 175–176; background
  154–157, 163–166; fairness in relation
  to access to services/treatment 159–160;
  fairness in relation to quality of care
  161–162; fairness in the workplace
  160–161; main barriers to fairness 163;
  overall perceptions of fairness 157–159
stakeholders 44–46, 105–106; and fairness
  42–44
Stansfeld, S. 109
Starmer, K. 169
statutory legislation xvi–xxix
statutory oversight 180–182
stewardship 38
Storr, A. 121
Strategic Health Authorities 81
strategy 38
streamlining 62
Stubblebine, W.C. 110
Sunak, Rishi 68, 81, 169
supporting leaders 92–93, 95
system design 106
System Improvement Board (SIB) 181, 182
Szreter 12

targets 182–184
taxation 184–186
Taylor, Louise 78
technical questions 192–193
technology 144–145
Thatcher, Margaret 66, 73, 79–80, 116n5,
  174
Thatcher, Margaret 79, 80, 174
Thatcherite Community Charge 105
Thirlwall Inquiry 89
Thomas, M. 64, 71, 74, 78, 83, 85, 86,
  137, 140, 149, 178
Thompson, J. 156
Tobin, J. 100
trade-offs 193–194
training leaders 93
transparency 38
treatment *see* services/treatment

Treliske Hospital 166
Tsuchiya, A. 104

UK Parliament Health Committee 139
unequal health 3–8, *4–5*, 14–17, 169–171;
  economic imperative 9; imperative to
  uphold fundamental values of society
  9–10; lessons from history 10–12,
  13–14; moral imperative 8; policy
  imperative 8–9; and positive change
  12–13
unfairness 107
United Nations 44
Universal Credit (UC) 133

value creation 39
value of fairness 171–172
values 9–10
vertical fairness 105
virtues of hospitality 172–173
Vize, R. 126

Wagstaff, A. 113
Walzer, M. 115
Warner, M. 69, 73, 82
wealth 173–174
Webster, C. 111
Welfare State 3, 10, 12, 66, 170
Wellbeing of Future Generations (Wales)
  Act (2015) 46
Wenzel, L. 156
West, Michael 73, 83, 89, 91, 148, 150
West Cornwall Hospital Renal Unit 155,
  162, 163, 166
White, S. 9
Whitehead, M. 145
Whitehead Report 11, 170
White Papers 41
Wickens, C. 70
Wilde, D. 119, 172–173, 176, 179
Williams, E. 116
Woodward, A. 8
working conditions 164
workplace, fairness in 30–32,
  160–161
World Health Organization 142

Yaseen, Talib 50

Zaranko, B. 69, 73, 82
Zwarenstein, M. 112

Printed in the United States
by Baker & Taylor Publisher Services